S0-BAV-193

The Fifth French Republic

By the same author

THE FRENCH POLITICAL SCENE

FRANCE BETWEEN THE REPUBLICS

INTRODUCTION TO POLITICS

FRENCH POLITICS: THE FIRST YEARS OF THE FOURTH REPUBLIC

FRANCE: THE FOURTH REPUBLIC

The Fifth French Republic

INSTITUTIONS AND POLITICS

Revised Edition

by

DOROTHY PICKLES

FREDERICK A. PRAEGER, *Publisher*

New York

BOOKS THAT MATTER

Published in the United States of America in 1962 by
Frederick A. Praeger, Inc., Publisher
64 University Place, New York 3, N.Y.

This is the second edition, revised and enlarged, of the book first published in 1960 by Frederick A. Praeger, New York.

Library of Congress Catalog Card Number: 62-21938

THE FIFTH FRENCH REPUBLIC is published in two editions:
A paperback edition (U-527)
A clothbound edition

Printed in the United States of America

Contents

Part III

THE POLITICS OF THE FIFTH REPUBLIC

List of Abbreviations

A.L.N.	Armée de la libération nationale.
F.L.N.	Front de la libération nationale.
C.F.T.C.	Confédération des travailleurs chrétiens.
C.G.T.	Confédération générale du travail.
C.N.I.P.	Centre national des Indépendants et Paysans.
G.P.R.A.	Gouvernement provisoire de la République algérienne.
M.N.A.	Mouvement national algérien.
M.R.P.	Mouvement républicain populaire.
O.A.S.	Organisation de l'armée secrète.
P.S.U.	Parti socialiste unifié.
R.G.R.	Rassemblement des gauches républicaines.
R.P.F.	Rassemblement du peuple français.
U.D.M.A.	Union démocratique du manifeste algérien.
U.D.S.R.	Union démocratique et socialiste de la résistance.
U.D.T.	Union démocratique du travail.
U.N.R.	Union pour la nouvelle République.

Preface

The Constitution of 4th October 1958 does not merely break a great deal of new ground. It does so in ways that are exceedingly complex and difficult for the non-specialist to follow. Whatever may be said about its merits and demerits, it is certainly the most confused and obscure of France's many Constitutions since 1791. It is also, in a special sense, a *pièce de circonstance*. It was produced in the stress of a national emergency, when France had narrowly avoided a violent revolution, and under the inspiration of General de Gaulle who became the first President of the Fifth Republic. In the opinion of many of the critics of the new régime, it is unlikely to outlive his Presidency. But since it has already survived for more than a year and even on relatively pessimistic hypotheses may do so for several more, it seemed justifiable and perhaps useful to try to describe what its purposes were and how far they are being achieved, even though it has been in existence for too short a time to make any final judgement possible.

The account is brief and has two main aims. They are, first, to try to place this Constitution in its political context and to make clear why and where it was a subject of controversy before it was voted; and second, to describe as simply as possible the institutions that it provides for, including the essential provisions of the numerous *Ordonnances* and organic laws which filled in some of the gaps during the six months following the promulgation of the Constitution itself. This second task has involved a certain amount of repetition, in the interest of clarity, owing to the complexity of the provisions themselves. There are also, inevitably, a great many omissions. The present introductory study will need to be completed by much more detailed analysis and comment, as information becomes available on the actual working of the Constitution.

I should like to take this opportunity to thank M. Guy Mollet, M. and Mme Rosenfeld, M. Lucien Neuwirth, M. Léon Delbecque, M. Michel Massenet, M. Jacques Fauvet, M. Brilhac and Professor Gonidec of the University of Rennes for their kindness in answering questions, or supplying information on a number of points.

November 1959 DOROTHY PICKLES

PREFACE TO THE SECOND EDITION

When this book was originally written, it was possible to do little more than describe the provisions of the new Constitution and speculate on how they might be expected, or were expected by politicians, political scientists and constitutional lawyers, to work in practice. After nearly four years of existence, the 1958 Constitution must be looked at in a quite different perspective. Some questions asked then can now be answered. Some views must be modified in the light of experience. There has been already one constitutional revision, and there have been several controversies centring round interpretations of parts of the Constitution. I have, therefore, re-written a good deal of the original subject-matter.

More important still, the Fifth Republic has now a history and a personality of its own. I have, therefore, added four chapters, in which I have tried to assess as accurately as possible the nature of the evolution of "de Gaulle's Republic" and, in particular, the political climate that it has produced.

It is never easy to keep up with the rate of change in French institutions and politics and I apologize in advance for any errors of fact or of judgement.

July 1962 DOROTHY PICKLES

PART I

Background to the Constitution

CHAPTER I

The Republican Tradition

CONSTITUTIONAL EXPERIMENTS

No study of the French Constitution can make its intentions plain unless it takes account of the factor of heredity. For in the field of constitution-making the French hold a world record. It has often been said that, since 1789, France has changed her Constitution on an average every 12 years. Such a statement needs amplification, for the average covers extremes in time ranging from the 21 days of the *Acte Additionnel* of 1815 to the 65 years of the Third Republic, and extremes in content ranging from complete changes of régime to modifications no greater than some carried out by the normal processes of constitutional revision. Moreover, it is difficult to find an agreed definition on which to base the calculation. Should only written Constitutions be counted, although some ('those of 1793 and 1814) were not applied? Or, if only those Constitutions are counted which were actually put into force, should provisional régimes be included which were based on no written text (those of 1792–5, 1848, 1871–5, 1940–4 and 1944–6)?

THE THREE CYCLES

Perhaps a more useful way of looking at French constitutional experiments is to concentrate attention less on how often they happened, and on the specific changes that each introduced, than on the general picture of constitutional evolution over the 170 years since the French revolution. During this period, movement from one system to another seems to form a pattern, repeated in three distinct cycles.[1] It is essential not to distort the facts in order to make this pattern tidier or more consistent than it really is. But though the parallel is not complete the general resemblances are marked. Constitutional Monarchy gives way to Republic and the Republic in turn is replaced by some form of dictatorial government. The first cycle may be said to begin with the Constitution of 1791 which was that of a Constitutional Monarchy. In 1792, the Monarchy gave way to Republican government, and France was at war by the time the first Republican Constitution had been voted in 1793. It was never applied and, indeed, it has been argued that it was inapplicable. That of 1795 already reflected the reaction against the revolutionary Governments of the Convention. Its main aim was to protect France from popular rule of this kind and it, therefore, incorporated a number of checks and balances which made it, in practice, unworkable. There followed in rapid succession the Constitutions of the years VIII, X, and XII which reflected the rise to power of Napoleon, who became Emperor.

The second cycle may be said to begin with the return of Louis XVIII, after the defeat of Napoleon in 1815.[2] It presents some variants but the general course of evolution is similar. The monarchy, for instance, underwent a double evolution, becoming first less liberal under Charles X, and then more Parliamentary under the July monarchy. The change was political rather than constitutional, the text of the Charter of 1830 presenting few differences from that of 1814. The Second Republic, whose constitution lasted only three years, was followed by the *coup d'état* of 1851 and the Second Empire, which lasted from 1852 to France's defeat in the War of 1870. It was twice liberalized, the second time only a few weeks before the Empire collapsed.

The third cycle, beginning with the voting of the constitution of the Third Republic in 1875, presents some special features. First, it does not begin with Monarchy. But the second liberali-

[1] *v. Les Constitutions de la France* by Maurice Duverger (Presses universitaires de France, 1944) which develops this idea in considerable detail. M. Duverger, however, does not regard the period from 1875 onwards as constituting a third cycle.

[2] The choice of this date involves considerable over-simplification. It ignores the Senatorial Constitution of 1814, monarchical in all but name, which was never applied, and the Imperial *Acte Additionnel* which was; and it takes no account of the resemblances between the Senatorial Constitution and the Charter of the same year.

zation of the Imperial Constitution transformed it into something like a constitutional monarchy, and the 1875 Constitution is often described as one of *attente monarchique*. It was, in fact, drawn up by an Assembly which included a majority of Monarchists, and in such a way as to facilitate a transition from Republic to Monarchy – a transition which was never made. In other words, the period opens with a would-be monarchic phase, followed by over 60 years of Republican government. The Vichy régime which followed it in 1940 was provisional, and the German occupation of half the country up to 1942 and the whole country from 1942 onwards meant that Governments were largely dependent on the goodwill of the occupier. It would in all probability have been impossible to hold any elections. Nevertheless, the régime was dictatorial in the sense that its general principles reflected the known anti-democratic opinions of prominent sections of French society (though not exclusively – the collaborators also included progressive elements) and in that it was regarded by many French Republicans as being *la revanche de* 1936.

Though no Constitution was ever promulgated, a number of so-called 'Constitutional Acts' (in reality executive decisions) were put into force, and there were administrative changes, the whole constituting what was described as 'the National Revolution', whose motto was *Travail, famille, patrie* and whose aim was the creation of a kind of nineteenth-century paternalist and corporatist dictatorship.

It ended, this time, with the victory of the Allies in 1944–5. But the circumstances of that victory as they concerned France produced some of the reflexes of defeat. France was less a liberating than a liberated country; her armed forces played only a minor, if vital, role. Up to 1946, France felt that the other three great Powers were treating her as a poor relation. She suffered, therefore, for some years following the war, from an over-sensitivity that often looked very like the kind of inferiority complex produced by defeat. This affected the politics of the Fourth Republic and so affected the fortunes of the Constitution of 1946.

IS FRANCE ENTERING A FOURTH CYCLE?

If the Fourth Republic represents, as it certainly does in the minds of some Frenchmen, the beginning of a fourth cycle, the early stages are dissimilar from those of the first three, and the end of the cycle is still in the future. The first difference is that it has no monarchical or even would-be monarchical initial phase. On the contrary, the provisional Government, headed by General de Gaulle, set out in 1945 to draw up a Republican Constitution that would express the permanent victory of Republican and democratic Parliamentary government.

For what emerges from the preceding brief summary of France's constitutional experiments since 1789, even if the suggested cyclical pattern is rejected as an oversimplification or as a somewhat fanciful distortion of the facts, is that no régime has up to now succeeded in establishing itself firmly enough to feel immune from the danger of attempts to overthrow it. Even the three-quarters of a century of the Third Republic – the longest-lived of any régime since 1789 – has been described as:

> an epoch in which the idea of democracy never quite secures its letters of credit and the idea of reaction never quite dares openly to organize itself as a party seeking to overthrow democratic foundations.[1]

In 1940, with the aid of a war, the democratic foundations had been overthrown once again, but the two Constituent Assemblies of 1945–6 were overwhelmingly Republican and democratic in outlook. Even if the Communists are left out of account, the 544 Deputies who sat for metropolitan France included over 300 representatives of democratic and predominantly left-wing parties. They hoped to remove, at long last, from the field of political controversy the question of what political system was best suited to France, and to produce that degree of unanimity regarding the political machinery that Lord Balfour has described as essential to the effective working of Parliamentary government.

It soon became apparent that this aim was not to be achieved. For by 1951 almost one elector in two was voting for a candidate representing a party (either Gaullist or Communist) that rejected the Parliamentary system, at least in the form it took under the Fourth Republic. By 1953–5, right-wing extremist movements had made their appearance, some of which resembled the kind of anti-Republican and anti-Parliamentary challenge that had characterized the last

[1] H. J. Laski, in the preface to *France is a Democracy*, Louis Lévy (Gollancz, 1943), p. 9.

decade of the Third Republic, though one only – the Poujadist movement – could claim to have made any serious impact on opinion.

When the challenge did come, however, in 1958, it presented quite a number of unique features. The revolution that led to the collapse of the Fourth Republic broke out, not in Paris, but in Algiers. The immediate cause was less the situation in France than the impact of events in France on the future of Algeria, and the immediate threat to France came in the main from certain sections of the army, in particular from those who were serving, or had served, in parachute regiments in Algeria. The end of the régime came without bloodshed and by technically legal and constitutional processes. It could not with accuracy be described as a victory for the revolutionaries, since the new Government included most of the Ministers who had held office in the previous one, and was supported by a majority of all parties except the Communist Party. The new Constitution was intended by the majority of those who drew it up to be both Republican and democratic and was accepted by an overwhelming majority of the population in the referendum of the 28th September 1958.

Some opponents of the new régime argued that, whatever the intentions of those who drew it up, the constitution would prove unworkable, at latest, when General de Gaulle was no longer head of the State. For them, the new régime constituted a move away from the Republican tradition, the first stage of the journey along a familiar road. They saw 1958 as equivalent to 1799 or 1851, both of which were preludes to dictatorship. Others, again, argued that, whatever the merits or demerits of the Constitution, the future of the Republic depended on General de Gaulle who was now 'the sole remaining rampart between the Republic and Fascism'.[1]

These divisions of opinions are explicable only in two essential contexts. The first is that of the French Republican tradition, as it has evolved during these numerous constitutional changes. The second is that of the events which constituted the immediate prelude to the Fifth Republic.

[1] Jacques Fauvet in *Le Monde*, 29–30th June 1958.

THE REPUBLICAN TRADITION

It is not easy to describe with any degree of completeness or precision what really constitutes the Republican tradition, because it is not a series of dogmas but rather a number of beliefs and emotions about the kind of relationship that ought to exist between State and citizen and between Government and legislature. These beliefs and emotions go very deep because Frenchmen have had to fight and die for them so often in their history, because memories of the most recent eclipse of democracy and Republicanism are still vivid, at least in the minds of all Frenchmen over thirty, and because some Frenchmen are still far from convinced that they will not have to fight for them again in the near future.

But exactly what they have fought for, or will fight for, is something that defies exact analysis, primarily for two reasons. First, not all Republicans are agreed on the meaning to be attached to the term; and second, the language in which the feelings are expressed has become a kind of political shorthand, summing up episodes of French history and attitudes to significant events or conflicts. Some of the language has by now become symbolic. It is difficult to sort out the relative importance of history and politics in phrases and words like 'The Republic, one and indivisible', 'the sacred right of insurrection', 'the rights of man and the citizen', 'popular sovereignty', 'equal and secret ballots', 'a secular, democratic, and social Republic'. They are now symbols of a *mystique*. They form part of the picture that some Frenchmen have of the Republic. General de Gaulle began his memoirs as follows:

> All my life, France has had a quite special meaning for me, that is based on sentiment as much as on reason.

Every Frenchman's Republic has a quite special meaning for him, too. But it is not always the same Republic.

In the minds of most Socialists, and of some Radicals, the Revolutionary tradition – the belief that modern France dates from 1789 – is an integral part of the Republican tradition. André Siegfried described this attitude in the '30's:

> A century and a half after the Declaration of the Rights of Man, the French Revolution is still something on which there is

no unanimity. The differences have nothing to do with a Republican or a Monarchic régime; they go much deeper. Léon Bourgeois understood this perfectly when, after the Boulangist affair, he replied to a number of Royalists prepared for a *rapprochement* with the régime: 'It is not merely a matter of accepting the Republic. Do you accept the Revolution?'[1]

Some of the Constitution-makers of 1946 were very conscious of this Revolutionary inheritance. M. Mollet, for instance, when he became President of the Constitutional Commission in March 1946, stated that it intended to remain faithful to the Declaration of 1789 and had it constantly in mind, 'as it has the texts of 1793, of various allied countries, and that drawn up in 1936 by the League of the Rights of Man.' In the Socialist calendar, Whit Sunday, when the martyrs of the *Commune* are remembered at the *Mur des Fédérés*, is as important as the 14th of July, for, in the minds of French Socialists, Socialism and Republicanism are inseparable.

Radicals, whose ideal of political equality is also inspired by 1789, by no means always subscribe to all the social implications that appear to Socialists as the natural twentieth-century expression of the principle of equality. Radical Republicanism has tended to emphasize spiritual and intellectual equality, to support anti-clericalism and educational opportunity – *la carrière ouverte aux talents* – and to allow economic equality often to take a back seat. More right-wing politicians, such as Doumergue, Poincaré, or M. Coty, all of whom were Presidents of the Republic whose authentic Republicanism was never in question, were less concerned with general principles and more with techniques of government, and, in particular, with the need for strong government. In general, right-wing Republicans have tended to associate left-wing Republicanism with a liking for weak government.

In spite of these and other divergences, it is possible to single out at least three tendencies that are essentially characteristic of the French Republican tradition. The first is the insistence on the importance of the individual citizen and on his right to certain freedoms regarded as fundamental. In institutional terms this has shown itself in a predilection for complex electoral systems designed to reflect (though not always with mathematical accuracy) as large a

[1] *Tableau des Partis en France* (Paris, Grasset, 1930), p. 57.

gamut as possible of political opinions, and in the inclusion in Constitutions of tributes to a certain number of these freedoms. The use of the word 'tributes' is deliberate. For since the rights or freedoms in question are not easily guaranteed either by Constitutions or by Courts of law, some of them remain in the realm of hope, or of theory, rather than of fact. The Constitutions of 1791, 1793, 1795, 1848, 1946 and 1958 all included Declarations of Rights, either directly or by reference.[1]

The second tendency is one that seeks to exalt the popularly elected Assembly at the expense of both the Second Chamber and the Government. In its most left-wing or revolutionary expression it is a belief in Conventional government, or *gouvernement d'assembleée;* in its most right-wing expression it becomes little more than a defence of the prestige of Parliament and of the right of Deputies to play a more independent role and to take a greater share in legislative initiative, and in legislative processes generally, than would be acceptable to either Government or Opposition parties in the British Parliament. Republicans of both right and left wings hold that the essential role and the unchallengeable right of Parliament is to vote the laws and to decide what are suitable subjects for legislation. Within this framework, the function of the Government is to execute the laws. In the words of article 6 of the Declaration of the Rights of Man:

> The law is the expression of the general will. All citizens have the right to participate in legislation, either directly or through their representatives.

Gouvernement d'assemblée, the encroachment by Parliament on what might legitimately be considered to be the executive sphere, has been responsible, more than any other single factor, for the weakness and incoherence of French Governments and so has led

[1] They usually reaffirm the rights contained in the 1789 Declaration of the Rights of Man, which was incorporated in the 1791 Constitution, though the 1795 Constitution shows a marked lack of enthusiasm for rights and a strong consciousness of duties. The 1946 and 1958 Constitutions go farther than the 1789 Declaration, the former adding a number of social and economic rights, such as the right to strike, to employment, to join the trade union of one's choice, to social security and educational opportunity, the latter subscribing in general to all of these, without special mention of any. The Consultative Constitutional Committee had proposed in 1958 to subscribe also to the rights mentioned in the Universal Declaration of Human Rights of 1948, but the Government rejected this amendment.

to reactions against it, some of which have rejected the Parliamentary system along with its weaknesses. But although there is always a danger that a movement for strong government may develop into a challenge to the régime, and always a fear in the minds of some Frenchmen that such movements will do so, because it has happened in the past, it is important to emphasize that the distinction between what have been called, for convenience, the left-wing and right-wing Republican traditions is by no means clear or consistent. Some left-wing Prime Ministers of the Fourth Republic, in particular, M. Mollet and M. Pflimlin, were in favour of amending the constitution of the Fourth Republic in order to strengthen Governments. M. Pflimlin succeeded in getting some of these amendments voted on the day preceding his resignation, and these two Ministers are popularly credited with the responsibility for the inclusion in the 1958 Constitution of provisions remarkably similar to two of them.[1] On the other hand, though the supporters of a Presidential or quasi-Presidential system have been in the main on the right, it has also found eminent supporters on the left, even if only temporarily.[2] When the 1958 Constitution was in preparation, during the discussion of the Standing Orders of both Assemblies, and throughout the period discussed in this book, some right-wing Deputies and Senators showed themselves to be no less fervent defenders of the rights of Parliament than their colleagues on the left.

What tends to separate Right and Left is often less the content of specific measures than the undertones for which history is responsible. The Left, for instance, remembers that the Directoire was followed by Napoleon, the second Republic by Louis Napoleon and the Third by Pétain, and is afraid of history repeating itself; the Right is conscious of the overlapping of Republican and Revolutionary traditions on the Left, of the fact that the first Republic developed into the Convention and the Terror, that Socialism was associated with the Second Republic and that the Third was heralded by the Commune, and so is equally afraid of history

[1] Articles 41 and 49; *v. infra*, pp. 110-13.

[2] Léon Blum wrote in favour of a Presidential system for France in 1946, but very shortly changed his mind. In 1956 there were a number of discussions of this question by politicians and political scientists, some on the left being attracted by it. Professor Vedel and Professor Duverger have both continued to defend certain forms of Presidential Government.

repeating itself in a different way. It can also, for instance, be generally assumed that on a certain number of issues, in particular those involving the rights of Catholic schools and of Parliament, the desirability of State control of the economy and a generous system of social security, or the merits of this or that electoral system, a majority of each tendency will be found in opposite camps.

Whether this pull between right- and left-wing Republicanism remains within the régime or leads to an attempt to overthrow it depends on a number of factors; on their relative strength, for instance, and on the extent to which each side can achieve some internal unity, instead of being split by issues like anti-clericalism or nationalization, which today cut across the traditional divisions between Republicans more than in the past. It also depends on external circumstances. External danger has always made it easier for right-wing Republicanism to slide into acquiesence in extremism. The defeat of both the First and the Third Republics was assisted, if not brought about, by war. In 1958, war also played a part in bringing the Fourth Republic to an end, though it was a rebellion in Algeria and not a foreign war. It also depends on the way in which Republican Constitutions are applied. And this is a factor which explains some of the uncertainty in the minds of many Frenchmen regarding the future evolution of the Fifth Republic.

The oscillations characteristic of French constitutional and political history over the past 170 years have in themselves contributed to the growth of a third Republican tradition which might be more accurately described as a constitutional attitude, characteristic of Republicans and anti-Republicans alike. It is an attitude of political rigidity, or intolerance, which is caused by the sense of constitutional instability. The fact that no régime is sure of its capacity to survive leads each in turn to look to its defences from the start, to seek to strengthen the régime by turning the Constitution into a strait-jacket for potential wreckers. It does so by concentrating attention on known and familiar dangers and by trying to make hard and fast rules to deal with them.[1] In practice, this has often turned out to be a plan for winning the last war. For each régime brings its own problems, which are often quite different

[1] Cf. M. Duverger, *Les Institutions de la Cinquième République,* in *Revue française de Science Politique*, March, 1959, p. 101. 'Every Constitution is a political weapon, used by a victorious party in order to consolidate its victory.'

from those of its predecessor. It was often said, for instance, that those who drew up the 1946 Constitution were haunted by de Gaulle and by the ghosts of the two Napoleons, Boulanger and Pétain. But the strait-jacket designed for them proved ineffective against the real challenge, which came from a quarter that had not been foreseen in 1946. The 1946 Constitution provided a complex procedure designed to prevent the deadlock between the Senate and the directly elected Assembly that had been one of the acknowledged weaknesses of the Third Republic. In case of conflict the Assembly's will was to prevail. But, in practice, this will was itself often paralysed by divisions which the constitutional machinery could do nothing to eliminate. The Constitution of 1946 was, in theory, flexible and the amending process simple. In practice, it took four years to achieve some minor, mainly technical, reforms and there followed three years of deadlock during which agreement was not even reached regarding the amendment of the amending process itself. It is no coincidence that the longest-lived of France's Republican Constitutions was the shortest and most flexible, though not because its authors were more confident of the régime's capacity to survive but, on the contrary, because they were trying in advance to leave elbow room for the Monarchy that they hoped would replace it.

It is not only that Constitutions cannot guarantee to safeguard the future. There are also some ills for which Constitutions have no cure and among them are deep and bitter political divisions. For most of the life of the Fourth Republic a large number of both its electors and its Parliamentary representatives on the Right and on the Left were bitterly opposed both to each other and to the régime. The Communists, it is true, did not in theory object to the Constitution, but in practice they prevented it from working properly. And even the parties that were attached to the régime were often so divided that the Assembly and Governments were alike powerless to act. Among the problems that gave rise to these divisions, the inadequacies of the Constitution were probably the least important. If Parliaments had known where they wanted to go, they might well have been able to agree on the reforms needed to make the Constitution a more efficient instrument for getting them there. As it was, the problem of constitutional reform, which ought to have been merely a minor irritant, became a major time-waster and added one more to the list of unsolved and insoluble problems that finally killed the régime.

This was not, of course, the view of General de Gaulle. He had opposed the Constitution from the start, resigned from the premiership and retired from politics before it came into force. It was only natural that on his return to power 12 years later he should have refused to accept institutions that he had always considered deplorable. Besides, by that time, many Frenchmen, too, had come to treat the Constitution as the scapegoat for the failings of the Fourth Republic.

This is not to say that the majority of Frenchmen thought that the kind of Constitution that General de Gaulle had in mind would be an improvement. In the prolonged debate on constitutional reform that took place in Parliament and press from 1955 onwards, the proposed remedies had followed, in the main, more conventional lines. Comment on the provisions of the new Constitution from August to the referendum on the 28th September 1958 was largely hostile, only the Gaullists being wholeheartedly approving. Yet 79.25 per cent of the voters in metropolitan France, and an even higher proportion in Algeria and the Overseas Territories, voted YES. It is essential, therefore, to consider briefly the events which led to the end of the Fourth Republic and which persuaded so many Frenchmen to accept without question a Constitution whose most criticized provisions were out of harmony, if not in conflict with, the Republican traditions as expressed in the Constitutions of earlier Republics.

CHAPTER II

Prelude to the Fifth Republic

Though a crisis of the régime had been predicted for a long time, the event that finally sparked off the explosion in May 1958 did not at first appear to present an immediate danger to the régime. A demonstration by the European population of Algiers, intended to prevent the Government then in process of formation in Paris from contemplating any form of negotiation with the Algerian nationalists, was nothing new. There had been demonstrations with similar aims on 6th February 1956, when M. Mollet visited Algeria, and in March and April 1958. Nor could a riot, or even a revolution, in Algeria, have constituted by itself a threat to France. Algerians were dependent on the French army to protect them from terrorist attacks and the army was, in turn, dependent on France for its supplies. It was generally estimated that Algeria could have been starved into submission within a fortnight.

THE IMPORTANCE OF PUBLIC OPINION

At least four circumstances combined to turn the demonstration into a fortnight-long campaign for a Government headed by General de Gaulle – a campaign which ended in victory. The first was the absence on the part of public and politicians alike of any real will to defend the Fourth Republic. Disillusionment and cynicism had been growing since 1949, largely owing to persistent deadlock in the Assembly and to the consequent instability of Governments and their inability to take urgent and necessary decisions. Deadlock over the Indo-Chinese war and over E.D.C. had been followed by deadlock over Tunisia and Morocco. From 1955 onwards, there had been deadlock over both constitutional and electoral reform and over the future of Algeria, where a nationalist rebellion had broken out in the Aurès mountains at the end of 1954. By 1958, the rebellion showed no signs of being overcome, though it was by then costing between £1 and £2 million a day, keeping the bulk of the French army in Algeria, creating problems for France in N.A.T.O., in the United Nations and in her relations with Morocco and Tunisia. From September 1957 to April 1958, three Governments fell, directly or indirectly owing to North African problems, and primarily to the Algerian rebellion. The effect of all these deadlocks was to create a growing disrespect on the part of the public for Parliament and for politicians.

The predominant atmosphere in France was one of political apathy. In the ranks of the army and the higher Civil Service there was some positive opposition. The Minister of the Interior in M. Pflimlin's Government, M. Jules Moch, revealed later that, when faced on the 13th May with an insurrection in Algiers, followed by an insurrection in Corsica, planned and carried out by participants in the Algiers movement, the Government had discovered that it could no longer rely on the loyalty of a number of army leaders, of the police, and of civilian officials. Some of these rebellious elements were Gaullist, others were not. There were also some Gaullists among French Deputies, though it is generally admitted that, when the insurrection began, there was not sufficient active support in the French Parliament to enable General de Gaulle to be voted into power constitutionally. The majority of the civilian population, both inside and outside Parliament, was certainly neither Gaullist nor anti-Republican. But neither politicians nor public showed any sign of readiness to die on the barricades for the French Republic. M. Mollet is said to have remarked during the crisis:

> There is talk of firing our last shots, but we have not yet fired our first.[1]

Those first shots never were fired.

There are a number of possible explanations of this state of affairs. Economic prosperity had helped to increase political apathy; even if large sections of the army had been loyal to the régime, to add a war in France to the existing war in Algeria would have been militarily risky and psychologically difficult; there was no real

[1] Quoted on p. 312 of *Les 13 Complots du 13 Mai*, by Merry and Serge Bromberger. (Paris, Arthème Fayard, 1959.)

political leadership, no faith in the success of resistance and no agreement on how to set about it; the facts of the situation were confused and most people (including members of Parliament) had little real knowledge of what was happening. All this adds up to one conclusion. There may be doubts regarding the real strength of the movement that threatened France with a *coup d'état*. There can be none regarding the real weakness of the Republican will to resist. As more than one commentator pointed out, the Republic was not murdered; it committed suicide.[1]

THE IMPORTANCE OF THE 13TH MAY

The circumstance which helped to make General de Gaulle's return possible was the transformation of the Algiers demonstration into a movement in which settlers and army leaders in Algeria combined to demand a Government of Public Safety, headed by General de Gaulle – a movement which, as time went on, won growing support in France.

This was the work of the different 'plotters' – 'Colonels' or civilians – about whom so much has since been written. Whether there were, in reality, '13 plots of the 13th May' is unimportant. There were certainly three distinct attitudes, which had to be focused on General de Gaulle if the insurrection was to succeed.

The interest of the extreme right-wing settlers – the 'ultras' – was concentrated on Algieria, on the need for Algeria to remain French. They were determined to prevent Algeria from going the way of Morocco and Tunisia and becoming an independent State. The European minority would then have to choose between leaving the country, which was impossible for the majority, made up of small tradesmen or officials, and becoming citizens of a backward Moslem country. The settlers were not Gaullist and had not even been Gaullist during the war, when General de Gaulle's provisional Government had its headquarters in Algiers.

The aims of the army – or more accurately of those of its leaders and officers who were opposed to the policies of Governments of the Fourth Republic, a small number of whom were also involved in

[1] *v.* for instance, Sirius, *Le suicide de la IV*[e] *République* (Editions du Cerf, 1958) and Jean Ferniot, *Les Ides de mai* (Plon, 1958), p. 1, 'The Fourth Republic . . . died alone, with no friends at the bedside'

more or less subversive organizations – were much more complex They shared the opposition of the 'ultras' to negotiation with the Moslem nationalists, though for different reasons. After so many humiliations in Indo-China, Morocco and Tunisia, army leaders wanted a victory. Many of the junior officers who had been responsible for the protection of the Moslem population from terrorist attacks had also come to the conclusion that military victory alone would not be enough to keep Algeria permanently bound to France. They believed in an extensive programme of economic and social reform in order to raise the standard of living of the Moslems and to make them 'first-class' Frenchmen (*des Français à part entière*). This was the policy known as 'integration'.[1] Although the settler population had for years resisted strenuously attempts to give the Moslem population something nearer to real equality, they accepted this programme in May 1958, partly as the necessary price of army support, without which the insurrection must necessarily fail, and partly because they would fear equality less in an Algeria administered as if it were part of metropolitan France. It is also true, as became evident later, that, for some of the settler organizations, the acceptance of 'integration' was a temporary expedient, and that, once their primary aim of *l'Algérie française* had become accepted French policy, the implications of 'integration' could be reconsidered.

Some of the army leaders, who, as part of their task of protecting the Moslem population, had been carrying out a whole series of administrative functions, had come to the conclusion that the best solution for Algeria would be for the army to rule. They were contemptuous of the quarrels of French Parliaments and the vacillations of French Governments, which, as they saw it, had already cost France most of her former Empire and were now threatening the loss of Algeria. They resented being called on to fight a war in conditions which seemed to them to prevent a military victory and, at the same time, to undermine the army's efforts to win over the

[1] The objective of integration has been defined as: 'the indissoluble union of former colonial peoples and the former mother country within a single political entity, with the aim of establishing equality of rights and duties, and, in the long run, an equalization of the standard of living'. (P. F. Gonidec, *Droit d'Outre-Mer*, Paris, Editions Montchrestien, 1959, p. 331.) If the real aims of the 'ultras' were to be judged by their actions over the previous ten years, it was evident that where the equalization of the standard of living was concerned, 'the long term' was likely to be very long indeed.

civilian population. In particular, they rejected even the suggestion of possible negotiations with the rebels, partly because of their determination not to be cheated of a military victory, but partly because they regarded negotiations as a betrayal of the loyal Moslem population. This last opinion was especially strong among young Captains in the S.A.S. (*Sections administratives spéciales*) who had been working and living with Moslems in the villages, acting as teachers, doctors, magistrates, engineers and administrators. Their argument was a simple one. Negotiations meant victory for the rebels. That would mean torture and death for Moslems who had been co-operating with the French and who had relied on the French army to protect them. It could not be expected, therefore, that Moslems would continue to trust the French, if there were to be talk of negotiations. The war was psychologically lost in advance if the French were not determined to win it. And if civilian Governments were not capable of this determination, then it was for the army to replace them.

This view was not characteristic of the army as a whole. Indeed, there is no such entity as 'the army'. In a country such as France, in which military service is traditional, the army is a cross-section of the nation. In 1958, it was a service apart from the nation, for many of its regular officers had been engaged overseas since the end of the war, and it was among the regular *cadres* that most of the subversive elements were to be found. But there was no unanimity. The army, too, has its Republican traditions, among which that of *la grande muette* – the view that the army's function is to leave politics to the civilians – is still strong. Probably only a small minority wanted power for the army; the rest wanted power, instead of weakness, to be the attribute of the French State. Some held that only a Government headed by General de Gaulle could guarantee this.

Army leaders and 'ultras', then, were agreed that French victory in Algeria was essential and that French Governments were too weak and divided to guarantee it. They were not agreed on the kind of Government that *was* needed in France, nor on the methods by which a change of Government could be achieved.

The third element in the revolution of 13th May was made up of what are generally called 'Gaullists'. They were in agreement with the two objectives of military victory and the retention of

Algeria as part of France and, in addition, convinced that only a French Government headed by General de Gaulle could be relied on to achieve them. Some believed also in 'integration'; others believed it to be a totally unrealistic and Utopian dream, both psychologically and economically impossible, but constituting, nevertheless, an invaluable instrument of propaganda, capable of rallying European and Moslem Algerians, together with the army, to support for General de Gaulle. They proved to be right – or, perhaps more accurately, the efforts of a number of able politicians were successful in turning it into such an instrument.

The important point is that this third element regarded Algeria as a means rather than an end. The aim of the Gaullist conspirators – for there was a conspiracy, indeed several, involving a number of Gaullist politicians and army officers – was to change the system of government in France. But beyond the aim of getting rid of the Fourth Republic and securing General de Gaulle's return to power, there was no unity between different personalities and movements. Some supporters of the revolution of 13th May were frankly Fascists, in the tradition of the early '30's; some were nearer to the reactionary conservatism of the Algerian 'ultras' or of M. Poujade; some were, or claimed to be, socially progressive; some were pinning their faith to new institutions, others to the leadership of General de Gaulle; some were concentrating on methods, on the first step, which was the success of the Revolution, and leaving the rest for later consideration; some were conspirators, active plotters, others disillusioned Republicans or former resisters with a nostalgic hangover from the years of underground fighting; some were idealistic Gaullists, others hard-headed politicians.

During the fortnight from 13th May to 1st June, these different currents of opinion were concentrated on achieving two things: a new Government, headed by General de Gaulle (it being assumed by those who were determined that Algeria should remain French that General de Gaulle shared their views); and the acceptance by such a Government of the policy of 'integration', in order to win over Moslem opinion to France. This result was achieved partly thanks to preparatory work carried out for some months by French politicians in Algeria, in particular by M. Delbecque, then a member of the *cabinet* of the Minister of Defence, M. Chaban-Delmas, who was himself a Gaullist; partly thanks to spectacular demonstrations of 'Franco-Moslem fraternization', which convinced a number of sceptics regarding the possibility of *l'Algérie française* that 'integration' might after all be a practical policy; partly by threats of an imminent military *coup d'état* in France and by an actual landing in Corsica, both of which convinced many people of the reality of disaffection in the army and the Civil Service; and partly by the oratorical gifts of M. Soustelle, a Gaullist Deputy and a former Governor-General of Algeria, extremely popular with the Algiers population, who landed in Algiers on 17th May, having evaded a police guard on his house in Paris.

The degree of unity between all these different tendencies, whether in France or in Algeria, was limited to the two objectives already mentioned. Each had its own conception of what General de Gaulle would, or ought to, do. None knew for certain the conditions on which he would agree even to assume power.

THE IMPORTANCE OF GENERAL DE GAULLE

General de Gaulle emerged from his retirement to make three public statements during the crisis. The first, on 15th May, expressed his readiness 'to assume the powers of the Republic'; the second, on 19th May, was a press conference at which he stated that he would do so only by legal means; the third, on 27th May, stated that he had 'set in motion the regular procedure necessary for the establishment of a Republican Government capable of ensuring the unity and independence of the country'.

The effect of these statements was to encourage support for him both in the army and in the French Parliament. The former felt that he agreed with the army's point of view (he had explicitly praised the army's work in Algeria at the press conference, while making no reference to the landing in Corsica, which was, of course, a *coup d'état*) and that victory was at hand. Parliamentarians were reassured regarding his intention to respect Republican legality. On the issue that above all divided the country nothing was said at all, which enabled Frenchmen, from Socialists to extreme Right, to come to quite contradictory conclusions regarding his policy for Algeria. General de Gaulle was really given a blank cheque on Algeria, though he had not been intended to have one, for once he had come to power, those who found that their assumptions were incorrect had to put up with the situation, at least for a time. Revolutions cannot be made every month.

THE IMPORTANCE OF PARLIAMENT

The last obstacle, the *investiture* of General de Gaulle as Prime Minister, was the most formidable. Three things helped to overcome it: a message to both Houses of Parliament by the President of the Republic, threatening to resign if General de Gaulle's candidature to the Premiership was not accepted; concessions by Parliament and concessions by General de Gaulle.

General de Gaulle's readiness to 'assume the powers of the Republic' was conditional on the grant of special powers to govern by decree for six months, during which period his Government was to draw up a new Constitution to be approved by a referendum. Parliament was to go into recess ('the session could not constitutionally be closed as it had not lasted for the seven months required by Article 9). Parliament was, of course, free to accept or reject both his *investiture* and these conditions. The difficulty, from General de Gaulle's point of view, was to prevent Deputies from debating and seeking to amend them, as he had no intention of becoming involved in the political bargaining normally characteristic of both *investiture* and legislation. On the other hand, *investiture* by the, National Assembly, the revision of Article 90 of the Constitution, governing the amending process (the procedure that had been envisaged by General de Gaulle was not in accordance with that laid down in the Constitution), and the passage of a law granting the special powers were the only legal and constitutional ways by which his conditions could be met.

What happened was that, after a brief declaration by General de Gaulle, the *investiture* debate took place in his absence, though he was present during the debate on the Bill to revise Article 90 of the Constitution. Parliament agreed to vote the Bill without amendment, and General de Gaulle's Government undertook, in drawing up the Constitution, to respect five basic conditions: the principle of universal suffrage, the responsibility of the Government to Parliament, the separation of legislative and executive power, the independence of the judiciary, and provision for the possibility of 'organizing the relations between the Republic and the associated peoples'. General de Gaulle also gave further reassurances to the Assembly in person, in particular that, in the new Constitution, the offices of President and Prime Minister would remain distinct.

All the same, the investiture vote was not obtained easily. Nor do these concessions in themselves explain why so many Deputies on the non-Communist Left voted for General de Gaulle on 1st June and why they advised their supporters to vote for the Constitution on 28th September. Most parties except the Communists were divided and the Socialist Parliamentary group debated for a whole day before deciding, by 77 votes to 74,[1] to support General de Gaulle's *investiture*. Even this narrow margin was achieved only after a visit to Colombey-les-deux-Eglises by M. Mollet, M. Auriol and the leader of the Socialist group in the Assembly, M. Deixonne. The *Mendésiste* section of the Radicals and the U.D.S.R. leader, M. Mitterand remained opposed, as did, of course, the Communist party. In the end, though 329 Deputies voted for General de Gaulle, 229 voted against, including 49 of the 96 Socialist Deputies.

The later decision of the majority of the non-Communist Left (Socialists, Radicals and M.R.P.) to vote for the new Constitution was governed by three factors, none of which was really relevant to the merits or demerits of the Constitution. The first was the fear of a military dictatorship. This argument was put forcibly during the referendum campaign by a number of leaders, from M. Reynaud on the Right to M. Mollet on the Left – the choice was '*de Gaulle ou les paras*'. For some this fear was twofold. It was that a military dictatorship would be merely a first stage, leading to a Popular Front. Those who opposed this argument, in particular M. Mendès-France, objected to a vote which they held to be 'under duress'. M. Mendès-France argued later[2] that General de Gaulle, instead of constituting a protection against a military dictatorship was in danger of becoming, against his will, the prisoner of the forces that wanted one. The weakness of the opposition was that it was small, divided, leaderless and without any concerted policy or plan of campaign.

The second factor was the conviction in the minds of many

[1] These figures include the Socialist Senators. Of the Deputies, 51 voted against and only 44 for.

[2] *v.* for instance, his lecture at Chatham House on 25 February 1959, reported in *International Affairs*, July 1959.

Frenchmen that General de Gaulle alone in France had sufficient prestige to be able to achieve some solution of the Algerian problem and to restore the authority of the State over the dissident elements in the army and the public service. Some trusted him to find *a* solution, whatever it might be; others to find a progressive solution; others to win the war and maintain *l'Algérie française*.

The third factor was the conviction that General de Gaulle had progressive views regarding the evolution of the Overseas Territories. This opinion was, perhaps, more than anything else responsible for the decision of the majority of the Socialist party to support the Constitution. It was indubitably decisive in the territories themselves. In July, a number of political leaders in the Overseas Territories had openly expressed their disappointment that the first draft of the Constitution had included no recognition of their right to independence. A Congress of the *Parti du Regroupement Africain* had passed a resolution in favour of immediate independence. General de Gaulle's promise that France would not prevent any Territory from seceding, and the provision in the definitive text of possibilities of evolution, not excluding independence, decided the leaders of all but one Territory to vote in favour of the Constitution.

In all these arguments, the actual content of the Constitution was, more often than not, left out of account altogether. This is not to say that there was no discussion of the Constitution itself. On the contrary, press and periodicals in France were full of comment; political parties discussed its weaknesses; political scientists analysed it. In general, as has been said, opinion was unfavourable, with the exception, naturally, of Gaullist opinion. But there is no doubt that the referendum of the 28th September 1958 was not, in reality, a vote for a Constitution, but a vote for General de Gaulle. The Constitution was, for most of those who thought about it at all, merely part of the price that had to be paid for his continued presence at the head of affairs.

All these happenings and conflicts of opinion help to explain why, once again, Frenchmen were divided from the start in their attitudes towards a new régime. Their attitudes towards the Constitution were coloured by their reactions to the revolution that brought it into being. The second President of the Fourth Republic, M. Coty, described it as 'a necessary and a constructive revolution', as one that was 'effected in calm, and in respect for the very laws that had to be reformed'. This was true of the actual transition from the Fourth to the Fifth Republic. But the real revolution was by then over. Even though it was a bloodless one, even though it led to decisions that were taken in accordance with all the constitutional and Parliamentary rules, and were ratified by the massive approval of the nation, it remained for many Frenchmen, by no means all on the Left, a revolution whose leaders were seeking to impose their will, in defiance of the Republican authorities. For a small minority on the Left the new régime represented a setback in the permanent battle for the victory of the Republican tradition; for some, it represented what they hoped would be a temporary emergency; for others it represented an experiment in a Republican tradition different from that of the Fourth Republic.

CHAPTER III

The Nature of the Constitution

The Constitution of the Fifth Republic has been described as 'tailor-made for General de Gaulle', 'quasi-Monarchical,'[1] quasi-Presidential, a Parliamentary Empire, unworkable, 'the worst-drafted in French constitutional history',[2] and ephemeral, to mention only a few of the French verdicts on it, almost all of which have been unflattering.

It is, in fact, a Constitution whose general characteristics are difficult to summarize, partly because the constitutional text is, more than most, an incomplete description of the system of government, partly because it is difficult to situate the Constitution politically in relation to its immediate predecessors. There has been a tendency on the part of writers, therefore, to single out one or more of its characteristics and label it accordingly – as Monarchist, Orléanist, Republican or Presidential. The truth is that it is a hybrid, an attempt to combine two constitutional principles, the possibility of whose peaceful co-existence has yet to be proved after several years of experience.

UNCERTAINTY AND CONFUSION

Since all Constitutions are necessarily modified in practice, it is always unrealistic to base deductions about the nature of a régime

[1] *v.* for instance, M. Duverger's description of it as *Orléaniste* in *Revue française de Science Politique*, March 1959, and in *La Ve République* (Presses Universitaires de France, 1959).

[2] Quoted by R. Capitant in the preface to L. Hamon's *De Gaulle dans la République* (Plon, 1958).

solely on the provisions of written texts, though it is useful to study them as a help to understanding what the leaders of a new régime are trying to do. The Fifth Republic has made this task very difficult by omitting from the text of the Constitution of the 4th October provisions for a number of extremely important institutions. The electoral laws, for instance, the institutions of the Community, the composition and some of the rules of functioning of the two Houses of Parliament, the organization of the Judiciary, the functions of a number of organs such as the Economic and Social Council, the Higher Council of the Judiciary, as well as a number of other matters, are dealt with in a series of Ordinances, promulgated in no logical order, between October 1958 and February 1959. Some of these have the status of organic laws; in other words, a special legislative procedure is required to revise them; others are ordinary laws. Some deal with relatively trivial detail; others with questions of major importance. Some, in particular the Ordinances providing for the institutions of the Community, were completed by Presidential '*décisions*', appearing from time to time in the *Journal Officiel*.

This is, then, to begin with, an untidy Constitution. It is also one which is in some places vague, and in others ambiguous. The difficulty of deciding the precise meaning of a number of articles is increased by the circumstances in which the Constitution was drawn up. That of the Fourth Republic was debated in Parliament for months, so that the precise shade of meaning given to this or that word, or article, by politicians of different parties was in no doubt and could be quoted later if difficulties of interpretation arose. The drafting of the Constitution of the Fifth Republic was the responsibility, not of Parliament but of the Government, and was done in private. A small Ministerial Committee presided over by General de Gaulle drew up a first draft which was approved by the Cabinet and then submitted to a Consultative Committee, mainly composed of Members of Parliament, and to the *Conseil d'Etat*, before being finally approved by the Cabinet. Interpretations have had to be based on the original text, together with the text as amended by the Consultative Committee, and the final text, together with reports of verbal explanations of some articles given in private session by General de Gaulle. Evidence as to the intentions of the authors on some points was provided by the publication, in

1960, of some of the '*Travaux préparatoires*'.[1] Such evidence is normally important, since it is regarded in France (and indeed generally by continental jurisprudence) as a legitimate aid to the interpretation of legal provisions, whereas British practice is to look no farther than the text of the law. In this case, the evidence was unhelpful, for either the Government ignored it and adopted its own interpretation or, where an issue was submitted to the Constitutional Council, this body, which is not a judicial organ, was free to adopt its own criteria of interpretation, since its decisions are subject to no appeal.

There is, too, an additional difficulty in describing the institutions of the Fifth Republic. Some changes of régime have been much more wholesale than others. The Constitutions of both the Third and Fourth Republics left the administrative and judicial organization of the country untouched. Indeed, local government organization has changed very little during the present century and it is often said that the general framework of French administration remains today much as it was under Napoleon. The Fifth Republic set out to have a thorough spring-cleaning. Under the special powers conferred on the Government, first by Parliament and then by Article 92 of the Constitution, over 300 Ordinances were promulgated between June 1958 and February 1959. Some of them dealt with purely administrative matters, such as the reorganization of the Paris markets, or of the medical service. Others provided for profound changes, some of them long overdue. The reorganization of national defence and of the Law Courts, the reform of criminal procedure, Local Government reforms, including modifications of the system of municipal elections, administrative changes affecting the status of Civil Servants and of the radio – all these, as they are applied, have modified and will modify considerably the administrative and judicial framework in which the Constitution is applied. Some have come or will come into effect only slowly; some may never be applied at all.

[1] *Avis et Débats du Comité Consultatif Constitutional.* (Paris, Documentation française, 1960.) Nothing has been published on the Ministerial discussions, or on the opinions of the *Conseil d'Etat.*

REPUBLICAN AND PRESIDENTIAL CHARACTERISTICS

It has already been said that the Constitution is the expression of two very different, and probably conflicting, principles. The first is the principle of Republican Parliamentary government. The Constitution is in many ways a reaction against certain habits and institutions of the Fourth Republic, in particular those which are associated with what has been called in an earlier chapter the left-wing Republican tradition. But it is nevertheless an indubitably Republican Constitution and, in accordance with the undertaking given by General de Gaulle's Government on taking office, it provides for a democratic and Parliamentary system of government. The head of the State and the head of the Government remain in theory distinct. The Prime Minister appoints and dismisses his colleagues and is responsible to Parliament (in practice to the National Assembly only). The two Houses of Parliament are democratically elected. The judiciary is independent. The organization and activities of the political parties remain unaffected, as do the fundamental liberties of the citizen.

The Constitution does seek, however, to reverse the tendency towards *gouvernement d'assemblée*, characteristic of the Fourth Republic, and indeed, deliberately encouraged by certain of the innovations of the Constitution of the Fourth Republic. Thus, the Senate's legislative powers are co-ordinate with those of the Assembly, except where the Government decides to give the Assembly the last word; Prime Ministers have both procedural and constitutional means of dominating the Assembly; and Parliament's role is both quantitatively and qualitatively diminished. Under the Fourth Republic, the Assembly was really in charge of legislation, the Government being obliged as a general rule to fight as best it could, for its Bills or its life, with the vote of confidence as almost its sole weapon.[1] Under the Fifth Republic, the Government is in charge of legislation, and even effective criticism by Parliament is difficult, unless the National Assembly is prepared to go to the length of defeating the Government.

These changes need not have implied any fundamental break with

[1] Prime Ministers of the Fourth Republic could dissolve the Assembly only in certain carefully defined circumstances, which in practice arose only once, in 1955.

Republican tradition. They represent a reaction towards more right-wing tendencies than those that were mainly responsible for the 1946 Constitution. Some changes in Parliamentary procedure were also acceptable to elements on the Left, and had actually been included in proposals for constitutional revision put forward in 1958. They are evidence of a desire on the part of some Parliamentarians, and in particular on the part of those who had held office under the Fourth Republic, to ensure more Governmental stability than the Parliamentary system had provided under either the Third or the Fourth Republic. They are evidence, too, of a Gaullist effort to achieve Governmental stability by laying down strict constitutional rules. It may be doubted whether constitutional or procedural rules can ever be an effective substitute for the unwritten agreement between Government and Opposition regarding the rules of the Parliamentary game, which is the real safeguard of Governmental stability and which, even more than the two-party system, explains the success of the British system. But that this was the intention of the authors of the Constitution is quite clear.[1]

One change, however, though not necessarily incompatible with Parliamentary government, is in conflict with the Republican tradition, as it has been described in earlier pages. The 1958 Constitution reverses the traditional relationship between the legislative and the rule-making authorities. Hitherto, though Parliament has always been free to delegate legislative powers to the Government, these have been 'special' powers, granted, and withdrawn, at the will of Parliament. The principle of the legislative supremacy of Parliament has remained intact. Henceforth, power to legislate is defined limitatively by the Constitution and, outside these limits, powers belong to the rule-making authority, that is to the Government.

The second principle, which might be described as that of personal leadership, is more than an innovation in French Republican Constitutions. It is a break with Republican tradition which led some Frenchmen to fear that this Constitution would be misused in order to install some form of personal rule. A number of its provisions justify the description of being 'tailor-made for General de

[1] *v.* for instance, on this, M. Debré's speech to the *Conseil d'Etat on* 27th August 1958. (*Revue française de Science Politique,* March, 1959, pp. 7–29.)

Gaulle' in at least three ways. General de Gaulle was himself largely responsible for their inclusion. His interpretation of their meaning will undoubtedly prevail, as long as he holds office. And the events described in the preceding chapter led both democrats and anti-democrats, Republicans and anti-Republicans, to agree to their inclusion, with the essential difference that, in the minds of those faithful to Republican tradition, they were justified only by the emergency. They trusted General de Gaulle, as they would have trusted no one else, not to misuse them, and all the more so after the election to the Assembly of some 200 U.N.R. Deputies of whose political instincts they were profoundly suspicious. Since the emergency powers were conferred not only on General de Gaulle but also on any future President, they were anxious, however, lest at some time in the future, a President less scrupulous than General de Gaulle was believed to be might interpret and use these powers for quite different ends.

The powers in question were first defended by General de Gaulle in 1946, in a speech at Bayeux. He then argued, first, that the head of the State should be a representative of the nation rather than of Parliament (that is, elected by a college larger than that consisting of the two Houses of Parliament) and that his functions should be those, not of an impartial figurehead, which is what Presidents of the Third and Fourth Republics usually were, but of a representative of the continuity of the State – an 'arbitrator' (*un arbitre*) 'above the accidents of political life'. As an arbitrator, he should, in normal circumstances, stand aloof from and above parties, and yet, at the same time, advise and guide Governments. Exactly how he could combine these two functions, the God-like and the human, was not clear, but General de Gaulle was certainly the only man whom democratic Republicans would have trusted to try.

This principle of a President whose role is positive – who, though he does not govern, does more than reign – was expressed in the 1958 Constitution by means of a division of executive power between President and Prime Minister that was not precisely defined. The President's function as an 'arbitrator' could, in normal circumstances, be primarily that of an adviser of the Government. His real importance in the State, therefore, became an imponderable, a resultant of the impact on each other of the respective personalities of President and Prime Minister and of political circumstances on both.

The nature of this impact during the first years of the Fifth Republic is discussed later.[1] All that needs to be noted here is the element of both confusion and uncertainty that this partial duality of the executive introduced. A President *may* remain in the background, as previous Presidents have done, using his new powers – the right to negotiate treaties, to dissolve the Assembly, to send messages to Parliament – in accordance with precedents, or on the advice of the Prime Minister. On the other hand, he may, as President de Gaulle has done, interpret these rights, or certain of them, in such a way as to lead him to govern, instead of reigning, in fields where responsibility for policy belongs constitutionally to the Prime Minister.

In one field in particular, the danger of conflict seemed at first, very great. In his capacity as *ex-officio* President of the Community, the President of the Republic was given explicit and extensive powers of decision in a body – the Executive Council of the Community – in which the Prime Minister of France was represented ostensibly on the same footing as the Prime Ministers of the 12 other member-States. The various organic laws and decrees governing the organization of the Community were silent on the methods by which the policy of France (directed by the Prime Minister) and that of the Community (influenced, if not directed, by the President of the Community) could be harmonized, and the risk of Presidential split-personality avoided. As it turned out, even if conflict had not been prevented by the Prime Minister's unwavering loyalty to the President, it was soon to be eliminated by the rapid transformation of the Community into an association of sovereign States.

The Presidential functions mentioned up to now are exercised in normal circumstances. In times of national crisis, the President becomes even more important. In a grave national emergency, the head of the State should, in General de Gaulle's view, assume full powers.

> It must be his duty, if it should happen that the country fall into danger, to be the protector (*le garant*) of national independence, and of the treaties concluded by France.

The 1958 Constitution did more than give the President the right to

[1] *v. infra*, pp. 125-7 and 136-46.

exercise such powers. It also made him both judge and jury, since he alone is constitutionally empowered to decide when such circumstances exist, and what measures are to be taken to restore normality.

Presidential powers in an emergency as defined by article 16 of the Constitution and the problems that the vague and obscure wording of the article were to create were responsible, in 1961, for acute divergencies of opinion between the President and a majority of the Deputies during the five months of emergency rule that followed the April insurrection in Algeria. These helped to intensify the doubts that had already existed in the minds of many Frenchmen in 1958 regarding the possibility of an effective combination between Parliamentary government as most French politicians understand it and Presidential leadership as General de Gaulle understands it.

THE INCOMPATIBILITY RULE

The third important innovation in the 1958 Constitution is certainly in conformity with General de Gaulle's views. It is the separation of legislative and executive powers, including the rule making Ministerial office incompatible with membership of Parliament. As expressed in 1946 and since, General de Gaulle's argument is that:

> It goes without saying that executive power should not emanate from Parliament – a Parliament which should be bi-cameral and should exercise legislative power – or the result will be a confusion of powers which will reduce the Government to a mere conglomeration of delegations. . . . The unity, cohesion and internal discipline of the French Government must he held sacred, if national leadership is not to degenerate rapidly into incompetence and impotence.
>
> But how, in the long run, can this unity, this cohesion and this discipline be maintained if executive power is the emanation of the very power that it ought to counter-balance, and if each member of a Government that is collectively responsible to the representatives of the whole nation conducts himself, in his Ministerial post, as the delegate of a party?

To British minds, this argument is unconvincing and unrealistic. And it must be added that it also fails to convince large sections of

French opinion. But on this issue there is no clear-cut division of opinion between orthodox Republicans and supporters of a Presidential, or quasi-Presidential system. Though French Republican Constitutions have always rejected both the right of the judiciary to intervene in disputes between the citizen and the administration and also judicial review of the constitutionality of legislation, there has never been the same degree of unanimity regarding the separation of executive and legislative functions.

Governments of both the Third and Fourth Republics were normally made up of members of Parliament. But it was not unusual for a Government to include Ministers who were not. Indeed Léon Blum's Government in 1936 included three women Under-Secretaries, though women were not then eligible for membership of either House. War-time and post-war Governments included non-Parliamentary 'technicians' from time to time. Since French Ministers are, by virtue of their office, entitled to attend and speak in either House (though not, of course, to vote, except in the House of which they are members) these exceptions did not create the kind of difficulty which arises in England when a Minister holding important office is not a member of the House of Commons. Some previous French Constitutions, however, have made Governmental office incompatible with membership of Parliament.[1] And during the discussions on the Constitution that preceded the 1958 Referendum, the majority of the Socialist Parliamentary group and also of the party's *comité directeur* expressed their approval of the incompatibility rule.

On the other hand, there was opposition to it on both the Right and the Left. The Consultative Constitutional Committee, for instance, suggested an amendment to the rules, as formulated in the Government's draft Constitution, which, in effect, constituted a repudiation of the principle.[2]

[1] *v.* for example, 1791 (*Titre* III, Chapter 1, Section III, articles 3 and 4), 1793 (Girondine) (*Titre* III, Section III, article 25), 1795, (articles 47 and 136).

[2] The amendment proposed (*a*) that (in conformity with traditional practice) Ministers should be chosen either from inside or outside Parliament; and (*b*) that during their period of office they should cease to be members of political parties, should engage in no party-political activities and should be suspended from membership of Parliament. Unless the intention was to sabotage the incompatibility rule, this seems a pointless gesture. In virtually all cases Ministers' political opinions would be known and their eventual return to party politics taken for granted.

OTHER CLAIMS TO ORIGINALITY

(*a*) **Parties.** In addition to its quasi-Presidential aspects, the 1958 Constitution includes at least three innovations justifying its description as being in a category of its own – *hors série*. The first is its explicit recognition (in article 4) of the role of political parties. For the first time, a Republican Constitution not merely mentions parties, but acknowledges them as a normal constituent of political life. During his 12 years in the political wilderness, General de Gaulle's public utterances usually included attacks on them. Under the Fifth Republic, the formation of parties and their freedom of action are constitutionalized, on one condition. They are required 'to respect the principles of national sovereignty and democracy'. This article is generally assumed to be intended less to encourage the formation of democratic parties than to make it possible for the Communist party, whose loyalty to France and respect for democracy are not generally apparent, to be banned, should necessity arise.[1] But whatever the ulterior motives, the article does, at least implicitly, make legal imposition of one-party government unconstitutional and, explicitly, make respect for democracy a constitutional requirement.

(*b*) **The Constitutional Council.** Though the 1958 Constitution does not provide for anything that could be described as judicial review, it does create a body which, within certain specific and narrowly defined limits, has the function of deciding on the constitutionality of Governmental or Parliamentary acts. The Constitutional Council replaces the Constitutional Committee of the 1946 Constitution. This had the very restricted function of pronouncing on the constitutionality of any Bill challenged conjointly, on that ground, by a majority of the Senate and the President of the Republic. It was called on to act only once, and then on a relatively minor technical matter.

The Constitutional Council's role is more important. It has four distinct functions. First, it supervises the regularity of the elections of the President of the Republic and of referenda, announces the results, is responsible for declaring the Presidency vacant if for any

[1] In fact, the Government was able to ban the Communist party altogether in 1939, and in Algeria throughout the rebellion, without the aid of such an article. Its value, other than as a declaration of principle, is therefore problematical.

cause the President cannot carry out his duties, and decides cases in which the regularity of Parliamentary elections is contested. Second, it *must* be consulted on the conformity with the Constitution of organic laws and the Standing Orders of both Houses. The Council merely pronounces on the question of constitutionality, leaving the Government or Parliament, as the case may be, to take the appropriate steps to regularize the situation. Its decision is final. Third, it acts as an advisory body to the President if he is contemplating the assumption of emergency powers. It *must* be consulted by him regarding both the existence of such an emergency (on which its opinion, with reasons, must be published) and the measures that he proposes to take to deal with it. But the President is not constitutionally obliged to accept its advice. Fourth, the Council's ruling *may* be sought by the President, the Prime Minister, or the President of either House as to the conformity with the Constitution of an international agreement or a law about to be promulgated (other than an organic law, on which it *must* be consulted) and on certain conflicts which may arise between the Government and Parliament regarding the delimitation of executive and legislative competence.

The Council has no general responsibility for ensuring respect for the Constitution. It can express its opinion only if consulted on the matters enumerated above and on the initiative of the persons mentioned. It has no power to enforce its decisions. If President, Government and Parliament were to agree to refrain from consulting the Council on a matter where consultation is optional, then there is no means by which the Council could make its views known. The citizen cannot appeal to it nor can any Courts of Law. It is not, therefore, in any sense comparable to the Supreme Court of the United States.

Nevertheless, on matters on which it must be, or is, in fact, consulted, the Council can have and has had great influence in determining the interpretation to be placed on a number of provisions of the Constitution.[1]

[1] *v.* pp. 115, 152, on the Council's decisions. The Council has nine members, appointed in equal numbers by the President of the Republic, the President of the Senate and the President of the Assembly. Councillors sit for nine years and are not eligible for a second term. Former Presidents of the Republic are members *ex officio*. The President of the Republic appoints the President of the Council from among its members. The President does not require a counter-signature in making these appointments.

(*c*) **The Community.** The concept of the Community, its organization and its evolution, are discussed in more detail in a later chapter. It is perhaps relevant, however, at this stage, to emphasize the fact that the 1958 Constitution is the first one in French history to abandon explicitly (except in the case of the four Overseas *départements* and five – later six – small Overseas Territories) the assimilationist principle that has dominated French thinking in this field since the Revolution. It opened the way to a relationship between Madagascar and the African Territories on the one hand, and the French Republic (including, at that time, Algeria, the Sahara and the Overseas *départements* and Territories) on the other, which was intended to be something between a Federation and a Commonwealth: a relationship which the Constitution declared to be susceptible of further evolution, not excluding independence for any member, on terms negotiated with France. The word 'independent' was used for the first time in a French Constitution with reference to the organization of former overseas dependencies.

The originality of these provisions did not lie merely in the proposal for some kind of federal relationship – an objective which was already that of General de Gaulle in 1946. Speaking of the coming (1946) Constitution, he said, in his Bayeux speech:

> The future of the 110 million men and women under our flag lies in a federal form of organization that time will determine little by little, but whose beginning must be recognized and whose development must be provided for in our new Constitution.

It lay also in the methods provided for in the 1958 Constitution for implementing the promise of evolution. By 1956, the evolution of the Overseas Territories had gone beyond anything contemplated or even authorized ten years earlier, on a strict reading of the Constitution. In the view of some Frenchmen, the 'outline-law' of 1956 could be regarded as constitutional only by a somewhat generous interpretation of the provisions of Title VIII of the Constitution and any further evolution was impossible without a revision of this section, which governed the organization of the Overseas Territories. The 1958 Constitution specifically laid down that any future change of status of the member States of the Community, even one involving the grant of independence, could be made without the need to revise the Constitution.[1] It may well be that the retention by the President of important powers of decision in the organs of the Community reflected, as well as his confidence in his own ability to adapt to the rapidly evolving situation in Africa, his determination not to allow reforms granted on paper to be sabotaged in practice by administrative or political conservatism, as has so frequently happened in the course of French colonial history and in the history of Franco-Algerian relations.

ADVISORY AND JUDICIAL ORGANS

Of the two advisory bodies set up under the 1946 Constitution, the Assembly of the Union and the Economic Council, only the latter survives, under the title of the Economic and Social Council. Both its composition and its functions are somewhat changed.[2] Its field of advice is now restricted to matters on which it is consulted by the Government, except for any suggestions it may make regarding either social and economic reforms necessitated by technical changes, or the Republic's contribution to the economic and social development of the Community. Under the Fourth Republic, it was free to study and report on any matters within its field of competence and could be consulted by the Assembly as well as by the Government. Its sessions are no longer public and much of its work is done in technical sections, to which outside specialists are co-opted. These changes indicate that, under the Fifth Republic, the Council is primarily a technical adviser. Under the Fourth Republic, its debates were often influenced by political considerations and it often divided along orthodox political lines.

[1] *v. infra*, pp. 162-3.

[2] The law of 30th December 1958 gives it 205 members, chosen for five years by appropriate professional organizations or by the Government, to represent the following interests and areas:

45, manual and black-coated workers,
41, private and nationalized industry and commercial concerns,
40, agriculture,
20, Algeria and the Sahara,
10, the Overseas *départements*,
10, economic and social interests Overseas,
15, various economic, social and cultural interests,
15, various social activities, including housing, co-operatives, family associations,
7, various special interests,
2, the middle classes.

The Higher Council of the Judiciary remains, but also with restricted functions and somewhat different methods of appointment. Its function is to advise the Government on appointments to a limited number of higher judicial posts, to act as disciplinary Court for judges, and also to advise the President on his exercise of the right of pardon.[1] Henceforth, on questions of reprieve, it is consulted as of right only where the death sentence is in question.

Under the Fourth Republic it had also been responsible for the general organization of Courts of Law and for ensuring the independence of judges. The purpose of the Fourth Republic in handing over these last-mentioned functions to the Higher Council had been to prevent political influence in promotions. Complaints began to be heard, however, alleging political bias in some appointments by the Higher Council and some overlapping with the Ministry of Justice. These functions were returned, therefore, to the Ministry of Justice. Under the special powers granted to the Government by the Constitution from October 1958 to February 1959, a number of Ordinances and decrees provided for a comprehensive reorganization of criminal procedure, for redistribution of Law Courts, and for improvements in the status and training of judges, designed to improve their quality.

The function of the High Court of Justice is, as it was under the Fourth Republic, to try Presidents of the Republic on charges of high treason. It also tries Ministers and their accomplices on charges of plotting against the safety of the State. To bring individuals before it, both Houses must pass identical motions by an absolute majority of their members. The vote is public. Ministers are 'penally responsible'[2] for their actions *qua* Ministers, provided that the offences were punishable at the time they were committed.

[1] The Higher Council of the Judiciary is composed of nine members, sitting for four years and re-eligible for a second term only. They are appointed by the President of the Republic (with the counter-signature of the Prime Minister). The President of the Republic and the Minister of Justice are members *ex officio,* the former acting as President, the latter as Vice-President. Seven of the nine members are chosen from different branches of the legal profession, from lists submitted by the relevant directing bodies.

[2] 'Penally responsible' appears to mean liable to trial in ordinary courts. Yet, in February, 1962, the *doyen* of the *juges d'instruction* of the Seine declared himself incompetent to consider a case against the Minister of the Armed Forces, on the ground that it must go to the High Court. He based his case on a purported

The only changes of importance in the method of functioning of the Court are, first, that decisions to bring an individual before the Court must now be taken by both Houses instead of by the National Assembly alone, as was the position under the Fourth Republic; second, that the vote is no longer secret, and, third, that the sentence on a President of the Republic found guilty of high treason (the only offence with which he can be charged in the exercise of his functions) is no longer to be determined on the basis of rules laid down in the penal code. This requirement is retained, however, in the case of all other offenders dealt with by the High Court.[1]

CONSTITUTIONAL REVISION

Like the 1946 Constitution, that of 1958 includes a special procedure for revision. It is relatively simple – simple that is, as far as the constitutional requirements are concerned, though not necessarily politically easy to apply. A proposal for revision (which can come either from the President of the Republic, at the suggestion of the Prime Minister, or from private Members) must, to be effective, be voted first in identical terms by both Houses of Parliament and then ratified by a Referendum, or, if the President decides otherwise, by a three-fifths majority of both Houses, meeting as Congress.[2] The Republican form of government is not subject to revision.

Under the Fourth Republic, the requirement which enabled the Assembly, if necessary, to dispense with the consent of the Senate

[1] The High Court of Justice is composed of 24 members, 12 chosen by each House from among its members, following a general election in the case of Deputies, and a partial renewal in the case of Senators. They hold office until the following election or partial renewal.

[2] Revision of the articles of *Titre* XII (the Community) constituted an exception, requiring only ordinary legislation. Such laws had to be voted, however, in the same terms by the Senate of the Community.

---

quotation from article 68 which, in fact contained some added words. For comments on this decision, *v.* Professor Duverger's article in *Le Monde*, 15th February 1962. In April 1962, however, a Court held itself competent to try a case against another Minister. The problem arises from the following sentence: '*La procédure définie ci-dessous leur est appliquée* [i.e. to Ministers] *ainsi qu'à leurs complices dans le cas de complot contre la sûreté de l'Etat.*' In the absence of a comma after either '*appliquée*' or '*complices*', its meaning is uncertain. Does it mean, a) that this procedure is applicable to Ministers – and in cases of plotting against the State to their accomplices as well, or b) that in cases of plotting against the State, and only in such cases, is the procedure applicable to Ministers? The second seems more probable.

was a two-thirds majority in the National Assembly, a condition that the National Assembly was frequently unable to fulfil. Under the Fifth Republic the Senate has an effective veto and the first stage of revision might, therefore, be difficult to complete.[1]

THE CONFLICT OF CONSTITUTIONAL OBJECTIVES

The attempt to combine the two principles of Parliamentary and Presidential government constitutes the specifically Gaullist element in the 1958 Constitution, whether or not General de Gaulle was himself personally responsible for the formulation of any of its provisions. But those who drafted the Constitution were responsible for at least three other influences which left their mark.

The two former Prime Ministers who were members of the Ministerial drafting Committee were left-wing Republicans who had really two aims. The first was to produce a democratic Constitution preserving the essential principles of traditional Republican and Parliamentary government. Neither had any real quarrel with the principles of the 1946 Constitution, in the drafting of which M. Mollet had certainly taken an active part. Both were preoccupied, however, by the practical difficulties that they had encountered in trying to govern in the conditions which prevailed throughout most of the life of the Fourth Republic. M. Pflimlin's Government had succeeded in introducing proposals for constitutional revision, intended to strengthen Governments, but the Fourth Republic fell

[1] It was suggested by M. Duverger (*v. Revue française de Science Politique*, March 1959, pp. 138–9) that the wording of the article governing revision (article 89) is ambiguous in that it does not make clear whether the President's decision not to submit a proposed revision to a Referendum renders the first stage (a vote in both Houses) unnecessary, or is taken only when this has been completed. Both logically and linguistically the second interpretation seems the only acceptable one. M. Duverger also raised the question as to whether the President can decide not to hold a Referendum only in the case of proposals made by the Government, or whether the origin of the proposals is immaterial once the proposals have been voted in both Houses. The use, at this stage, of the word *projet* only would support the first interpretation, which was generally accepted.

There are also a number of other ambiguities. The article gives no information regarding the procedure governing the 'voting' of a proposal for revision. Article 126 of the Standing Orders makes it clear that the ordinary legislative procedure is to be used, but it is still not clear whether the procedure would be the same in Congress as in the two Houses. The revision of articles 85 and 86, in June 1960, did nothing to clear up ambiguities, since revision was carried out by the procedure laid down in article 85 as being applicable to Title XII. There was disagreement regarding the constitutionality of the procedure as applied to this particular case, *v. infra*, pp. 162-3.

before they had become law. The essentials of these proposals were, therefore, included in Article 49 of the 1958 Constitution.

No doubt, in their Ministerial capacity, left-wing Ministers of the Fourth Republic could welcome, too, the reduction of Parliamentary sessions to five and a half months. The practical objective of most French Prime Ministers since the war has been well described as that of persuading Deputies to take long vacations, an objective often achieved under the Third Republic by the system of *décrets-lois*, though not under the Fourth, which had to rely on devices such as special-powers Acts and the practice of legislation in the form of outline-laws. The ex-Ministers and their party supporters appreciated restrictions on Parliament much less, however, when they went into opposition.[1]

They fitted in very well, however, with the conceptions of the Minister of Justice, M. Debré, who was responsible for organizing the work of the Ministerial committee and for drawing up the working draft. There is considerable evidence to suggest that the 1958 Constitution owes more to M. Debré than to anyone else.[2] He had spent fifteen years, beginning in the underground resistance movement, working out the constitutional reforms that would help to give France the kind of government she needed. It probably owes to him some of the most unworkable of its provisions – the effort to constitutionalize Parliamentary procedure, for instance, and to define and limit the sphere of activity of Parliament by rigid rules, described by one legal expert as 'the pure and simple organization of anarchy'.[3]

M. Debré shared neither the revolutionary inheritance nor the Parliamentary outlook of the left-wing Ministers. He was a loyal Gaullist, a didactic speaker, and a most unpopular Parliamentary

[1] The Socialist party's interpretation of the principle of Parliamentary sovereignty has, in practice, led to a tendency to favour *gouvernement d'assemblée*, and the Catholic M.R.P. which is in many ways very close to the Socialists, has a similar outlook. It was however, an M.R.P. Minister – M. Lecourt, a former Minister of Justice – who was primarily responsible for the complex proposals whose essential purpose was realized in article 49. They owe little to theory and practically everything to the hard school of ministerial experience.

[2] *v.* the excellent piece of research on this subject in *Revue Française de Science Politique*, March 1959, by Nicholas Wahl, *Aux Origines de la Nouvelle Constitution.*

[3] G. Morange, *La hiérarchie des textes dans la Constitution du 4 octobre 1958 Recueil Dalloz hebdomadaire,* 28th January 1959, p. 26).

performer, an intelligent and precise lawyer and a highly respected *Conseiller d'Etat*, a doctrinaire reformer and a frustrated pedagogue. His aim as a constitution-maker was to discipline Deputies and, by showing them who was master, lead them to a better way of life.

Lastly, there was discernible in the Constitution the faint protest, the sigh of regret, of orthodox, mainly right-wing, Republican and Parliamentary opinion, represented by members of the Constitutional Advisory Committee, presided over by M. Paul Reynaud. Whatever their feelings about the political situation in 1958, and its necessities, their spiritual home remained the Parliamentary traditions of the immediately preceding régimes.

These four schools of thought were all, to some extent, looking backwards. General de Gaulle, too, remembered 1940 and was anxious that in any future national emergency the continuity of government should be better provided for than hitherto. The left-wing Ministers wanted stronger Republican Governments than they had headed under the Fourth Republic. M. Debré wanted to make a new place for Parliament and to see that it kept to it, and the members of Parliament whose advice was sought on the new Constitution were trying to salvage what remnants they could of the Parliamentary rights and habits of the Third Republic.

The result was a Constitution whose provisions are often ambiguous or obscure and whose purposes are sometimes confused and contradictory. It was ironical that one of the chief victims was the Prime Minister himself, since the duality of the executive resulted in the spectacle of the first Prime Minister, M. Debré, playing understudy to the first President, and often apparently working from a different edition of his part. In the long series of French Constitutions, that of 1958 is unlikely to be remembered as a model of either the logic or the clarity of thought and expression on which the French (often rightly) pride themselves.

PART II

Institutions and Parties of the Fifth Republic

CHAPTER IV

The Electoral System and French Electoral Habits

ELECTORAL STABILITY AND INSTABILITY

It is a prevalent British opinion that the French are addicted to systems of proportional representation, that their electoral behaviour is characterized by great fickleness, and that an electoral system designed to discourage the formation of small splinter parties would do a great deal to cure the Governmental instability from which France has suffered since the beginning of the Third Republic. In fact, except for a brief period in 1945 and 1946, France has never had fully proportional representation and all the evidence shows that, at least up to the end of the second world war, French electorates presented a striking picture of stability. Studies of electoral behaviour have shown, not only that the overall electoral strength of certain basic political tendencies varied very little up to 1939, but that in certain regions political convictions remained surprisingly consistent for nearly a century. André Siegfried noted this fact in 1930:

> The same political orientation, expressed by virtually the same majorities, can be found often in a *département* or a *canton* over a period of fifty years or more. Beneath changing political labels that deceive the superficial observer, these fundamental tendencies constitute a firm basis for political evolution.[1]

François Goguel estimated that, between 1877 and 1928, the relative strengths of what he termed the forces of movement and those of

[1] *Tableau des Partis en France* (Grasset, 1930), p. 52.

order, or what are usually referred to more loosely as the forces of Left and Right, varied by only 0.5 per cent.[1]

General stability of opinion is not, of course, inconsistent with changes in the electoral complexion of certain regions. These are often due to changes in economic structure, changes which, over the country as a whole, often cancel each other out. Nor is it inconsistent with considerable fluctuations in the number of seats held by different parties or tendencies, often brought about by changes in the electoral system, or by electoral alliances affecting the working of electoral systems. For if Frenchmen have tended to stick to their principles or their parties in successive elections, they have certainly not stuck to one system of election. Between 1875 and 1958 France changed her electoral system eight times. And of the five different systems used during that period, only one was used for more than two successive elections. Of the 22 elections between 1875 and 1958, however, only three were conducted on a wholly proportional system, and they all took place between October 1945 and November 1946.

Nor does a study of French electoral systems in relation to party or Governmental instability bear out the thesis that the electoral system has encouraged instability. The elections of 1924, 1936 and 1946, for instance, were held on different systems. All resulted in large majorities for left-wing coalitions, yet in every case the coalition had broken down long before the end of the Parliament.[2]

[1] *La Politique des Partis sous la IIIe République* (Paris, Editions du Seuil, 1946), p. 20.

Cf. also R. Aron in *Preuves* (February 1959, p. 9): '75 per cent of the French who voted in November and December 1958 were faithful to their traditional preferences. They were almost as stable as British electors, 10 per cent of whom, by changing their party, can bring the Labour revolution or a Conservative return to power. The difference is that France changes her régime or her Constitution and that, within the Parliamentary system, the French vote for so many parties that they give a mandate to none.'

[2] In case this example should be taken to justify the thesis that left-wing Governments are more unstable than right, the following examples could also be quoted: from 1917–24 right-centre Governments had an average life of eleven months; the 1924–8 and 1936–40 left-wing or left-centre Governments had an average life of eight months; the 1946–51 left-centre coalitions (for the most part excluding the Communists) had an average life of seven and half months; the 1951–55 centre-right coalitions had an average life of eight months; and the 1956–8 centre-left coalitions had an average life of about eight and a half months. The electoral system that produced the 1924 Chamber was different from that of 1936; that of 1946 differed from that of 1951.

It has been estimated that, between 1919 and 1957, the average life of Governments was six and a half months during Assemblies elected by proportional or quasi-proportional systems, and five months during those elected by majority systems (*v.* M. Massenet, *L'Angoisse au Pouvoir*, Plon, 1959, p. 5).

What does seem generally true of French electoral systems is first that, even during the brief post-war period during which proportional representation was tried, they have been deliberately designed to produce some degree of disproportion between votes and seats, with the aim either of reducing the number of small and undisciplined splinter groups or of obtaining, in spite of them, an Assembly in which there would be a coherent majority, or sometimes with the specific aim of reducing Communist, or Communist and Gaullist, representation. In two elections, those of 1919 and 1924, the system chosen was intended to produce gross distortion, and did so.[1] That introduced in the elections of 1951 was intended to reduce Communist and Gaullist representation. This it did, producing in 1951 considerable disproportion between votes and seats. In 1956, however, it produced much less disproportion, owing to changes in party structures, and still more in party alliances.[2]

French electoral systems and the numerous proposals for electoral reform that have been put forward since the war also reveal a distinct preference in the minds of many politicians for involved systems. In 1951 eight, and in 1955 11 different proposals were debated in the Assembly, a number of them highly complicated and ingenious combinations of majority or proportional principles, with one or more ballots and list or individual voting.

[1] The 1919 system was a hybrid. Candidates stood either as individuals or as members of lists, and electors had as many votes as there were seats to be filled, though they were not obliged to use them all. They could not give more than one vote to a single candidate, but they could vote for candidates on different lists. The *département* was usually the constituency. Seats were allocated in three stages. Candidates receiving an absolute majority of the votes cast were elected. Remaining seats were allocated, first proportionally by the application of a quotient, but with preference given to list candidates, any further vacant seats going to the list with the highest average. The result was a gross over-representation of majorities.

[2] The 1951 system was also a hybrid. Voting was for party lists at a single ballot, any list receiving an absolute majority of the votes cast in the constituency taking all the seats. Parties could also form alliances, which were announced on the ballot paper. Allied lists took all the seats if they received an absolute majority of the votes cast, allocation between them being proportional to the number of votes received. Where no list or group of lists received an absolute majority, allocation of seats was proportional, but the allied group still counted as a single list for this purpose, by a method which over-represented large blocks of votes; within the group the allocation of seats was proportional to votes received. In 1951, alliances between non-Communist and non-Gaullist parties effectively reduced representation of Communists, though the Gaullists did well. In 1956, the Gaullists had virtually disappeared and the multiplicity of alliances prevented all but 11 alliances from obtaining an absolute majority. The result was, therefore, much closer to proportional representation.

Finally, the French are deeply divided about the electoral system itself. It has been said that what they are looking for is:

> a system that would produce assemblies that accurately reflected the divisions of the electorate and parties that were stable, disciplined and responsible. Experience has shown that in France an electoral system can yield the first result but not the second.[1]

Experience has also shown that political divisions prevented any serious or prolonged attempt to achieve one of the above results at the cost of sacrificing the other. Either electoral systems have been designed to meet a particular emergency or to produce a particular result, in which case they have been speedily abandoned once the conditions responsible for their creation ceased to exist, or else they have been compromises in which electoral principles have been adapted in order to meet the requirements of majority parties with conflicting electoral interests. No system has succeeded in satisfying a sufficient number of politicians for long enough to enable the problem to be removed from the field of political controversy. Sooner or later, those who lost by the system have wanted to change it.

This electoral instability has itself contributed both to Parliamentary deadlock and to Governmental instability. Assembly and Government have at times wanted to change the system, but have been powerless to do so, owing to party divisions on the electoral issue. Yet it is only natural that parties should oppose the adoption of systems whose effect would be to weaken them. The Catholic M.R.P. and the Communist party have always believed that they fare better under a system of proportional representation than under one involving alliances, for the latter is isolated, and the former finds that Socialist parties in some constituencies are reluctant to ally themselves with a clerical party. The Right, traditionally indisciplined and liable to form small, often ephemeral, groups, has tended to fear both proportional representation and the single-member system with two ballots, since it has been at a disadvantage compared with large disciplined parties. It has tended, therefore, to prefer one of the more complex systems, involving both majority

[1] Peter Campbell, *French Electoral Systems and Elections* 1789–1957 (Faber, 1958), p. 45. The first part of this excellent study provides a well-documented refutation of the thesis that the electoral system is responsible for political instability.

and proportional systems and allowing a good deal of free play for manoeuvre within the constituency. The Socialists have been divided, being attracted in principle to the proportional system, but conscious of their need of alliances in practice. The Radicals have remained faithful to the single-member system with two ballots, which is associated *par excellence* with the Third Republic, when the Radical party was at its peak.

French electoral habits since the war have differed from those of the Third Republic in two major ways. First the distribution of votes between the traditional parties has changed. It is no longer true to say that the average French elector votes Radical. This party, which dominated the Third Republic's political life, is now both small and divided. Whereas, in 1932, over 19 per cent of the votes were cast for the Radical party, in 1946 the proportion was only 13 per cent, in 1956 13·5 per cent, in 1958 11 per cent, divided between three different tendencies. There has been a move to the Left on the part of the electors. This tendency was already observable before the war. The Radical party was then losing ground to the Socialists. During the year following the war, the Socialist party reached its peak, with almost 18 per cent of the votes, But the victory was short-lived, for the real shift of opinion was farther left. In 1946 the Communist vote reached 28·6 per cent, and, until 1958, Communist strength was consistently in the region of 25 per cent.[1]

The second change is the sudden appearance and disappearance of new and important parties. In 1945, the M.R.P. (*Mouvement républicain populaire*), a progressive Catholic party formed during the resistance period, polled 4¾ million votes. In 1946, with 5½ million votes, it became the largest party, polling nearly half a million more votes than the Communists. In the following election, a few months later, the Communists moved up to first place and by 1951 the M.R.P. vote had fallen to 2¼ million. It has since remained at round about that figure. The position of second largest party was filled in 1951 by another newcomer, the Gaullist R.P.F. (*Rassemblement du peuple français*), founded in 1947. This movement polled over 4 million votes. By 1956 it had disappeared. A small Gaullist

[1] It is often stated that a quarter of the French electorate votes for the Communist party. This has never been true. From 1946 to 1958 about one elector in five and one voter in four did so. About 75 per cent to 80 per cent of the French electorate normally vote.

rump polled something under a million votes and a third newcomer, the extreme-right Poujadist movement, received over 2½ million votes. In the 1958 election, the Poujadist and extreme-right vote together amounted to only about half a million, but a new formation polled 3½ million votes. It was Gaullist, in the sense that its members acknowledged General de Gaulle as their leader, though he himself had no public links with them and forbade any party to use his name in the electoral campaign.

The rise of four new formations attracting between an eighth and a quarter of the total vote, and the fall of three of them, all within the space of 13 years, during which six elections were held, does not seem to indicate a high degree of electoral stability. Yet in a sense it does. Although these four movements represented a great many different, and sometimes conflicting, political tendencies, they did have something in common. The extremist tendency which was present in at least three of the four movements has been a recurrent phenomenon in Republican France. The eighties saw the Boulangist movement. The first decade of the twentieth century saw extreme nationalist movements, of which the most important was the *Action Française*. The thirties saw the formation of a number of para-military groups with views ranging from corporatism to Fascism and tactics ranging from anti-Parliamentarianism to the terrorism of the *Cagoulards*. The fifties again saw the formation of extreme Right groups. The electoral strength of most of these was negligible, because, as opponents of the Parliamentary system, they often refused to take part in elections.

Those who voted for the four above-mentioned formations also included many who could not be classed as anti-Republican or anti-Parliamentary. They had in common a certain dissatisfaction with traditional political parties, a desire for something new. Three of the formations (not the M.R.P.) also expressed dissatisfaction with the system of Parliamentary government under the Fourth Republic. In other words, there has been in post-war France a consistently high 'disgruntlement' vote. On the Left, it tends to be cast in favour of the Communist party; on the Right, or among the non-politically minded, it tends to be cast for new formations, either attacking the 'system', or looking to personal leadership, or both.

THE ELECTORAL SYSTEM OF THE FIFTH REPUBLIC

(*a*) **The National Assembly.** Though, by 1955, there was general agreement that the electoral law of 1951 ought to be revised, political divisions and conflicting electoral interests prevented the revision from being achieved during the life of the Fourth Republic. The new régime took the matter out of the hands of Parliament. The Constitution gave the Government full powers, until 5th February 1959, to legislate by Ordinances having the force of law, and specifically authorized it to determine the electoral system. This does not mean that Parliament's traditional right to vote and revise the electoral laws has been lost. On the contrary, electoral laws are included among the matters enumerated in article 34 of the Constitution as belonging to the legislative sphere. But until Parliament decides to change it, the electoral system laid down in the *Ordonnance* of 13th October 1958 remains that of the Fifth Republic.

That system is, for elections to the National Assembly, the single-member system with two ballots, the simplest of all French systems and the one which had been used for 13 of the 21 previous elections. Though this choice is reported to have been made by General de Gaulle himself, it was not popular with the Gaullists, who preferred a majority system with list voting and two ballots, as being more likely to favour a large and (for the time being) united party. The single-member system with two ballots was not used, however, for the election of all the 552 Deputies of the first National Assembly. In all four systems were used:

(i) In the 90 *départements* of France and Corsica 465 Deputies, and in the four Overseas *départements* ten Deputies were elected on this system.[1]

(ii) The five Overseas Territories elected six Deputies. Four constitute single-member constituencies, the fifth a two-member constituency. There was one ballot only.[2]

[1] The four Overseas *départements* are Guadeloupe, Martinique, Réunion and Guyana.

[2] The five Overseas Territories are St Pierre-et-Miquelon, Somaliland, New Caledonia, Polynesia and the Comoro archipelago. The last-mentioned is a two-member constituency. In December 1959, the French-protected islands of Wallis and Futuna, with a population of some 11,000, voted in favour of their transfer to the status of an Overseas Territory. A law of July 1961 recognized this status. The Territory is to be represented by one Deputy and one Senator.

(iii) Algeria elected 67 Deputies, of whom 46 were required to be Moslem and 21 European or assimilated Moslems.[1] In each of 18 constituencies, parties presented lists including Moslem and European candidates in proportions decided on the basis of the population, though not in proportion to the relative strengths of the two communities. There was one ballot only, and any list receiving a relative majority was declared elected. Electors, whether European or Moslem, could vote only for a whole list.

(iv) The two Saharan *départements* of Oasis and Saoura elected four Deputies. Saoura elected one; in Oasis voting was for lists of three candidates. In both *départements*, candidates could be either European or Moslem.[2]

To be elected on the single-member system with two ballots, a candidate had to obtain either a minimum of 50 per cent plus 1 of the votes cast at the first ballot, and a number of votes equal to a quarter of the electorate, or head the poll at a second ballot held a week later.

In metropolitan France, in 1958, only 39 of the 465 candidates were elected at the first ballot. Traditionally, during the period between the two ballots, discussions are carried on between the parties contesting the election, with a view to deciding whether all candidates shall stand again, or whether one or more shall stand down, either retiring and leaving the field clear for the others, or retiring with the recommendation that supporters shall vote for one specified candidate among those left. In pre-war elections, the second ballot sometimes became a straight fight between Right and Left. Radicals, Socialists and Communists sometimes concluded agreements to the effect that two of the three party representatives should stand down in favour of the one who polled most votes at the first ballot. Sometimes the agreement was tacit or partial only. Since the elector was free to ignore the advice given, there was never any absolute guarantee that such undertakings would be honoured. In pre-war elections, too, it was possible for new candi-

[1] On the distinction between Moslems and Europeans *v. infra*, p. 175 n.1.

[2] From July 1962, as a result of France's recognition of Algerian independence, the seats of the 71 Deputies for Algeria and the Sahara were abolished, thus reducing the membership of the National Assembly to 482 (including the representative for Wallis and Futuna.

dates to intervene at the second ballot and this could put all the calculations out. This is now forbidden.

The general conditions governing the eligibility of candidates and the qualifications of electors have been similar, whatever the electoral system.[1] Electors must be French, over 21 and in possession of their civil and political rights.[2] Their names must be included in the electoral register and, in *communes* of over 5,000, they must produce satisfactory proof of their identity to officials in the polling booths. They may not vote in more than one constituency. If they can qualify as electors in more than one constituency, they must choose to be registered in one only. Postal votes are permitted for certain specified categories (the ill and aged, for instance, commercial travellers, lighthouse keepers, servicemen away from home . . . etc.). Proxy votes are permitted in the case of servicemen overseas, and of officials or French citizens resident abroad.

Candidates are elected for five years. They must be French and over 23. They may not stand in more than one constituency.[3] They are required to pay a deposit of 100,000 francs, reimbursable if they receive 5 per cent or more of the votes in either ballot.[4] They have the right to a certain amount of free publicity, or rather the

[1] In 1958 there were some differences, both in the conditions governing candidates and in voting practice in Algeria. Owing to the backwardness of the country and the need to protect voters from reprisals threatened by the F.L.N. (which boycotted the election) the army was in control of the arrangements and elections were staggered over three days, to enable elections to be held in safety. Moslem electors, most of whom are illiterate, voted by means of coloured cards and there were special polling booths in some areas for Moslem women, who were voting for the first time. Civilian control commissions had representatives in each constituency, to supervise the regularity of the elections. There were, nevertheless, criticisms of the army's conduct of affairs and allegations of political propaganda by the army, though General de Gaulle had issued specific instructions that everything was to be done to enable all political tendencies to express themselves freely.

[2] Among those disqualified are certain categories of the insane, declared bankrupts, those convicted of certain penal offences . . . etc. Some penal sentences specifically disqualify the person convicted from voting.

[3] Civil servants and serving officers are disqualified from standing in constituencies in which they hold office or have held office within periods ranging, in different cases, from six months to three years. An additional limitation was placed on candidates in Algeria in 1958; certain high officials and all soldiers having served in Algeria within the previous year were precluded from standing.

[4] Candidates not receiving 5% of the votes cast are ineligible to stand at the second ballot. If a candidate dies between the two ballots, he is replaced by his substitute.

cost of this publicity is reimbursed to those who obtain 5 per cent of the votes cast. It includes posters on official hoardings and the printing and postage of election addresses and election cards. The purpose of this concession is to provide something like equality between candidates. In theory, no other posters or correspondence are permitted. In practice, this rule is easily evaded. Unofficial posters often appear, and candidates can send so-called private letters to their electors in sealed envelopes. It is even possible to launch a newspaper for a short period, for there is no maximum permitted expenditure in France. In metropolitan France, parties with candidates in at least 75 constituencies also have the right to a certain amount of radio and television time. In 1958, 12 parties qualified for this right.

Men and women may be both electors and candidates on exactly the same terms.

The most important innovation under the Fifth Republic is the requirement that all candidates, or all lists, where voting is by list, must nominate a substitute[1] who will replace them if, after election, they die, or become disqualified from sitting owing to the new incompatibility rules – that is, if they accept Government office, or paid employment as an official of a trade union or other professional association, or appointment to the Constitutional Council, or membership of a Government mission lasting more than six months. In these cases, the substitute replaces the member until the following elections. If the member resigns, or becomes ineligible for any other reason, his seat is filled by a by-election.

The substitute is a 'shadow' Deputy. He is subject to the general rules governing candidature and must be qualified to vote. His name appears on the ballot paper along with that of the candidate, and the elector, in voting for the candidate, also votes contingently for his substitute. The substitute has certain privileges; for instance, he has none of the financial responsibilities for the campaign and is not obliged to take part in it, though he often did in 1958. He has also certain disabilities; if he does, in fact, replace the Deputy, he cannot oust him from his seat by standing against him at the following elections. Deputies may not themselves act as substitutes for

[1] In Algeria, lists included one European and one Moslem substitute. In the Oasis *département*, however, all three candidates were required to name a substitute.

Senators, or *vice versa*,[1] nor may any substitute act for more than one Deputy.

In practice, in 1958, the substitute often tended to be used by the candidate as an adjunct in the electoral campaign – and one rather more useful than the candidate's wife usually is in England, since the candidate was free to choose his substitute at the time of the election. Candidates often did so in 1958, with the specific intention of attracting, or placating, certain sections of opinion, without involving themselves in any definite commitments to them.

Perhaps the best way to give some idea of the numbers and types of candidates contesting constituencies is to choose a few examples. In the *département* of the Eure, for instance, there were in the 1958 elections 24 candidates standing in four constituencies. They included 16 different political labels, and six distinct political tendencies (Communist, Socialist, Radical, Gaullist, Right, extreme Right; there were no M.R.P. or U.D.S.R. candidates); seven of the candidates were either Mayors of their *commune* or local Councillors. This is a typical *département*, since the average over the whole country was six candidates per constituency. The lowest number of candidates was two (in only one constituency), the highest 15. In Paris, the third Sector (the Latin quarter) had 11 candidates representing six political tendencies (Communist, Socialist, three Gaullists, three Right, extreme Right and the right-wing Catholic movement, *Démocratie chrétienne*; there were no Radical or M.R.P. candidates).

It is necessary to emphasize that this first election since 1936 held under the single-member system with two ballots was in many respects unique in French history and that comparisons with the results of previous elections under this system are not likely to be very illuminating. It was held in an atmosphere of crisis in which the dominant issue was that of confidence in General de Gaulle, a confidence expressed by the overwhelming majority of the candidates, many of whom were opposed to each other on everything else. General de Gaulle associated himself with no party and forbade his name to be used 'even as an adjective', but this rule was extensively and ingeniously evaded. It was, indeed, often very difficult to

[1] Those who drafted the electoral law had apparently not thought of this method, by which some Deputies and Senators could have ensured their membership of one House or the other, and a special Ordinance had to be promulgated forbidding its use.

grasp from candidates' speeches or addresses what their policy was. Thus, to take one example, in St Gaudens (Haute Garonne), the candidate elected, an 80-year-old Radical, M. Hyppolite Ducos, who had represented the region for 40 years, was one of six candidates, all of whom expressed themselves in favour of peace in Algeria, none of whom expressed themselves in favour of Algerian independence, and five of whom (that is excepting only the Communist) supported General de Gaulle.

It was also an election in which constituency boundaries were all new, and in which the system was also new to all electors under 40 and to two of the main parties, the U.N.R. and the M.R.P. There had been great population changes since 1936, and the Government, therefore, redrew boundaries on the basis of one representative per 93,000 inhabitants, and of a minimum representation of two Deputies per *département*. In accordance with French tradition, constituencies included, where possible, both rural and urban areas. These criteria resulted in the over-representation of the smaller *départements*, and also in some odd juxtapositions. Thus, for instance, the fashionable, and conservative, *commune* of Neuilly formed part of a constituency including the working-class, and Socialist, *commune* of Puteaux.

In the circumstances, accurate prediction of the results was impossible and they turned out to be a surprise for everybody, not least for the Ministry of the Interior. The Gaullists, who disliked the system, won a sweeping victory; Socialist Parliamentary strength was halved; Communist Parliamentary representation was almost wiped out; Radicals, who had been in favour of the system, fared badly; the M.R.P., which had always feared and disliked it, maintained its position.

There was, however, a striking disparity between the votes cast for the different parties and their Parliamentary representation, a disparity which resulted largely from political factors that had not been present at elections held under this system during the Third Republic. There was, first, the presence of some 2½ million 'floating' votes, that had been cast for the Poujadist party in 1956; there was the presence of the M.R.P., a left-wing Catholic party, whose two million and more votes did not fit into the normal 'Left versus Right' pattern that had developed in pre-war elections under this system; there was an unbridgeable gulf between the two Left-wing parties, Socialists and Communists, who, in the thirties, had been in the habit of combining against the Right at the second ballot; there were three Radical groups, where during the Third Republic there had been only one; and there was the totally unknown newcomer, the U.N.R., whose popularity was unknown and whose relations with the orthodox Right were confused and contradictory.

In theory, the single-member system is designed to strengthen moderate parties, since it puts at a disadvantage any party unable or unwilling to combine with others at the second ballot. In 1958 the Left *could* not combine, since Socialists and Communists had been in conflict since 1947; the Right in many cases *would* not. The result was that a larger number than usual of candidates maintained their candidature at the second ballot. In addition, either because parties or electors were not used to the discipline of the second ballot or because the gravity of the circumstances was such that they considered it inapplicable, many of the electors ignored the recommendations of candidates who did stand down. Whatever they were advised to do, large numbers of electors belonging to all political tendencies (even including Communists) voted at the second ballot for the Gaullist candidate – that is, for the U.N.R., whose 'Gaullism' was its *raison d'être*.

It is clear that the electoral system could not in these circumstances have produced a representative Assembly. It produced what was probably the most unrepresentative Assembly in French history. Fifty Deputies represented the 7 million electors who voted for Socialist and Communist candidates while the 3½ million electors who voted for the U.N.R. were represented by over 200 Deputies.

It was also an Assembly politically unique in that the 200 or so U.N.R. Deputies had no policy other than fidelity to General de Gaulle, nor did they evolve a policy during the following years.

(*b*) **The Senate.** In accordance with the practice of the two preceding régimes, the Senate is indirectly elected, mainly by local Councillors. It is, therefore, necessary to describe its electoral system in two stages; first the election of the electoral college itself, and second the system by which the Senators were elected in 1959.

In metropolitan France, (including Algeria, the Sahara,[1] and the

[1] From July 1962, as a result of France's recognition of Algerian independence, the seats of the 34 Senators for Algeria and the Sahara were abolished, thus reducing the membership of the Senate to 274 (including the representative for Wallis and Futuna).

four Overseas *départements*) Senators were elected by a college consisting, in each *département*, of:

(i) the Deputies representing the *département*,

(ii) the Councillors representing the *département*,

(iii) Municipal Councillors, whose number varies according to the population;

(*a*) *Communes* with populations of 9,000–30,000, and the 60 *Communes* of the Seine, irrespective of their population, are represented by all Municipal Councillors.

(*b*) *Communes* with populations of over 30,000 have, in addition the right to an additional delegate for every 1,000 inhabitants over 30,000.

(*c*) *Communes* with populations of under 9,000 (that is 37,518 of the 38,000 *communes*) choose from among their Municipal Councillors from one to 15 delegates, according to their population.

In the five[1] Overseas Territories, each of which elected one Senator, the electoral college was similarly composed, except that special arrangements had to be made for representatives of *communes* that did not yet have fully elective Councils.

Four different systems were employed in the election of the 307 Senators.

(i) In *départements* represented by one to four Senators, that is in all but seven of the 90 *départements* of France, in the four Overseas *départements* and the five Overseas Territories, election was by the majority system, with two ballots. To be elected at the first ballot, candidates had to obtain an absolute majority of the votes cast and a number of votes equal to at least a quarter of the electorate. At the second ballot a relative majority only was required. 209 Senators (195 metropolitan Senators, seven for the Overseas *départements*, two for the Sahara and five for the Overseas Territories) were elected on this system.

(ii) In the seven heavily populated *départements* of France[2] which

[1] Now six.

[2] These are: Nord, Pas-de-Calais, Rhône, Seine, Seine Maritime, Seine-et-Oise and Bouches-du-Rhône.

had five or more Senators, election was by proportional representation (the highest-average system). Sixty metropolitan Senators were elected in this way.

(iii) In the eight Algerian constituencies, electing 32 Senators, the system was also that of the majority system with two ballots, but voting was for lists on which European and Moslem candidates were represented in fixed proportions; ten represent the European and 22 the Moslem communities. Any list obtaining an absolute majority of the votes at the first ballot was declared elected. A relative majority only was required at the second.

(iv) The six Senators representing French residents abroad are chosen in the first instance by the High Council of French residents abroad, composed of *ex-officio* and elected members and of members nominated by the Ministry of Foreign Affairs, from names submitted by its different regional sections. The Council's choice must be ratified by the Senate. If 30 Senators oppose any nomination, a secret ballot takes place on all. A relative majority only is required for election.

Senators are elected for nine years, a third retiring every three years.[1] Candidates must be aged at least 35. Other qualifications are the same as those required for election to the Assembly, including the obligation to name a substitute.[2]

This system is criticized for the same reasons as were those governing elections to the Second Chamber of both the Third and Fourth Republics. The fact that election is for nine years (six under the Fourth Republic) and that the electors themselves may have been elected from four to six years earlier means that there is a danger of Senators being out of touch with public opinion. The electoral college over-represents small rural areas. Over half of the

[1] Exceptionally, in 1959, all Senators were elected at the same time. The 307 are divided into three 'series', A, B, and C, each including a third of the Senators. It was decided by lot that series A should be renewed in 1962, series B in 1965 and series C in 1968.

[2] In *départements* where election is by proportional representation, the candidate coming next on the list following the last elected candidate acts as the substitute. Substitutes called on to replace Senators used to hold office only until the following partial renewal. They now hold office for the full remaining terms of their predecessors.

Senatorial electors represent villages with fewer than 1,500 inhabitants. Towns with populations of 10,000 and upwards are represented by only just over a fifth of the Senatorial electors, though they constitute over 40 per cent of the population. The provision that every *département*, however small, has at least one Senator, and the general over-representation of the smaller *départements*, help to increase the unbalance. Thus, the *département* of the Lot, with a population of 147,000, has one Senator. Those of Basses Alpes and Hautes Alpes, with populations of between 80–90,000, each have one Senator. At the other end of the scale, the Seine *département*, with a population of almost five million, has 22, and the Nord, with a population of two millions, has 9 – one for every quarter of a million.

In essence, this is the system by which the Council of the Republic was elected under the previous régime.[1] It is, therefore, not surprising that the first elections of the Senate of the Fifth Republic should have resulted in the election of a high percentage of personalities of the Fourth. Of the retiring Senators standing, 84 per cent were returned. And among the 85 new Senators, 35 were former Members of Parliament; 29 were Deputies who had lost their seats in the elections of November 1958 including party leaders such as MM. Edgar Faure, Mitterrand, Deferre, Duclos, Bonnefous. It was suggested that the Senate, with its practised Parliamentary performers, might attract more public interest than the Assembly. In fact, neither parties nor Parliament have interested the public, political interest – what little there was – being reserved for the activities of the President.

[1] The main changes are the reduction of the number of *départements* in which election is by proportional representation from 11 to seven (from those with four Senators to those with five or more), and the slight increase in the representation of large towns. Electoral colleges under the Fourth Republic included additional delegates only for towns of over 45,000 inhabitants, and only one delegate for every 5,000 inhabitants over that figure.

CHAPTER V

Parties

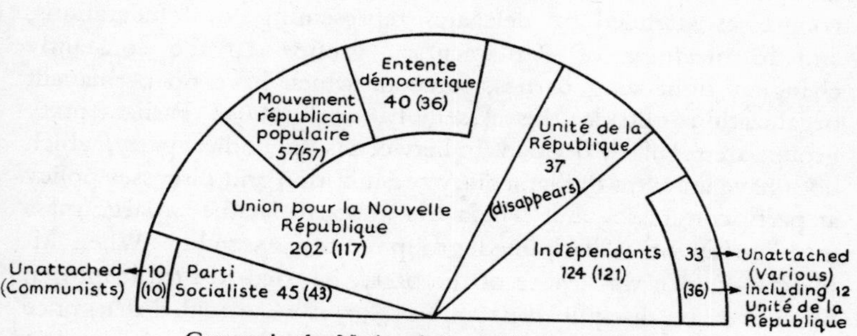

Groups in the National Assembly in June 1962 (including affiliates.[1])
Figures in brackets are for July 1962, immediately after the announcement of the Algerian independence.

PERMANENT CHARACTERISTICS OF THE PARTY SYSTEM

The French party system has a number of permanent characteristics, some of which appear inconsistent with each other. The first is the multiplicity of parties. In a general election, what could be called 'national' parties number anything from 12 to 20, and there are also a varying number of less important formations, some local, some ephemeral, some consisting of little more than a label attached to some personality or special interest. Between nine and 15 groups are normally represented in the Assembly, some of them with smaller affiliated groups, and some with closely related organizations outside the Assembly.

There is also a great diversity in both their organization and their

[1] Four seats were vacant before, and two after the announcement of Algerian independence.

politics. They cover a range extending from Communism on the Left to anti-Parliamentary and even Fascist groups on the extreme Right. Some attach great importance to political principles and doctrines and will expel members who stray openly or continuously from the orthodox path. Others appear to have no general principles and some have no coherent policy. Radicalism, for instance, has been described as a state of mind, while French conservatism is, more than anything else, a collection of special interests, often in conflict with each other. Party organization varies from the organized and disciplined parties on the Left, whose policy is formulated at party congresses attended by delegates representing local federations, and in meetings of Parliamentary groups, to the constantly changing right-wing parties, some of which have no permanent organization outside the Assembly, and whose Parliamentary groups are regularly divided. In between is the Radical party, which does have an extra-Parliamentary organization and discusses policy at party congresses, but which has never had either a large mass membership or a disciplined group in the Assembly. When M. Mendès-France was leader of the party, he tried to turn it into an organized and disciplined party. In 1957, it was decided that, once the Parliamentary group had taken a decision, members must respect it; they were entitled to abstain, but not to vote against. A fortnight later, the group decided to vote for M. Mollet, who was then trying to form a Government. In the event, 21 voted for, eight abstained and 13 voted against. This is an average sample of a Radical vote in the Assembly.

There is no French party that is comparable with any of the three British parties. Until the fifties there was no large conservative party. There were extra-Parliamentary organizations, such as the pre-war *Fédération républicaine*, and a number of independent and shifting Parliamentary groups. Even now, the *Centre national des Indépendants*, which includes the bulk of the Parliamentary conservatives, is not a party, but a federation loosely held together. It is not responsible for policy and has no unified organization in the country.

Nor has there ever been in France any political formation remotely resembling the British Liberal party. France has Radical parties and parties of social reform; many of her parties are internationalist and individualist; but the special combination of Radicalism, free-trade, international idealism and social reformism, Protestantism, individualism and love of liberty that goes to make up Liberalism has never been found in a single party, and some of the elements – Protestantism and free-trade, for instance – are virtually non-existent.

The French Socialist party has a divided inheritance, in which the reformist and humanitarian idealism of Jaurès is allied to the doctrinaire and theoretical approach of Guesde, and the pluralist and syndicalist views of Proudhon exist alongside, but mix ill with, the 'scientific' Socialism of Marx. Though it uses the vocabulary of a class party and pays lip service to the concept of the class war, its members include a high proportion of middle-class intellectuals – teachers, and civil servants in particular – and of black-coated workers. It suffers, as does the predominantly Catholic M.R.P., from the organizational divorce between political parties and trade unions which exists in France.

Another characteristic of French parties is their fluidity. Parties come and go in bewildering numbers, sometimes within a very short time. It was pointed out in the last chapter that the six elections since the war had seen the spectacular rise of four new, major parties, and the equally rapid disappearance of two of them. A glance at the list of political groups in the Assembly, over the same period of time, would show that well over 20 new Parliamentary formations made their appearance, of which 15 or more disappeared after one or two sessions. Many of these never had any existence outside the Assembly, but at least half a dozen did, and others were formed in the country but were never represented in Parliament.

Yet, as has also been pointed out in earlier chapters, one of the most striking characteristics of French politics is the stability of political tendencies. Since the war, three electors in four have voted regularly for one of six tendencies, of which three – Conservative, Radical and Socialist – go back over half a century, and the fourth – Communist – over a quarter of a century. Of the other two, the progressive Catholic M.R.P. has existed since the war, and some small pre-war groups also represented a similar point of view. Only Gaullism is a wholly post-war product, and that, too, includes elements whose inheritance goes some way back in history.

The combination of stability of opinion and instability of political organizations has no single or simple explanation. Parties are divided, partly owing to the highly developed individualism of the French character, partly owing to the relatively more important role played by personalities in French politics than in systems like the British. Divisions are encouraged by the interplay of economic interests on the Right and doctrinal conflicts on the Left. The divisions lead to splits and splinter groups, instead of subsisting as tendencies within a party, partly because the existence of a multi-party system tends, in itself, to remove the electoral incentives to unity that characterize a two-party system like the British; partly because France's economic stability enabled her, up to the second world war, to indulge in the luxury of political and party squabbles that a more economically vulnerable country could not afford; partly, too, because of the greater number of issues on which divisions were bitter and intransigent, and because of the length of French political memories.

THE IMPERMANENCE OF PARTY ALIGNMENTS UNDER THE FIFTH REPUBLIC

From time to time in French history the permanent tendencies just described have been jolted out of their familiar ruts by a national crisis or controversy, which, for a time, has either split the country in two, as the Dreyfus affair did, or as the division between resisters and collaborators did during the war, or which has dominated political thinking to the exclusion of almost anything else, as the controversy on German rearmament did between 1952 and 1954. Since French political memories are long, some of these controversies survive as political issues long after the original problem has become part of history, as the anti-clerical issue has done.

The events of 13th May 1958 were caused by a crisis and in turn provoked a controversy of the kind just described. During the first years of the Fifth Republic the attitudes of French parties were dominated by their approach to the problems of Algeria, General de Gaulle's role, and the provisions of the new Constitution. The result of the apparent insolubility of the Algerian problem, and of its relation to the other two, was that new parties appeared, seeking some new approach, and that old parties were divided within themselves or actually split on these issues. Almost all French parties except the Communists had breakaway or minority sections, whose differences from the majority of the party were due entirely to the crisis, and whose separation was not necessarily permanent. The breakaway Socialists were opposed to the régime, to its Algerian policy and to the leadership of M. Guy Mollet, who was associated in their minds with both. M. Bidault's *Démocratie chrétienne* was opposed to the M.R.P.'s Algerian and foreign policies. The U.D.S.R. split into pro- and anti-Gaullist sections. The *Mendésiste* Radicals disagreed with the *Valoisien* party mainly on this problem, though there were also both personal and political points of friction. Most of the 71 Deputies for Algeria had no policy on any issue except that of Algeria.

Since the normal business of government had to be carried on, parties were inevitably obliged to take stands on other problems in the course of a Parliamentary session. But the first sessions of the Fifth Republic were naturally occupied for some time in setting up the new organs provided for in the Constitution and in drafting the Parliamentary Standing Orders. The legislative programmes were slight and, on the whole, relatively non-controversial. The budgetary debates revealed the familiar divisions on economic and financial policy. While the Algerian problem dominated everything else, the situation was bound to remain abnormal and unstable, and parties were, to a much greater extent than usual, unorientated, seeking new orientations, and when they failed to find them, either biding their time in the hope of being able to go back to old orientations, or frankly falling back on traditional behaviour. Familiarity is, after all, a common substitute for security.

THE STATIC RIGHT

The last-mentioned attitude was, comprehensibly, the predominating characteristic of the orthodox right-wing parties. It will be clear from what has already been said that there is no such thing as a right-wing policy. But there are right-wing attitudes. In economic affairs, the French Right is opposed to State control of industry and to State intervention in the interests of a planned economy, but in favour of State action to assist producers, often small and uneconomic producers. Right-wing Deputies have regularly supported price-fixing in the interests of farmers, subsidies to the wine-growers of the south and to the beetroot producers of the north, and fiscal privileges to agricultural producers and to several millions of home distillers. In social matters, right-wing groups have defended Catholic claims to State aid for Catholic schools. In the political field, they have favoured nationalist foreign policies (*la politique de la grandeur*) though, when it comes to budget debates, they are usually unwilling to foot the bills and call for economies in State expenditure. They have been opposed to what they term 'abandonment' of French possessions overseas and they accepted with great reluctance any move towards limited home rule in Algeria and the Overseas Territories. For a time, the majority supported the policy of integration, summarized by the slogan *Algérie française*. In the 'fifties' a small right-wing anti-colonialist tendency developed, arguing (with truth) that the French overseas possessions were a financial liability. This tendency was small, however, and remained wholly without influence.

In 1949, following the failure of the post-war *Parti républicain de la liberté* to build up a strong conservative party, a loosely organized federation of right-wing groups was founded, with local branches in the *départments*. The *Centre national des Indépendants et Paysans* (C.N.I.P.), as it was called, steadily increased its strength in Parliament and was represented by some 120 Deputies in the 1959 Assembly. The organization in the country consists largely of Members of Parliament, local Councillors and local notabilities, has no co-ordinated policy or real control over its members and is, in fact, little more than an electoral organization, meeting also from time to time in Congress, or in smaller 'study groups' in order to discuss political problems and vote resolutions which in practice do not have binding force.

As a Parliamentary group, the C.N.I.P. has been important, not only because it was the second largest group in the 1959 Assembly, but because it represented orthodox Conservatism and included elder statesmen, such as MM. Pinay and Reynaud.

At first, the group somewhat grudgingly supported General de Gaulle, though there was always little love lost between the *Indépendants* and the Gaullists, for whose ideas of political 'renewal' the former had little sympathy. They liked even less the fiscal reforms and increased taxes introduced by the new régime. Indeed, this is essentially a party belonging to and representative of '*le système*', and conscious of nostalgia for the traditional ways. Even the leader (up to the end of 1961) of its reactionary wing, M. Duchet, agreed with moderates, such as M. Reynaud and M. Pinay, in deploring the replacement, under the Fifth Republic, of 'the dictatorship of Parliamentary assemblies by the dictatorship of Civil Servants and technocratic advisers'.[1] A so-called 'little Congress' of members and local notabilities voted unanimously in January 1962 against any proposal that might be made for the President to be elected by universal suffrage – though this was probably less the affirmation of a political principle than the declaration of a vested interest, for the constitution of the Presidential electoral college, as laid down in article 6 of the Constitution, might be expected, in normal circumstances to result in the election of conservative Presidents.

From the end of 1959 onwards, the *Indépendants* were seriously divided on the President's Algerian policy, the moderates (MM. Pinay, Reynaud, Rochereau, Giscard-d'Estaing, for instance) supporting 'self-determination', M. Duchet, the Secretary-General, and his supporters, opposing it. After the insurrection in Algiers in January 1960, M. Reynaud resigned from the party, saying that 'the National Centre has fallen into the hands of the ultras' – by which he meant M. Duchet, who had supported the insurrection.

The Parliamentary group remained, however, more cautious and non-committal than the local elements of the party. For instance, 84 of the 119 Deputies voted in favour of General de Gaulle's policy at this time. A year later, no directives were issued by the party regarding the way *Indépendants* should vote in the referendum, but it was openly asserted that, though they disliked Algerian self-determination, the majority of the Parliamentary group privately hoped that General de Gaulle would succeed, thus saving them from the responsibility and from the inevitable unpopularity that association with the policy of self-determination would involve. '*Le non est un alibi*' as M. Mollet succinctly put it.[2] For the local notabilities voted overwhelmingly, even as late as January 1962, for 'the maintenance of Algeria and the Sahara in the Republic'.

There was within the Parliamentary group an increasingly vocal section whose sympathies were even extended to the O.A.S. (*Organisation de l'armée secrète*).[3] In November 1961, 25 Deputies

[1] Quoted in *Le Monde*, 19th May 1959.

[2] In *Démocratie* 61, 5th January 1961.

[3] *v. infra*, pp. 220-25.

voted for the so-called 'Salan amendment' in the debate on the Defence estimates – an amendment whose wording reproduced some passages taken from ex-General Salan's letter of 11th September to Members of Parliament. The 80 Deputies who voted for this amendment were generally considered to represent the hard core of O.A.S. supporters.[1]

Fundamentally, the *Indépendants* dislike and distrust General de Gaulle and all that he stands for, though they recognize and welcome the increase in French prestige, both in Europe and in the West, which his Presidency has brought. Moderate elder Statesmen such as MM. Reynaud and Pinay, both convinced 'Europeans', while prepared to trust the President on Algeria, regret the President's rejection of European integration in a supra-national community and his non-co-operative attitude in N.A.T.O. The bulk of the party, however, provides a classic example of the political irresponsibility of parties under the Fifth Republic. They were content to deplore and to attack, not daring, however, to risk a defeat of the Government or a major conflict with the President while the Algerian problem remained unsolved; not daring to come out openly for or against the O.A.S., simply waiting until such time as they could reasonably hope to go back to their familiar Parliamentary occupation – the defence of local and sectional interests. They represent the 'littleness' of French political conservatism, its old-fashioned parochialism, its old-fashioned attitudes to economic planning (even conservative planning), economic expansion, the dynamic tendencies which have been responsible for France's ability to stand up to competition in the Common Market.[2] They have still the attitudes and reflexes of a pressure group rather than a party, defending the (often out-of-date) claims of small farmers, ex-service men, local wine-growers, distillers . . . etc. The Algerian problem was too big for them and, by the end of 1961, was threatening to disrupt the fragile and superficial bonds that had held *Indépendants* and *Paysans* precariously and inadequately together for the previous twelve years.

[1] In the vote on the Algerian estimates the previous day, a considerably larger number of *Indépendants* had voted with the 'ultras', one of whom openly prophesied that 'in six months, this Assembly will make Salan Prime Minister'. *v. l'Express*, 16th April 1961.

[2] M. Reynaud has always been a significant exception where economic policy was concerned.

THE EXTREME RIGHT

Small, extremist, right-wing groups, whose numbers and influence fluctuate according to the political situation, have always been a feature of French political life. Groups such as *Jeune nation, Le Front national français, Réconciliation française, le Parti nationaliste,* and the *Mouvement du* 13 *Mai* have all been in existence at some time during the Fifth Republic. Little is known of the membership figures of those that exist in more than name, but they are certainly small. The influence of such groups is normally negligible, but they could have become important in the event of some new 13th May, which they would have supported as some of them supported the first. Thy agreed in opposing the liberal element of General de Gaulle's policy, their general attitude being that of the Algerian 'ultras'.

This is also the position of what remains of M. Poujade's movement. Most of the two and a half millions who voted for Poujadist candidates in 1956 seem to have supported orthodox right-wing candidates in 1958. The movement is now small, disunited and has no representation in Parliament, and no real influence in the country.

In July 1959, some 50 of the 71 Deputies representing Algeria formed the group known as *Unité de la République*. This represented the 'ultra' point of view and was more of a pressure group than a party, since it had no coherent policy except support for *l'Algérie française*. A number of its Moslem members left the group after the insurrection of January 1960, and by the middle of the year it numbered about 30 (including only eleven of the Assembly's 48 Moslem Deputies). These Moslem defections were in part counter-balanced by the coming-in of most of those U.N.R. Deputies, accurately described as 'more 13th May than Gaullist', who were expelled from the party (or resigned) as a result of the President's open declaration in favour of self-determination, or of their support of the January insurrection. With Algerian independence the group disappeared.

M. Jacques Soustelle remained an enigmatic and elusive figure, committed to the policy of *Algérie française*, but evasive regarding his attitude to the O.A.S. After his expulsion from the U.N.R. he formed a new movement, the *Regroupement national*, described by him as being not a party but an association in favour of *l'Algérie française* and having also a broad programme of social reform and economic expansion. He then joined the movement founded in Algeria in April 1961 by two 'ultra' European Deputies, MM. Marçais and Lauriol, the R.N.U.R. (*Rassemblement national pour l'unité de la République*), better known by the name of its executive committee the *Comité de Vincennes*, whose President was M. Bidault. This movement, which included extremists such as the Deputies MM. Delbecque and Le Pen and the former Poujadist Deputy and ex-Police Commissioner Dides, openly attacked the head of the State, whose Algerian policy was described as 'treason'. It was finally banned at the end of 1961.

As far as could be seen, M. Soustelle played no active role in the movement. From mid-1961 onwards, he was domiciled outside France, but succeeded in giving secret interviews from time to time, and even a press conference in Paris in December 1961. He steadfastly maintained that he was not a member of the O.A.S., and did not believe in violence, though he refused to respond to M. Maurice Schumann's request to him to dissociate himself openly from it. He claimed that European Algerians would fight to prevent the application of any agreement that France might reach with the F.L.N. for the establishment of an Algerian Algeria, dismissed the concept as an illusion, and described the Fifth Republic as a dictatorship.[1]

The precise relationship between these extremist movements and the various subversive terrorist organizations, described loosely as the O.A.S., which became active in 1961, was not clear, nor were the relations of different O.A.S. organizations with each other. They did not regard themselves as parties and the O.A.S. could certainly not be regarded as a party. But the orthodox parties had their O.A.S. sympathizers in the Assembly, prepared to justify the activities of the O.A.S.[2] They were estimated to number about 80, including 34 members of the group *Unité de la République*, 25 *Indépendants*, and some 16 Deputies attached to no group.

[1] *v.* reports of a secret interview in November 1961, of a secret press conference in Paris in December 1961, and extracts from *Le Journal du Parlement* quoted in *Le Monde*, 11th January 1962.

[2] *v. infra*, pp. 220-25.

THE DYNAMIC RIGHT. IS GAULLISM CONSERVATIVE?

Gaullism does not lend itself to precise definition. Gaullists in the National Assembly have been united by their loyalty to General de Gaulle and by their belief in the need for a national 'renewal' (*le renouveau français*). General de Gaulle, however, has consistently refused to be associated with any party (though his refusal to allow the movement to describe itself as Gaullist applied only to the period of the electoral campaign). For six years, during the Fourth Republic, the Gaullist Rally of the French People had both a leader and a programme. But the movement was disbanded in 1955, General de Gaulle's association with it being officially severed. His association with Gaullist members of Parliament had already been severed two years earlier. Gaullism under the Fifth Republic has had neither a party leader nor a programme.

In 1958 Gaullism included half a dozen tendencies. The so-called Gaullist party, the Union for the New Republic (U.N.R.) was formed only a few weeks before the 1958 election, by the fusion of four Gaullist movements of very different political complexions. The Social Republicans constituted the sole remnant of the pre-war Gaullist organization, represented in the 1956 Assembly by some 20 Deputies. The Union for French Renewal (*Union pour le renouveau français*) was founded by M. Soustelle, himself a Social-Republican Deputy, as an extension into France of an Algerian movement representing the settler point of view. M. Soustelle, a former Governor-General of Algeria, was very popular with the European population of that country. and a firm believer in the policy of '*Algérie française*'. His part in the revolution of 13th May was to maintain enthusiasm for the policy of 'integration', following the demonstrations of Franco-Moslem fraternization from 16th May onwards, and he made a number of speeches on this subject. The other two constituent groups were the Republican Convention, led by M. Delbecque, who also played an active role in the events (and even more in the preparation) of 13th May, and the Workers' Committee for the support of General de Gaulle. Both were formed to support General de Gaulle in the campaign for the referendum.

Once the election of 1958 was over, the Parliamentary group of over 200 Deputies belonging to the U.N.R. had to work out a policy. It found itself divided on questions of leadership and organization, as well as on questions of policy. When the party's first Secretary-General, M. Frey, became a Minister, he was succeeded temporarily by M. Chalandon, a liberal economist, who believed in economic expansion, a progressive social policy and a 'liberal' solution for Algeria. The U.N.R. was in his mind, a dynamic, but not a conservative party.

M. Chalandon's approach was that of a technocrat, for whom the party ought to consist of *cadres*, whose function should be to carry out faithfully the policies of General de Gaulle.[1] Both on policy and on organization he found himself in conflict with the tendency represented by M. Soustelle and M. Delbecque, who believed that the party's electoral popularity had depended almost entirely on its association in the minds of the electors with General de Gaulle, and that what was needed was its transformation into a mass party with a modern organization.

By the end of 1961, the U.N.R. had still not formulated a policy, but it had, at least, become more homogeneous. The President's announcement of the policy of self-determination for Algeria led to the departure of nine members including the most active and vociferous supporters of the ideas of 13th May and *l'Algérie française* (MM. Delbecque, Biaggi, Battesti, Arrighi, Thomazo), most of whom joined the group, *Unité de la République*. The Algiers insurrection of January 1960 led to the dismissal of M. Soustelle from the Government and to his expulsion from the U.N.R. Some of those who remained in the party (according to some estimates, almost a third) still believed in integration – the President's third choice of '*francisation*' – but responded to the Prime Minister's

[1] M. Chalandon had expressed views consistent with both the conception of the party as an agent for General de Gaulle and that of a centre party. Cf., for instance, 'General de Gaulle is our clandestine leader. We are rather like secret agents, owing total obedience to their military leader, who will not hesitate to disavow them if things go badly' (quoted in *Le Monde*, 21st July 1959), and the following extract from an article in the Gaullist press bulletin: 'We are a party movement and, consequently, the negation of traditional conservatism. . . . We are also a liberal party. . . . We have strengthened the power of the executive, but in order to safeguard essential liberties. . . . Lastly, we are a Governmental party. . . . We are bound to support Governments, of whatever kind, to be the pivot of majorities; they will be perhaps Left, perhaps Right, but, in any case, we shall be there.' (Quoted in *Le Monde*, 19th May 1959.)

On the policy of Gaullism under the Fourth Republic, *v.* Philip Williams, *Politics in post-war France* (Longmans, 1954) and, for a brief discussion, the author's *France: The Fourth Republic* (Methuen, 1958).

appeal to the party to leave things in the hands of General de Gaulle.

For the following two years the 208 to 211 Deputies of the party provided solid and disciplined support for M. Debré's Government. When, at the party conference in November 1959, M. Chaban-Delmas asserted the President's 'constitutional responsibility' within what he called the 'Presidential sector', comprising defence, Algerian, Community and foreign affairs, this totally unconstitutional expansion of the President's powers went unchallenged at the time and was not challenged later. The party's *raison d'être* continued to be its association with, and fidelity to, General de Gaulle. When M. Debré resigned in April 1962 and was replaced as Prime Minister by M. Pompidou, many commentators wondered whether U.N.R. loyalty to the Government would continue to be as staunch.

By 1961–2, the Parliamentary group had at least developed some of the reflexes of a genuine Parliamentary party. Members of the older Parliamentary parties must have derived some ironic satisfaction at the U.N.R.'s reaction to what they had predicted would be one of the weaknesses of the 1958 Constitution. For, by the middle of 1961, not only were U.N.R. Deputies protesting against the technocratic character of the Government and calling for 'the rehabilitation of the function of Parliament', but the Prime Minister himself was complaining of the 'isolation' that power had brought with it.[1]

Outside the ranks of the U.N.R., there are the left-wing Gaullists. At the time of the 1958 election some 80 candidates stood, polling about half-a-million votes, but winning no seat. Several tendencies united in 1959 to form the *Union démocratique du travail* (U.D.T.) which included an ex-ambassador, M. Grandval, some ex-Deputies (MM. Louis Vallon, de Lipkowski and René Capitant) and an ex-Senator, M. Léo Hamon.[2]

Unlike the U.N.R., the U.D.T. has a programme, the general

[1] *v.* for instance, the following extract from his speech to delegates of the Conference in Paris of the International Political Science Association:
"..... *le pouvoir meurt de sa solitude; il lui faut donc un cortège de sympathies et d' amitiés*". (Figaro, 27th September 1961.

[2] A movement with this title was founded in 1955 by M. Louis Vallon, and the general social and economic policy of the two movements is similar. There was a breakaway shortly after the foundation of the movement in 1959 of some former members of the tendency represented by the *Centre de la réforme républicaine*.

character of which is indicated by the fact that its members are sometimes called *Mendésistes de droite*. The party differs from the orthodox Left on two points. It is prepared to work within the framework of the new institutions and accepts General de Gaulle's leadership in general, not only in the field of Algerian policy; and it is specifically in favour of the referendum and the dissolution as genuine democratic instruments. It agrees with the general economic and social policies of the non-Communist Left and also refuses any co-operation with the Communist party.

The U.D.T. is numerically small and apparently without influence in the country, but attracts a certain number of intellectuals. Though perhaps less Gaullist than Left, it would still be unlikely to survive if the U.N.R. did not.

The future of Gaullism is still unpredictable. It does not seem to have established any firm hold in the countryside (nor, indeed, did the R.P.F.) and once the threat of insurrection disappears, and with it the need to rally round the President in defence of the Republic, the movement might break up,[1] or even cease to exist, particularly if General de Gaulle disappears from the political scene. Throughout the first Parliament of the Fifth Republic, the U.N.R. was neither dynamic nor conservative, but merely a reflection of Presidential and Governmental requirements, a twentieth-century manifestation of the kind of party loyalty described by Bagehot a century earlier as 'the finest brute vote in Europe'.

THE STATIC LEFT. HAS RADICALISM A FUTURE?

The Radical party is the oldest French party, but its influence has been declining since the thirties, when the Socialist party became a serious rival in the traditional Radical strongholds. It almost disappeared during the early post-war years, but by 1955 had recovered to the extent of having some 75 Deputies (including associates and the U.D.S.R.), and of having provided eight of the 16 Prime Ministers who had held office since the beginning of the Fourth Republic. From 1955 onwards, it was weakened by three successive splits. M. Edgar Faure's *Rassemblement des gauches républicaines* (R.G.R.) was an electoral coalition, re-formed as a

[1] There were reported to be serious divisions in the Government at the end of 1961, mainly on Algerian policy.

party after his expulsion from the Radical party, along with several others, following the 1955 dissolution. The R.G.R.'s differences from the parent party were personal rather than political. In 1956, the *Centre républicain* was formed, consisting of a dozen or so of the more right-wing representatives in the Assembly, including two former Prime Ministers, MM. Marie and Queuille. It differed from the orthodox Radicals in continuing to support '*l'Algérie française*'.[1] In 1958, M. Mendès-France and a handful of his supporters on the left of the party were deemed to have excluded themselves, owing to their refusal to resign, on the instructions of the party, from the left-wing electoral alliance, the *Union des forces démocratiques*. The Radicals (all tendencies) lost about half a million votes in the 1958 elections. The party's main achievement under the Fifth Republic has been the partial reunification of the movement and the reform of its internal organization. In the 1959 Parliament, two main tendencies, Deputies of the orthodox, or *Valoisien*, tendency, and *Libertés démocratiques*, including left-centre members of various shades – united to form the Parliamentary group called the *Entente démocratique*.[2] The right-wing dissident-Radical *Centre républicain*, which had comprised eleven members of the Assembly at the beginning of the Parliament, was reduced to two by the autumn, and M. Edgar's Faure's dissident group also disappeared. He himself, along with several other dissidents, was readmitted to the party at the 1961 Congress.[3] By the middle of 1959, 26 of the local federations affected by the splits had already returned to the fold. The Congress of that year was described as one of 'convalescence'. By 1961, the patient was much healthier.

To begin with there had been some rejuvenation. The elder statesmen had either died (M. Herriot in 1957, M. Baylet in 1959) or, having joined one of the dissident groups, returned to occupy back seats. The most prominent and the most disturbing influence,

[1] This group did not constitute a separate Parliamentary group in the 1958 Assembly and had virtually disappeared within a year.

[2] The two tendencies are usually distinguished in voting lists published in the press as the '*Section radical – socialiste*' and '*Liberte's démocratiques*'.

[3] The *Centre républicain* continued to exist outside Parliament. The leader M. André Morice had not been re-elected.

M. Edgar Faure became a Senator in 1959. He used these years during which he was in a political wilderness to write a book on Turgot and to present himself for the *agrégation* in Roman Law, taking first place in the autumn of 1961.

M. Mendès-France, was no longer a member. Of the new leaders, M. Gaillard was in his early forties, and M. Maurice Faure, who became President in 1961, was still under forty.

The party remained politically on the Left and, attached as it was to the traditional forms of Parliamentary government in France, deeply suspicious of the new institutions, which its members regarded as 'half-Parliamentary in law, but wholly Presidential in fact'.[1] Radical Deputies signed the censure motions introduced both in 1960 and in 1961, though not all members of the group voted in favour of them. No directive was finally issued by the party regarding the vote in the 1961 referendum, the Executive Committee having been in favour of voting 'No', but with a large minority in favour of 'Yes'. In other words, the party remained on the fence, disliking the régime, but avoiding attacking it directly,[2] sympathetic to the President's Algerian policy, but critical of the progress of the negotiations, anti-clerical, but less fervently than in the past,[3] opposed to the President's policy of an independent atomic 'striking force' and critical of his attitude within the Atlantic alliance. This was, to all intents and purposes the 'constructive opposition' of the Socialists, except for the disagreement between the two parties (and particularly between Socialists and the more conservative Radical elements of the South West) on social and economic policy. Under the Fifth Republic, no less than under its predecessors, Radical pocket books continued to be carried on the Right rather than on the Left.

THE CATHOLIC LEFT

In matters of social and economic policy, the M.R.P. (*Mouvement républicain populaire*) is definitely farther to the Left than the majority of the Radicals. But, though it is firmly Republican and democratic, the movement has found it difficult to establish itself as an authentic left-wing party, for several reasons. It has existed

[1] Quoted in *Le Monde* 16th June 1959.

[2] *v.* for instance, M. Gaillard's closing speech at the 1960 Conference, in which he defined the position of the party as being Governmental without necessarily offering its services. In fact there had been no Radical Minister since early 1959.

[3] A resolution calling for a battle for '*la laïcité*' was defeated at the 1959 Congress.

only since the war and has not yet managed to get a firm hold in the traditionally-minded country areas except in the predominantly Catholic *départements* of Eastern and Western France. Though by no means all its members are Catholics, it is strongly influenced by Catholicism, as are the numerous youth and women's organizations associated with it. And on the question that is almost a test of left-wing *bona fides*, the Catholic-schools problem, the M.R.P. shares the views of the Right. It has often been supported by electors who are more conservative than the majority of its leaders. As a predominantly Catholic, anti-Marxist, anti-class-war party, preaching the virtues of family life, a party whose loyalty to General de Gaulle in the early post-war period gained for it the description of *le parti de la fidélité*, the M.R.P. has been, from a right-wing point of view, a respectable substitute if, for any reason, right-wing candidates were unacceptable in a constituency. For the same reasons, the M.R.P. tended to be unacceptable to the Socialists. The battle over the *loi Barangé*, which, in 1951, provided a small State contribution to Catholic schools, led to the alienation of the M.R.P. and Socialist parties from each other throughout the second Parliament of the Fourth Republic.

The success, in the 1956 elections, of a number of younger candidates, whose views reflected those of the strong Catholic Trade Union Confederation, the C.F.T.C. (*Confédération des travailleurs chrétiens*) and the removal of some of the more right-wing elements from the party with the formation of M. Bidault's *Démocratie chrétienne*[1] after the events of 13th May, helped to strengthen the leftward orientation of the party. Its internal organization, which is democratic, was modified, from 1958 onwards, in order to give to rank-and-file representatives, and especially workers and peasants, half the places in the executive organs of the party.

The M.R.P.'s policy in relation to Algeria has, at times, appeared to be more progressive than that of the Socialist party. The movement has favoured a negotiated settlement, but has had confidence in General de Gaulle's intentions regarding Algeria. It also favours a policy of aid to under-developed areas, often advocated by General de Gaulle in his speeches up and down the country. In foreign

[1] *Démocratie chrétienne* has been 'integrationist', in favour of *Algérie française*, of a strong French foreign policy in general and of French firmness in the intermittent and apparently endless negotiations on Franco-Tunisian relations.

affairs, it is the only party to have been consistently and unanimously in favour of the policy of European integration and has been, more than any other section of opinion, responsible for France's moves in that direction. In internal affairs it believes in a policy of economic expansion and deplores the social inequalities resulting from the Government's economic policy. It is also suspicious of the technocratic tendencies of the Fifth Republic and shares the general criticisms of the Left regarding the evolution of the régime towards a *de facto* presidential system.

Though no less critical than the Socialists of the Government's economic and social policies, the M.R.P. remained, up to 1962, a Governmental party, but not without uneasiness.[1] Belief in General de Gaulle as the only hope of solving the Algerian problem began to show signs of strain after the breakdown of the Melun Conference, in June 1960, and the party became increasingly anxious regarding the moral repercussions of a terrorist war, in particular the evidence of torture by the French army in Algeria, to which individual priests and Catholic organizations repeatedly drew attention. There was also disillusionment regarding the high cost of General de Gaulle's policies in other fields, and particularly in those of defence and European integration. As the originator and chief protagonist of European integration, the M.R.P. naturally opposed the President's nationalistic defence policy and his rejection of the principle of political integration in favour of '*l'Europe des Etats*'. The five M.R.P. Ministers included by M. Pompidou in his Government of April 1962 all resigned following General de Gaulle's press conference of 15th May 1962, owing to the tone of his remarks on European supranationalism.

By 1960, the situation which had existed during the early years of the movement, when the rank and file were to the right of the leadership, was reversed, perhaps in part owing to the deliberate democratization of the party's organization. For at the National Committee, held in the autumn, Ministers and ex-Ministers failed to persuade the rank and file not to vote a strongly worded resolution dissociating the movement from the President's policy and calling on the Parliamentary representatives to vote in accordance with the

[1] M. Lecourt resigned in August 1961, owing to disagreements with M. Debré and it was generally understood that M. Maurice Schumann had been offered, but had refused a Governmental post. The three remaining M.R.P. Ministers all occupied posts of a predominantly technical nature.

criticisms expressed. The M.R.P. remained conscious, however, that in the critical situation of the Algerian negotiations, anything that might weaken what remained of the authority of the State might remove the last hope of a solution and, therefore, did not withdraw its Ministers from the Government until after the agreement on a cease-fire in Algeria.

SOCIALISM AND 'CONSTRUCTIVE OPPOSITION'

After a brief post-war period of great prestige and influence, the Socialist party lost votes steadily until about 1955, from which point, up to the end of the Fourth Republic, it began to gain ground, though, in 1958, its membership figures were still not more than half those of 1946. The composition of the party was, moreover, increasingly middle-class and middle-aged.

The party had to face great practical difficulties throughout the Fourth Republic. With the passage of the Communist party into opposition in 1947, it had to compete for working-class votes with a party which could, and did, exploit to the full the opportunities for political irresponsibility offered by opposition, while the Socialist party was often compelled either to support or to participate in Governments, the majority of whose members were considerably to its right. Socialist party organization was ill-adapted to the needs of a party in office, being traditionally organized to give full expression to all tendencies within the party. M. Guy Mollet, who became Secretary-General in 1946, was largely responsible for making the party a disciplined organ of decision, but incurred great unpopularity with the numerically small but influential minority which had been opposed to the majority view on German rearmament, on Algeria, on General de Gaulle's return to power and on the Constitution.

The Socialist party's Algerian policy consisted of a three-point programme (known in the movement as the 'triptych') aiming at military pacification, free elections and negotiations. In essence, this was the programme that liberal opinion, including the Socialists, at first considered to be General de Gaulle's policy, with the difference that General de Gaulle decided to hold elections, in spite of the continuance of the fighting. Under the Fifth Republic, the party continued to advocate negotiations for a cease-fire and, subsequently or simultaneously, efforts to negotiate a settlement, but there were differences of emphasis, even within the majority, and more serious differences between the majority and the minority.

In September 1958, the minority broke away and formed an independent party, its candidates opposing those of the parent party in the elections. All the candidates of this 'autonomous' party were defeated. Ideologically, there is no real difference of opinion between majority and minority. Both remain faithful to anti-clericalism, and parts of the Marxist inheritance, these sentiments being particularly strong among the rank and file. On the problems confronting the Fifth Republic in its early years, the differences have been important. The majority party's position has been one of 'constructive opposition', by which is meant co-operation as far as possible with General de Gaulle in his efforts to save the Republic and to bring peace to Algeria, but opposition to specific aspects of the Government's policy, especially to its economic restrictionism and its fiscal and social policies, which, the party believes, places too big a burden on the working class. In foreign policy, the party has remained faithful to the policy of European integration, though being generally less united on it, and less interested in it, than the M.R.P. It is firmly opposed to any association, either electoral or on specific issues, with the Communist party.

In September 1959 M. Mendès-France and the majority of his small *Centre d'action démocratique* joined the autonomous party. In April 1960, after difficult negotiations, the party united with the *Union de la gauche socialiste*, itself a federation of small left-wing splinter groups, opposed to the régime and including fellow-travellers, ex-Communists and a number of left-wing intellectuals. The *Parti socialiste unifié* (P.S.U.), as it called itself, has proved neither united nor influential. Its programme was a restatement of traditional Socialist positions, combining nostalgia for the past, hopes for the future and irrelevance to present circumstances. Its first Congress in May 1961 revealed the persistence of the tendencies that had made the achievement of unity so difficult. The Keynsian pragmatism of M. André Philip and the more old-fashioned Marxism of M. Oreste Rosenfeld made uncomfortable bedfellows and anti-Mollet democratic Socialists, doctrinaire ex-Communist intellectuals, left-wing Catholics and working-class Marxist elements found it difficult to live together.

The voice of the P.S.U. has not, in fact, carried beyond its own meetings and, even there, enthusiasm apparently soon flagged. By the end of 1961 there were already rumours of an impending reconciliation between the majority and minority movements. M. Mendès-France has appeared to have little contact with the P.S.U. and no influence within it. He spent a great deal of his time outside the country on lecture tours and neither in these nor in the Press conferences that he gave from time to time did he appear to speak for anybody but himself. His conferences at least made news, which P.S.U. meetings did not, but he remained a voice crying in a political wilderness, a leader without followers.

Three things made the reunion of former Socialists in the P.S.U. with the orthodox Socialist party difficult. The first was the bitter personal hostility of some P.S.U. leaders to the leadership of M. Guy Mollet and, in particular, to his insistence on party discipline, as opposed to the pre-war traditional acceptance of '*tendances*'. The second was the P.S.U.'s hostility to the régime, whereas the orthodox party, though formally in opposition from the beginning of 1959, continued to insist that it must be 'constructive opposition', so long as any hope remained that the President could succeed in achieving a settlement in Algeria. The third was the P.S.U's willingness to accept some degree of common action with the Communist party.[1]

The orthodox party has had its own majority and minority problems, and though M. Mollet has weathered the storms successfully, Socialist influence in the country has been obviously weakened by the disunity and dissensions. The membership figures alone are eloquent: in 1957, nearly 110,000 members; in 1958, 94,000; in 1959, under 83,000.

There have been three main sources of division; Socialist attitudes to the régime, to doctrine and to Algeria. The section led by M. Albert Gazier, and including MM. Pineau, Dardel, Fuzier, Guille, Coutrot, is opposed to the régime and had no faith in the President's

[1] There was a meeting between M. Guy Mollet and M. Mendès-France in September 1961, but its purpose was to discuss the possibility of joint action by all democratic forces, in order to prevent a constitutional vacuum following the departure, for whatever reason, of General de Gaulle from the Elysée. There is no evidence that M. Mendès-France has ever considered joining the Socialist party and the personal incompatibility between the two leaders would make such a move extremely unlikely, even if ex-Socialist P.S.U. members were to return to their former party.

capacity to solve the Algerian problem, which was the majority's chief justification for the 'constructive' nature of its opposition. M. Gazier pointed out, for instance, in September 1961, in defence of his view, that General de Gaulle had then had more time to deal with the problem than all Governments of the Fourth Republic put together. He and his supporters have remained within the party, however, since they recognize that the overwhelming majority of the rank and file have consistently backed the position defended by M. Mollet.

M. Jules Moch is anxious to bring the party's Marxist basis up to date, by reformulating its economic policy, and in particular the policy of nationalization, in the light of changes in the class structure, of the evolution of modern capitalism and of the growing importance of technocracy. These views have met with little support from the rank and file.[1] The party remains on the whole backward-looking, as is evidenced not only by the caution (or is it perhaps lack of interest?) with which the movement treats any suggestion to do more than 'clarify' a Marxist framework which is traditional but hardly orthodox, or to modify in any way its traditional anti-clericalism. The only subject which really roused the party's passionate interest during the first three years of the Fifth Republic was the Education Bill of December 1959, providing on certain conditions for a system of regular State aid to Catholic schools. This was treated as a major break with the half-century practice of State neutrality in religious matters.

On Algeria, there have been four distinct tendencies. A small section, led by M. Max Lejeune, continued to believe in the possibility and desirability of putting the clock back and providing a status for Algeria, on the lines of the 1958 outline-law.[2] M. Gazier and his supporters and the majority of the *Comité directeur* were, in 1960, at the time of the breakdown of the Melun negotiations, in

[1] M. Moch who is a *polytechnicien* by training, and M. André Philip (who joined the P.S.U.) who is an economist, have both met with little response in their efforts to modernize the party's economics. M. Léon Blum met with no more success when he tried, in 1946, to introduce a modest change in the party's statement of its Marxist belief by substituting for the words 'class struggle' the term 'class action.'

[2] This was already so far out of touch with realities in Algeria that no attempt was ever made to apply it. Yet, in June 1960, M. Lejeune and M. Lacoste were among the signatories of the *Manifeste de la gauche pour le maintien de l'Algérie dans la République*. Other non-Socialist signatories included MM. Bourges-Maunoury, André Morice, and Jules Romains.

favour of simultaneous discussions on a cease-fire and self-determination – in other words, they believed that General de Gaulle was mishandling the problem. M. Gaston Defferre wanted an Algerian Government, that is, he had arrived at a belief in *l'Algérie algérienne* before General de Gaulle – or at least before the latter felt that he could safely put this forward to the French people as his policy. M. Guy Mollet believed then, as he continued to do up to the achievement of Algerian independence, that General de Gaulle must be given a free hand.

As Socialist criticisms of Presidential policy grew, the gap between majority and minority views narrowed. Both sides could agree to deplore what they regarded as Presidential and Governmental lack of respect for the Constitution, the evolution of the régime towards a Presidential system, the President's responsibility for divisions within N.A.T.O., the brakes on European integration, the social injustice of the Government's social and economic policies. At the special conference in September 1961, there was more unity than there had been since 1958, but it was a negative unity based on criticisms of the President. The Parliamentary group could vote unanimously for the motion of censure of December 1961, blaming the Government for its clumsiness, weakness, internal divisions and inability to deal with the threats to the Republic. But when it came to taking positive steps to look beyond the crisis conditions created by the Algerian situation, and beyond the régime, the divisions were seen to be still there.

The Socialist party has not, of course, been any more negative than other parties. Indeed M. Mollet's constructive opposition has been more statesmanlike and responsible than the opposition of other parties. And M. Mollet is one of the few political leaders who have not merely tried to look ahead, but have also tried to find some way of penetrating the political apathy characteristic of all parties under the Fifth Republic, whether on the Right or on the Left.[1]

THE COMMUNIST PARTY

Except for a few months in 1946, the Communist party has consistently polled more votes than any other party. Even in the 1958 elections, which resulted in the reduction of its Parliamentary

[1] On this *v. infra*, pp. 227-8.

representation from 142 to ten Deputies, the party polled 3,882,204 votes at the first ballot. This total showed a drop of over a million and a half on the 1956 figures, but it was still over 200,000 higher than the total of the votes cast for the Gaullist U.N.R.

The strength of Communism in a country like France, with a high proportion of craftsmen and small owner-farmers, and with a highly individualist and critical approach to politics, is perhaps, at first sight, surprising. In the context of left-wing Republican and Revolutionary tradition it is less so. Part of the Communist party's strength comes from its claim to be, at the same time, Republican and Revolutionary, whole-heartedly Marxist and the most left-wing party. Its position of permanent opposition, since 1947, has given it ample opportunity to demonstrate its interest in the workers. Its closely-knit internal organization, based on occupational 'cells' more than on local branches, and its real (though not, of course, admitted) control of the oldest and strongest of the Trade-Union organizations, the C.G.T. (*Confédération générale du travail*), have given it an efficient organization, able to back up its demands, by strike action if necessary.

Communism also has a strong ideological attraction for left-wing intellectuals, whose influence is strong in France in the numerous left-wing literary and political periodicals which are concerned with Communist doctrine as well as with current political problems. This element contributes to the spread of Communist propaganda, but at times has also constituted a weakness. The fact that some intellectuals insist on thinking for themselves has involved, of recent years, a number of tortuous doctrinal controversies and one or two spectacular departures from the party. And the events in Hungary, on which a number of Communist intellectuals openly attacked the orthodox point of view and some resigned from the party, dealt the Communists the most severe blow that they had received since the outbreak of war in 1939.

The Communist party reacted to the events of 13th May, first by calling for demonstrations of loyalty to the Republic, especially for strikes, and then by declaring its opposition to the new régime. Both the response to Communist appeals and the voting figures in the referendum and elections revealed, however, that, whether for political reasons (the persistence of the feeling regarding Hungary, or the unpopularity of its support for the Moslem rebels) or for economic reasons (the unpopularity of political strikes), the party had lost much of its former hold over its supporters.[1] In the referendum, only four and a half million electors voted *No*, whereas in 1956, five and a half million electors had voted for the Communist party. The result was that, for the first year or so of the new régime, apart from one abortive strike threat which was not of purely Communist inspiration, the Communist party remained very much in the background, advocating united working-class action. This has almost always been a sign of Communist consciousness of weakness. In Parliament, the party had no longer any influence, since its small numbers deprived it of both representation on Commissions and the possibility of introducing motions of censure. The Assembly also consistently refused to nominate Communists to other bodies, such as the Senate of the Community. The danger was, therefore, that the party would concentrate its attention on the industrial sphere where it still had considerable influence.

The fact that this threat did not materialise during the first three years of the régime could be attributed in the first place to the persistence of the factors which had led to the decline of Communist influence during the last years of the Fourth Republic. France was economically prosperous, and so Communist propaganda was deprived of its favourite weapon – the exploitation of grievances. The party was slow to recover the self-confidence shaken visibly by de-Stalinization, and less visibly, though perhaps as profoundly, by the Hungarian revolt. The one shook the party's faith in its leaders, the other, its faith in the working-class *mystique*. In the words of one commentator, by turning its guns on the workers, the U.S.S.R. had lost, at least for a time, 'its halo of proletarian sanctity'.

There were, however, more specific reasons for the party's embarrassment during the first years of the Fifth Republic. The heresy-hunting that had characterized so much of the 'fifties' was continued into the 'sixties'. But its causes, though not its pretexts, were now a direct result of the Presidential Algerian policy. The party's immediate reaction to General de Gaulle's announcement of his policy of self-determination for Algeria was to denounce it as a

[1] There was a sharp drop in the number and sales of Communist papers particularly in the provinces. This may have been partly due to the sudden fall in, Communist income owing to the reduction in the number of Communist party Deputies, all of whom contribute a considerable share of their income to the party.

'time-saving manœuvre'. It soon became clear, however, that the Soviet Union had its own reasons for approving the policy and so, while Mr Krushchev was speaking (temporarily) of the need for links between France and Algeria, French Communist leaders were obliged also to make a volte-face. They hurriedly ate their words and were rapped over the knuckles by M. Thorez (whose reputation was saved by the fact that he was out of the country at the time) for having been out of step.

When Mr Krushchev's Paris visit was over and the Summit talks had broken down, the breakdown of the Melun negotiations enabled the Communists to return to their former opposition to the Government's Algerian policy. But by then the majority of Frenchmen, including many Communist supporters, wanted above all to see peace in Algeria and were prepared to back General de Gaulle to obtain it. And so the familiar themes of Communist witch-hunts – the accusations of 'opportunism', of 'right-wing deviations', enveloped in the customary ideological jargon – failed lamentably to make an appeal. MM. Servin and Casanova (the latter a winner of the Lenin peace prize in 1960) were expelled from the Communist party *bureau* in 1960, ostensibly on grounds of 'opportunism', and both duly made their '*autocritique*'. But what they were really being blamed for was, first, their refusal to regard de Gaulle as being wholly an expression of monopolistic interests and personal power – which was the orthodox party line – and second, their refusal to treat Communist-sponsored peace organizations as being primarily intended to act as Communist propaganda machines.

During those first years of the Fifth Republic, the Communist party had to recognize that its appeal both inside and outside the movement was weak. At the 1961 Congress, the rapporteur, M. Waldeck-Rochet (whose unshakeable orthodoxy led him to be regarded as a possible successor to M. Thorez) freely admitted a further decline in membership figures.[1] But the French Communist party has frequently gone through similar periods of relative unpopularity and nothing about this one of necessity heralds any spectacular or permanent decline of the party's hold either on the organized industrial workers or on the voters.

[1] Between 1956 and 1961, official membership figures fell from 429,000 to 407,000.

CHAPTER VI

Parliament

The Constitution deals with legislative procedure in much more detail than previous Constitutions have done. A number of matters traditionally left for Parliament to decide are now constitutionalized. Parliamentary Standing Orders, for instance, must now be submitted to the Constitutional Council and declared in conformity with the Constitution, before they can come into force; Governments are specifically given control over matters previously controlled by Parliament. The Assembly's Standing Orders, too, have themselves prohibited devices much used by previous Assemblies (and also by the Senate) in order to harass and weaken Governments,[1] and have provided for a greater measure of control by the President of the Assembly, in order to prevent the indiscipline and disorder that have sometimes characterized debates in the Assembly. The result has been an Assembly diminished in power, in relation to the Government, and in prestige in relation to the Senate.

THE RIGHTS AND DUTIES OF MEMBERS OF PARLIAMENT

Members of Parliament enjoy certain privileges. In order that they may speak and vote freely, they are not liable, either during or after their membership of either House, to criminal or civil proceedings in respect of anything said or done by them in the House in the exercise of their duties. They remain responsible for anything said or published outside Parliament. While Parliament is sitting, proceedings may not be taken against them for anything said or done in their private capacity, unless the House of which they are members decides, by a vote, to suspend their immunity.

[1] *v.* below, pp. 115 sqq.

Exceptions to the rule are minor offences, the penalty for which would not prevent them for carrying out their Parliamentary duties, and serious offences in which the member is caught *flagrante delicto*. In the latter case, he may be arrested, though the House is still free to stop proceedings. When Parliament is not sitting, proceedings are possible but, except in cases where the arrest is *flagrante delicto*, or where a Court has made a final finding of guilt, or where arrest has been authorized in a previous session, the member may be arrested only with the authorization of the *bureau* of the House.

Members are also subject to certain obligations. Certain occupations are incompatible with membership of Parliament. Those which entail the member's replacement by a substitute have been mentioned in the previous chapter.[1] In the case of other incompatibilities, the member's resignation is followed by a by-election. Most of the incompatibilities existed also under the Third and Fourth Republics. They include directorships of nationalized and State-subsidized concerns, or of concerns carrying out public-works contracts. The Fifth Republic has added to the list that of the legal representation of concerns involved in actions against the State. Membership in an unpaid capacity of local Government authorities and of certain local non-profit-making concerns is specifically excepted from the list of incompatibilities.[2]

Mandatory instructions to members of Parliament (*le mandat impératif*) are null and void. The interpretation of this rule (article 27 of the Constitution) has given rise to some discussion, since Deputies and Senators who belong to an organized party clearly do vote in accordance with a mandate from their parties, and also with decisions of their Parliamentary group. It has not been used to interfere with the normal working of democratic party machinery. Its intention was rather to prevent the kind of party domination represented by the Communist party's habit of requiring Communist members to place a signed resignation form in the hands of the party, to be used as the party, and not the member, sees fit. In other words, the member is intended to be, as Burke maintained he was, a national representative and not merely a delegate of special interests.

[1] *v. supra,* pp. 56–57.

[2] Three traditional exceptions are also holders of university chairs (and now also of research chairs), members of Government missions (of under six months' duration) and ministers of religion in the three *départements of* Alsace-Lorraine, still governed in religious matters by the *Concordat*.

It is difficult, nevertheless, to see any practical utility in this prohibition, since, except in the case of a flagrant and generally known practice such as that quoted above, proof of compliance with mandatory instructions would usually be impossible. The demands of pressure groups, though not mandatory, can be similarly destructive of the real independence of the member. In his letter to the President of the Assembly of 18th March 1960, the President did, indeed, treat as mandatory, in the constitutional sense, what were in reality the normal proposals of pressure groups.[1]

The Constitution (article 27) also prohibits members from voting by proxy. Under the Fourth Republic, absenteeism was a regular thing. The French Parliamentary system makes no provision for pairing, and since the Assembly has been hitherto accustomed to voting a great many Bills every session, the obligation of personal voting would have been a much heavier burden on the French Deputy than it is on the member of the British House of Commons, though it would not have been so hard on his feet. Apart from votes by show of hands, or by standing, voting in the French Parliament has normally been by ballot, and proxy-voting used to be general. Either one member of the group cast the votes for the whole group (the Communist method), or members gave a number of signed voting papers to one or more proxies, who voted on their behalf. If more than one proxy voted for the same member the Secretaries detected it when the votes were checked. If the proxy voted in a way the member disliked, he could send in a *rectification de vote*. This did not affect the result, but it often enabled a Deputy to save face if his vote had been cast in a way that his electors would dislike. One result of this system was that debates which were in actual fact conducted before almost empty benches could be followed by votes including upwards of 75 per cent of the membership of the House.

The Fifth Republic tried to change all this. A member may now delegate his vote only for five reasons, duly notified in writing in advance. They are; absence on grounds of illness, accident or family circumstances; absence on a Government mission or on military service; absence from France on the occasion of a special session; or owing to representation of the Senate or the Assembly at a meeting of an international Assembly. No member may cast a

[1] *v. infra*, p. 141.

proxy vote for more than one of his colleagues at a time. *Rectification de vote* is now prohibited. Since 1959, the Assembly has had electronic voting, each Deputy having his own apparatus and key. In practice, some Deputies surrender their keys to group leaders.

Under the Fifth Republic, the member is required, not only to vote in person, but to vote regularly. Parliamentary salaries have been increased, but the total is now divided into two parts: a basic salary, and an 'attendance bonus' (*indemnité de fonction*), which is received in full only if the member's attendance is satisfactory.[1] Each House is free to decide exactly how members are to be penalized for non-attendance. The Assembly's Standing Orders provide that absence from three consecutive Commission sittings without valid explanation entails the member's resignation from the Commission and the loss of a third of the attendance bonus, until the opening of the following October session. Absence without valid explanation from more than a third of the votes by ballot in any month entails the loss of a third of the monthly attendance bonus. Two-thirds of the bonus is forfeited in the case of absence from more than half the votes.[2]

THE GENERAL ORGANIZATION OF PARLIAMENTARY BUSINESS

Members of Parliament are, in fact, being paid more for less work – or perhaps more accurately for shorter hours – since, under the Fifth Republic, Parliament sits for a maximum of five and a half months in the year, whereas during the later years of the Fourth

[1] The basic salary is the average salary of members of the highest category of the Civil Service (*hors échelle*). Under the Fourth Republic it was that of the *Conseillers d'Etat*. The attendance bonus is an innovation of the Fifth Republic. There was some criticism of the increased salaries, at a time when taxation was being increased and general wage increases discouraged. But it has been pointed out that the increased salary is taxed at a higher rate. Members are also not allowed to supplement their incomes, though certain exceptions are allowed, in particular the holding of military and civil pensions and receipt of the allowances paid to local-government representatives.

[2] During the first session (April to July 1959) from 75 to 100 Deputies were fined. French ingenuity was already finding ways of getting round this unpopular provision, however. It was remarked that poorly attended debates were often followed by an influx of voters, the qualification for the attendance bonus being presence for the *vote*, not for the debate. The 'valid explanation' proviso also enables Commissions to interpret the regulations very liberally.

Republic it sat for a minimum of seven months. The Parliamentary Commissions can meet when Parliament is not sitting, however. The first session, from the first Tuesday in October to the third Friday in December, lasts 74 days and is mainly concerned with the budget. The second, from the end of April to July, may not exceed three months and is mainly concerned with the legislative programme. Special sessions may be held only if convened by the President of the Republic, which should mean, in effect, by the Prime Minister, since the President requires a counter-signature, or on the request of a majority of the members of the Assembly, for a specific agenda. In the latter case, the session must be closed as soon as the agenda has been completed and, in any case after a period not exceeding 12 days.[1] In addiiton, Parliament meets as of right on two occasions; after an election, for a special session of up to a fortnight; and during a period of application of article 16, when it is entitled to sit for the duration of the emergency.[2]

At the beginning of the October session, each House elects the *bureau*, consisting of its President, Vice-Presidents (six for the Assembly and four for the Senate), Secretaries (twelve for the Assembly and eight for the Senate), who supervise the production of the official records and check the votes, and the *Questeurs* (three for each House), who are responsible for administrative and financial arrangements. With the exception of the President, the members of the *bureau* are, in effect, chosen by the leaders of the Parliamentary groups, the Assembly normally endorsing the list of names presented by them. The functions of the *bureau* as a collective body are to organize and supervise the different services in the Assembly, and, if required, to advise the President of the Assembly on a number of points, in particular on disciplinary matters and the admissibility of Bills or resolutions.

The President of the Assembly is elected at the first meeting of the session, which is presided over by the oldest member (*le doyen d'âge*) Formerly elected annually, the President is now elected for

[1] A final paragraph (article 29) states that a 'new session' may not be held until a month has elapsed after 'the closure decree', except on the request of the Prime Minister. On the constitutional controversy regarding the precise interpretation of these two articles, *à propos* of the request for a special session in March, 1960, *v. infra*, p. 141.

[2] *v. infra*, pp. 151-4.

the duration of the Parliament.[1] The Constitution makes no mention of the system of election, which is unchanged. The ballot is secret. For election at a first or second ballot, an absolute majority of the membership of the House is required, but a relative majority only is required at the third ballot. The President has certain new functions under the Fifth Republic. He must be consulted by the President of the Republic as to the existence of an emergency as defined by article 16. A private member's Bill or amendment which the President of the Assembly believes to be constitutional, but which the Government has challenged as unconstitutional, must be either submitted by him to the Constutitional Council or ruled out of order. For the rest, Presidents carry out the normal functions of Chairman. They do not have the unchallenged authority of the Speaker of the House of Commons, partly, though only partly, because they remain active members of their parties and partly, perhaps, because under the Fourth Republic they had to be re-elected annually by their colleagues, but they have a position of great prestige, the President of the Assembly ranking fourth in the order of precedence, immediately after the President of the Senate.[2]

Under the Fifth Republic, the Assembly's Standing Orders give somewhat more discretion to the President then his predecessors have had, particularly in calling Deputies to order, and in calling for the closure of debates.

French Parliamentary procedure has to take into account the existence of a number of Parliamentary groups not always classifiable as belonging definitely to the Government or to the Opposition side. Only organized groups, that is, groups with 30 members or more, are now represented at the *Conférence des Présidents* and on the Parliamentary Commissions into which each House is divided for purposes of legislation. The traditional method of evading the regulations of minimum membership, by tacking on a number of isolated members or small groups, for 'administrative purposes', is

[1] In the case of the President of the Senate, until the next partial renewal. In the main, the functions of the two Presidents are similar.

[2] It is the President of the Senate who now replaces the President of the Republic, if incapacitated, and not the President of the Assembly, as under the Fourth Republic. One reason for the change may be that, since the Senate is renewed partially, there is always a President of the Senate in office. It is the President of the Assembly, however, who presides over a meeting of the two Houses in Congress at Versailles, if this procedure of constitutional revision is chosen in preference to a referendum.

now prohibited.[1] Representation of groups on Commissions is proportional to their strength in the Assembly, including affiliates (*apparentés*). Isolated members can be members of Commissions only if elected by the whole Assembly to any vacancies remaining after the seats have been allotted to group members.

The Parliamentary timetable is drawn up every week by *la Conférence des Présidents* – a meeting of the President and Vice-Presidents of the Assembly, and of heads of Parliamentary groups, Presidents of Commissions, and the *rapporteur général* of the Finance Commission. Voting in this body is weighted in proportion to party strength. What influence the Government used to have on its decisions depended largely on the prestige of the Government and on the persuasiveness of the Government representatives. The Constitution now gives the Government effective control over the timetable by according priority to Government Bills and to those private members' Bills acceptable to the Government.

LEGISLATIVE PROCEDURE

Bills may be introduced and have their first reading in either House, except for Finance Bills which must be read first in the National Assembly. Private members' Bills are not in order if they involve a decrease in the revenue or an increase in expenditure. Once introduced, Bills are submitted either to one of the six regular Commissions, or, on the request of either Government or Assembly, to an *ad hoc* Commission whose members may not exceed 30. Commissions formerly numbered 19, each consisting of 44 members. The purpose of the reduction is twofold: to reduce the authority of Commissions, whose Presidents, when the field of activity of Commissions roughly coincided with that of a Ministry, tended to become shadow Ministers; and also to prevent the time-wasting process of submitting to several Commissions Bills whose scope is such as to interest more than one Ministry, the main Commission remaining responsible for the report, the others merely stating their

[1] Under the previous régimes, the required number was 14. In 1958, it was raised to 28, but the provision had not entered into application by the time the Fourth Republic came to an end. The system of affiliated members or groups benefited both affiliates (*apparentés*) and parent group, since it enabled both to enjoy the advantages of parliamentary groups without fulfilling the obligation to accept a common policy – which involved no more than subscribing to a vaguely worded declaration.

opinion. For instance, the Bill to ratify the E.D.C. Treaty in 1954 was submitted to the Foreign Affairs Commission for report, and also to four other Commissions for their opinion. Nevertheless, the Standing Orders also provide that the practice of submitting Bills to more than one Commission should be continued.

The Assembly normally sits on four days a week, Commissions holding meetings in the morning. The Friday sessions are normally reserved for questions. Debate on a Government Bill begins with a Ministerial declaration, followed by the Commission's report. Formerly, the Assembly debate normally[1] took place on the basis of the Commission's amended text, and not on the Government's Bill, and the Commission, not the Minister, was responsible for piloting the Bill through the House. The Government was even unable to propose its own counter-amendments, except by devious procedures such as issuing so-called 'corrected' versions of an article, or getting a Deputy to move an amendment from the floor.

The 1958 Constitution has changed all that. Henceforth the Minister pilots his own Bill when it comes before the House, and may propose amendments, and object to the proposal of amendments from the floor. The effect of these changes on the authority and stability of Governments is discussed in the following chapter. As far as legislative procedure is concerned, the right of Governments to refuse to consider amendments not previously submitted to the relevant Commission, to insist on a single vote on the whole or a part of the Bill, including only such amendments as have been either proposed or accepted by the Government, the further restrictions on amendments introduced by the Standing Orders and the right of the President to call for the closure, when, in his view, the case for and against has been adequately presented, could, if properly used, produce far more coherent and orderly debates, and consequently better drafted laws. The decline in the importance of Parliament, and the unambitious legislative programmes of the first Government of the Fifth Republic give no guidance as to how the rules might work if political interest and Parliamentary activity were to increase.

The Assembly first debates the general principles of the Bill,

[1] A great many Bills are adopted without debate, particularly private members' Bills. If there is a debate on these, it is still on the basis of the Commission's report and the Government spokesman takes part only if he so desires.

as presented by the Government and the Commission spokesman, and then votes on it article by article, finally voting on the text as a whole, as amended. This completes what is called the first reading. The Bill then goes to the Senate (or to the Assembly if it has been read first in the Senate) where it goes through a similar process. If passed by both Houses, it is promulgated by the President of the Republic and published in the *Journal Officiel* and is then law.[1]

During the debate, Ministers and Presidents of Commissions may intervene at any moment; Deputies may interrupt a speaker, with his permission, for a maximum of five minutes, or may rise on a point of order at any time. Ministers may be present at debates and speak in either House, as was the practice under previous régimes. The debate may be open or 'organized'. In the first case, would-be speakers notify the President, who chooses the order in which they are called. In the second case, the total time allotted to the debate and the share allotted to each Parliamentary group (which is proportional to its strength in the House) is rigidly worked out in advance (though often less rigidly adhered to). An innovation of the Fifth Republic is the requirement in the Standing Orders, so far widely ignored in practice, that Deputies shall not read their speeches. Before the vote is taken, spokesmen of groups who wish to explain why their groups have decided to vote one way or the other are normally allowed five minutes in which to do so (*l'explication de vote*).[2]

FINANCE AND ORGANIC LAWS

The voting of finance and organic laws is subject to special procedures laid down in the Constitution. An 'organic law' is one of two things, It is either one of the 19 which the Constitution provided for in order to complete a number of its provisions, and which were promulgated as Ordinances (*Ordonnances portant loi organique*) during the transitional period when the Government had full powers; or else it is that provided for under article 34, to 'complete and define' the legislative powers of Parliament and which at the time of writing had still not seen the light. This must be voted

[1] Promulgation takes place within 15 days unless, within that period, the President asks Parliament to reconsider the Bill. Parliament must comply with this request.

[2] On voting procedure, *v. supra*, pp. 91-92.

according to the procedure required for the amendment of all 20 organic laws. Though these organic laws may be amended, no new ones can be voted.[1] The differences between this procedure and the normal legislative procedure are that Bills must be tabled a full fortnight before they are debated and that, if the two Houses disagree, and the Prime Minister asks the Assembly to decide, the Assembly can override the Senate only by voting the law by a majority of its total membership. Organic laws affecting the Senate must be voted in the same terms by both Houses. Organic laws are promulgated only when the Constitutional Council has declared that they are in conformity with the Constitution.

The procedure for voting Finance Bills is designed to prevent the Assembly from using delaying tactics, as it did under the Fourth Republic, in order to bring pressure to bear on Governments. If the Assembly has not completed the first reading within 40 days, the Government sends the Bill to the Senate to be read within a fortnight. If the Bill has not been voted after 70 days, the Government may apply its provisions by Ordinance. If the Government has failed to introduce the Bill in time for it to be promulgated by the beginning of the financial year, it may ask Parliament to authorize taxation by decree and to authorize expenditure in respect of any estimates previously accepted by the Assembly. The authorization may be asked for in one of two ways. Either the Assembly is requested, ten days before the end of the session, to vote the parts of the law covering the collection of taxes and the general headings of expenditure, the text then being submitted to the Senate as a matter of urgency;[2] or else if this fails the Assembly is requested, two days before the end of the session, to vote a special Bill entitling the Government to collect taxes in anticipation of authorization by the finance law. This Bill also is treated as a matter of urgency.

These provisions cannot, of course, ensure that the Assembly will accede to the request, in which case the Government is no better off than the Governments of the Fourth Republic were at times – for instance, when the Assembly voted expenditure, but refused to vote the parts of the Bill providing for the necessary revenue. The moral here is, perhaps, that Governments should

[1] But amendment, of course, could be equivalent to voting a new organic law, providing that the Constitutional Council agreed.

[2] When a matter is declared 'urgent' the procedure is speeded up.

present their budgets on time![1] Nor can they ensure that the Assembly, if it does vote the Bill, will do so without amending it in ways displeasing to the Government, though, if the Government decides to make the issue a matter of confidence, the Assembly may hesitate to turn the Government out, particularly if the consequence may be a dissolution. The implications of these provisions, in the context of the general relationship between Government and Parliament, are discussed in the following chapter.

It will have been noted that Finance Bills are voted by the two Houses, though the Constitution (article 39) requires them to be voted first by the Assembly. There is nothing in French Parliamentary procedure comparable to the British system, which permits the House of Commons to override the House of Lords in the matter of Money Bills more easily than in the matter of ordinary legislation. In France, if the two Houses disagree on a Finance Bill, the procedure is the same as that governing disagreements on ordinary Bills.

RELATIONS BETWEEN THE TWO HOUSES

The 1958 Constitution does not permit the Assembly to override the Senate, as it could under the previous Constitution, unless the Government decides to intervene on the side of the Assembly. If the Government does not intervene, a Bill on which the two Houses disagree can go back and forth between Assembly and Senate – the process known as 'the shuttle' (*la navette*) – indefinitely. Second and, if necessary, further readings deal only with articles on which agreement has still not been reached. There is no provision in the Constitution for putting an end to persistent disagreement.

If, however, the Government does intervene, it may do so either passively or actively. In the first case, it may, after the Bill has been read twice in each House, require the setting-up of a Commission consisting of equal numbers (seven) from each House. If the Commission reaches agreement, the Bill may then be submitted by the Government to both Houses to be voted on (with only such amendments as the Government accepts). If the Commission does not agree, or if the Bill as agreed is rejected by either House, the two

[1] Governments have not always presented their budgets on time, but the first three of this régime were, at least, voted on time.

Houses may make further efforts to agree, or drop the Bill, or shelve it. Alternatively, the Government may intervene actively with a request, first, to each House to give the Bill a further reading and then, if the disagreement persists, to the Assembly to vote, either on the Commission's Bill, or on its own Bill, with or without any amendments proposed by the Senate. In order to override the Senate, the Assembly requires only an ordinary majority vote on the Bill, unless it is organic.

This means, of course, that, where the Government is not interested in a Bill, the co-ordinate relationship between the two Houses which existed under the 1875 Constitution is restored. The Senate can then effectively block legislation proposed by the Assembly, and has, indeed, done so.

Except for this contingent legislative equality and its effective right of veto over any change in its own status (which existed also under the 1946 Constitution), the Senate remains a subordinate legislative Chamber. The Government is not responsible to it. The prestige of the Senate is, however, increased in several ways, some of which have already been mentioned.[1] During the first years of the new régime, its prestige was derived, in practice, less from any constitutional provisions than from the election to the Senate of a number of Parliamentary personalities who had been defeated in the elections to the Assembly, at a time when the Assembly included an almost unprecedented number of rather nondescript newcomers.

[1] They include the right of the President of the Senate to replace the President of the Republic, if incapacitated, until the election of a new President; the obligation on the President to consult the President of the Senate before applying article 16, and before deciding on the desirability of a dissolution; the right of the President of the Senate to submit Bills in certain circumstances to the Constitutional Council and (like the President of the Assembly) to nominate three members of the Constitutional Council; the right of the Senate to equal representation with the Assembly in the High Court of Justice; the need for the Assembly to obtain the concurrence of the Senate before requesting a referendum; and the right of the Senate to receive Presidential messages.

The right of the Prime Minister to request the approval of the Senate at any time he so desires (article 49) existed also under the Fourth Republic. It is difficult to see why a Prime Minister should take advantage of the opportunity unless he is seeking to play off one House against the other, for, though the Government is not constitutionally obliged to resign if defeated in the Senate, not to do so would entail some loss of face. This view is borne out by several passages in M. Debré's speech to the *Conseil d'Etat* (*v. Revue française de Science Politique*, March 1959, pp. 8, 17, 26).

RESTRICTIONS ON PARLIAMENTARY SOVEREIGNTY

(*a*) **The Legislative Sphere.** One of the most important innovations of the Fifth Republic is the restriction of the scope of Parliamentary activity. This represents a break with the Republican tradition of Parliamentary sovereignty.

Parliament is henceforth regarded as having two functions: that of legislating within a circumscribed field and that of supervision and control of the Government.[1] The Government, on the other hand, while it retains the traditional functions belonging to the executive, henceforth deals, by executive action, with all matters not specifically reserved to the legislature and may also, with the permission of Parliament, take over, for a limited period, responsibility for dealing with matters defined by the Constitution as properly belonging to the legislature (article 38).

There is, of course, nothing new in the exercise of legislative functions by Governments. *Décrets-lois* of the Third Republic, *lois-cadres* and special powers under the Fourth Republic, were all instances of delegated legislation. The difference is that, hitherto, such delegated legislation has been regarded as exceptional, the rule of Parliamentary sovereignty being maintained in principle; it has also been temporary, Parliament being the final judge of the extent and the duration of special powers accorded to Governments to legislate by decree; and it has been subject to ratification by Parliament.

This is, in fact, the first serious attempt in French Republican history to define a 'legislative sphere' (*le domaine de la loi*). Certain matters have been, in the past, constitutionally reserved to the legislature, others have been so reserved by custom, or by virtue of special legislative provisions. For instance, the choice of electoral systems, the granting of amnesties, questions concerning the fundamental rights and liberties of the citizen, property, personal status, penal law, the principles of taxation, and so on, are all matters that the legislature has normally claimed the right to deal with. These traditions constituted restrictions of the executive's right to encroach on the legislature. The legislative domain was, up to 1958, anything claimed by Parliament as such.

[1] A third function should be mentioned: a declaration of war must be authorized by Parliament (article 35).

The sphere assigned to legislation by the Constitution and by custom is merely a minimum guaranteed sphere. Beyond, stretches an *a priori*, unlimited, and indeterminate field of action for the unfettered initiative of the legislator who, by legislating on any matter whatsoever, thereby incorporates it in the legislative sphere.[1]

To prescribe limits to legislative activity, leaving everything outside these limits to the executive, is, therefore, something quite new in Republican history.[2]

As defined by article 34 of the Constitution, the field of legislation now includes two categories. The first consists of the 'rules governing' certain enumerated subjects – the fundamental liberties of the citizen, civil status and civic rights, liability to taxation and national defence, the penal code, amnesty, declarations of war, electoral laws, the creation of nationalized industries . . . to quote the main ones listed. The second consists of the 'general principles governing' the organization of a further list of subjects – national defence, local government, education, property and commercial rights, labour, trade union, social security and finance laws (in conditions defined in an organic law) and 'programme-laws'[3] in the field of economic and social policy. . . . Everything else belongs to the executive field (article 37).

The list certainly still gives scope for a good deal of Parliamentary activity. Unfortunately, it has given scope for a great deal of argu-

[1] Georges Galichon, *Aspects de la Procédure législative en France* (*Revue française de Science Politique,* October–December 1954, p. 795). Cf. Pinto, *Eléments de Droit Constitutionnel* (Lille, 1952), p. 516: 'The Constitution does not define the legislative sphere. It does not limit the matters that can be dealt with by legislation', and also the following extract from a speech in the Senate by M. Léo Hamon on 25th January 1951: 'French law recognizes no such thing as a "law", in the sense in which it exists in a rigid Constitution of the American type, where a Constitutional Court ensures respect even by Parliament for the separation of functions. In this country, a law is not defined in relation to the matters with which it deals; the definition is juridically speaking, purely formal: a law is an act emanating from Parliament.'

[2] The law of the 17th August 1948 did attempt to define a field of activity that could properly be described as executive. But this was, in fact, a piece of special pleading designed to get round the Constitutional prohibition (under article 13) of delegated legislation, without having recourse to a revision of the Constitution.

[3] A 'programme-law' is an innovation of the Fifth Republic – it is a long-term project and Parliament is assumed to be morally committed to vote later instalments of expenditure in application of its provisions, as they turn up in subsequent budgets.

ment, both regarding the respective spheres of executive and legislative action, in general, and also regarding the distinction between general principles, which, in the second category, alone belong to the legislative field, and the detailed application, which is now a matter for the executive. Experience has shown that 'One man's detail may honestly be another man's principle.'[1]

There is scope for argument, too, regarding the respective functions of the two organs to which the Constitution entrusts decisions affecting the application of the new principles. These are worth mentioning because they raise important issues in themselves, and also because they illustrate very clearly the kind of uncertainty that has been created by the numerous omissions and ambiguities of this badly drafted Constitution. The title of 'the worst drafted article of a Constitution that does no credit to the French language'[2] has already been claimed for article 89, governing the conditions of constitutional revision. Articles 34, 37 and 41, have certainly equally strong claims to consideration.

The Constitution provides (article 37) that, in the case of laws passed *before* the new Constitution came into force, the *Conseil d'Etat* – the supreme administrative jurisdiction[3] – must be consulted as to whether or not they now come within the executive field. They can then be modified by decree.[4] In the case of laws passed *since* the Constitution came into force, the Constitutional Council will decide whether a matter has erroneously been treated as within the legislative field, when it would properly come within the executive field. Without the Constitutional Council's authorization, Governments cannot themselves act on this assumption and proceed to modify by decree what is, in form, a law.

So far the position, though complicated, is relatively clear. But how can the propriety of a Government's action be challenged, if it

[1] Martin Harrison, *The Constitution of the Fifth Republic*, in *Political Studies*, February 1959, p. 49.

[2] M. Duverger. op. cit., p. 138.

[3] On the functions of the *Conseil d'Etat*, *v.* the author's *France – the Fourth Republic*, pp. 105–10, 138–9, Brian Chapman, *The Profession of Government* (Allen and Unwin, 1958) and Charles E. Freedmann, *The Conseil d'Etat* (Columbia University Press, New York, 1961).

[4] The *Conseil d'Etat's* role, in other words, is purely advisory. On this, *v.* G. Morange, *La hiérarchie des textes dans la Constitution de 1958*, in *Recueil Dalloz hebdomadaire*, 28th January 1959.

proceeds to decide for itself to treat as a matter suitable for executive action something that might be regarded by others as falling within the legislative sphere? Article 41 permits the Government to object to a Bill or an amendment, on the ground that the subject is not a proper one for legislation, and if the President of the relevant House disagrees, the matter is submitted to the Constitutional Council. The President of the Republic, or the President of either Assembly, can submit any Bill for the Constitutional Council's ruling as to its conformity with the Constitution (article 51). There is no Constitutional provision enabling Parliament to object to a Government decree, on the ground that the Constitution required its subject matter to be dealt with by a law and not by a decree.

There has been a great deal of criticism of these two articles, in particular by lawyers. It is generally agreed that injured parties have redress *via* the normal channels of administrative law. The *Conseil d'Etat* can hear an appeal by a citizen against the application to him of a decree, on the ground that the Government was not constitutionally entitled to issue it. In such a case, the Government could challenge the decision by securing the passage of a Bill having the same effect as the decree, and then asking the Constitutional Council (under articles 37 or 61) to decide whether or not it belonged constitutionally to the law-making sphere. The Constitutional Council's decision in such matters is final and would, therefore, be binding on the *Conseil d'Etat* in future cases. It would be possible, however, in the view of some lawyers, for conflicting decisions to persist, for instance, on pre- and post-1958 laws dealing with the same subject.

There are, of course, the political remedies, namely, pressure on the Government or its defeat on a motion of censure. But this could be rendered ineffective by a dissolution, or the fear of one, or, more often, would mean using a steam hammer to crack a nut. Indeed, one of the chief criticisms of the 1958 Constitution is precisely that it overlooks the need to provide adequate safety-valves for opposition falling short of a desire to turn the Government out.

Hopes that some of the difficulties would be ironed out by the organic law provided for by article 34 have not been realized, since this had not been voted at the end of four years. The provision has, moreover, ambiguities and uncertainties of its own. Is the expression 'completed and defined' limitative, permitting only such changes in the original text as are required to clarify its intentions, or does the word 'complete' authorize additions to the list of legislative functions? These questions can presumably be answered only by the Constitutional Council, if and when the law is passed.

Two arguments in particular have been put forward in support of the restrictions on the legislative activity of Parliament. The first is that they reverse the tendency to *gouvernment d'assemblée* which, with a divided Assembly such as existed throughout most of the life of the Fourth Republic, meant that Governments had to fight inch by inch in order to survive, and that, more often than not, the price of survival was inaction. The second is that, in an age of wholesale Governmental intervention in economic and social life, some degree of delegated legislation is essential, and that French Parliaments have for too long resisted this necessary evolution. It was generally admitted by critics of the post-war Parliamentary system that Parliament legislated too much and that there was far too much detailed and unco-ordinated legislation.[1] A Radical Deputy wrote in 1956 that the Assembly was sovereign, chaotic and tyrannical, and by making everything its business failed to do anything properly. M. Debré accused Parliaments of the Fourth Republic of 'a two-fold deviation'. Since the war, in particular, he said, they had witnessed:

> a Parliament snowed under by Bills, and seeking to multiply interventions haphazard on points of detail, and a Government, on the other hand, dealing with the most serious national problems without interference by Parliament.

[1] During the first Parliament of the Fourth Republic (January 1947 to June 1951) 1,289 Bills were passed (of which 937 were Government Bills); during the first half of the second Parliament (June 1951 to August 1953) 452 (of which 299 were Government Bills). These figures alone do not give an accurate impression of the legislative activity of Parliament, since they leave out of account Bills that were defeated and the very much larger number (about half of those introduced) which never got beyond the stage of being considered by the relevant Commission. Mr. Lidderdale (*The Parliament of France,* Hansard Society, 1949, p. 179) estimates that in the 1946–7 session, only one in 17 of the private members' Bills reached the Statute Book. Mr. Harrison (op cit., p. 50) estimates that, towards the end of the Fourth Republic, about 1,800 Bills were presented during a session, of which 750 were rejected and 250 debated.

v. also André Philip (*La Crise de la démocratie française,* in *Preuves,* November 1958, p. 13) on this point. The Assembly, he says, passed about 300–500 Bills a year, for the most part dealing with matters more suitable to a *Conseil Général,* while no serious discussion took place on the plan for the country's general economic policy.

As will be seen later[1] the Fifth Republic has gone too far in the opposite direction and, by giving Parliament too little business, reduced both its incentive to efficiency and its capacity to ensure that of the Government in the fields in which the latter has replaced Parliament.

(*b*) **The Supervision of Standing Orders and Elections.** The Constitutional Council limits Parliamentary sovereignty in three other ways. First, its supervision of the regularity of elections and referenda and its right to decide cases of alleged irregularity withdraw from Parliament one of its traditional rights. This innovation might perhaps be regarded as an improvement, and, indeed, is so regarded by many, for French Assemblies have at times been guilty of both partisan and illogical decisions.[2] Second, the right of the Constitutional Council to ensure the conformity with the Constitution of Parliamentary Standing Orders removes Parliament's traditional right to control its own procedure. The Council has not only ruled out of order certain procedures to which the majority members of Parliament are attached, but has, in so doing, interpreted the Constitutional provisions in a way with which many members of Parliament disagreed at the time. Third, in the view of many Deputies, the partisan quality of its decisions has, in effect, added a further restriction. The responsibility of the Constitutional Council for deciding certain specific disputes arising between Government and Parliament, with a view to ensuring that each keeps within its allotted constitutional sphere, can withdraw from Parliament rights that, even within the limits laid down by the Constitution, Deputies and Senators feel that they still possess. Just as the judicial review of the American Supreme Court has been, at different periods of American history, liberal or restrictive in spirit, so, in its more limited sphere, the non-judicial French Constitutional Council can carry out its limited functions of review of constitutionality in a liberal or a restrictive spirit. Its decisions during the

[1] *v. infra*, pp. 115–25.

[2] For instance, after the 1951 election, when two cases of dispued electtion results (in the Bas Rhin and Seine inférieure respectively) were decided by the National Assembly on contradictory principles, in each case to achieve a specific political results. For the facts, *v. Année Politique*, 1951, pp. 154 and 175. Twelve Poujadist Deputies were also unseated after the 1956 elections, on valid grounds, but in an atmosphere that did no credit to Parliament.

first years of the régime were, in fact, always restrictive of what Parliament held to be its rights. The Constitutional Council played a not unimportant part in bringing about the worsening of relations between Government and Parliament which became one of the most characteristic features of the régime.

CHAPTER VII

The Relations Between Government and Parliament

THE PURPOSE OF THE CONSTITUTION

The 1958 Constitution deliberately seeks to change the focus of interest in French political life. Traditionally, the popularly elected Assembly has been the maker and breaker of Governments. Except for the rare occurrence of a dissolution, which happened only twice in 83 years, Deputies could count on remaining for the five years (or four, under the Third Republic) of their term of office, however many Governments came and went. Under the Fifth Republic, the focus of interest was intended to be the President of the Republic and the Government. The Constitution seeks to strengthen Governments, not merely by limiting the scope of Parliamentary activities, in the hope of reducing the number of issues and occasions on which Governments can come into conflict with the Assembly, but also by carefully defining and limiting the conditions in which Governments can be defeated.

Both these methods were essentially attempts to eliminate the symptoms of the disease of Governmental instability, without sacrificing the essential condition of Parliamentary government, the responsibility of the Government to the popularly elected Assembly. When Parliament is a framework within which one of two parties governs with the consent of the other, which hopes and strives to replace it, strong government and Parliamentary government can coexist harmoniously, because the Government is at the same time the leader and the emanation of the Parliamentary majority. That being so, there can normally be no conflict between Parliament and Government on the issues of policy that divide Government and Opposition, since 'Parliament' means the majority party, which is linked to the Government by common interests. Both Government and Opposition have a common interest, too, in accepting the same rules of the Parliamentary game.

This classic picture of the two-party system as it works in Great Britain has little, if any, relevance to the problems that beset French Governments in their relations with Parliament. The essential difference is not that France has a multi-party system. Multi-party systems are the rule rather than the exception in countries with Parliamentary government, and many countries have been able to combine strong government with a Parliamentary system. The French system has two essential characteristics which make the combination difficult and sometimes impossible. First, neither on the Government nor on the Opposition side do parties normally have sufficient common interest to hold them together for long. There is, therefore, no clear dividing line between Government and Opposition, and majorities can, and very often do, shift during the life of a Parliament, so that there can be first Left and then Right Governments within the life-time of the same Parliament. Second, the presence since the war of a large permanent opposition to the régime, including Communists on the one hand and anti-Communists, sometimes extremely right-wing, on the other, has often meant that a small – sometimes a very small – number of additional opposition votes could bring down a Government. But since the Opposition was both a temporary combination and a politically heterogeneous one, the defeat could not entail a wholesale change of either Government personnel or policy. The parties (or most of them) that formed the preceding coalition returned to office, either giving way to the majority on the particular issue that defeated them, or changing their political mixture just enough to enable them to obtain a majority. In either case, this situation involved domination of the Government by an Assembly in which opposition elements could combine to defeat Governments, but not to replace them.

The authors of the 1958 Constitution, and in particular, the first Prime Minister of the new régime, M. Debré, deliberately set out to overcome these obstacles to stable government by substituting for the common interest of disciplined parties a series of rigid rules.[1] Constitutional rules were designed to make it more difficult for Governments to be defeated; changes in procedure were intended to prevent Governments from being harassed and subjected to constant pressure by the Assembly; and the Government was given, in addition, weapons intended to enable it either to ignore Parliamentary pressure, or else to make its consequences unpleasant for Deputies.

THE CONSTITUTIONAL METHODS OF ENSURING GOVERNMENTAL RESPONSIBILITY

The Constitution lays down three methods of enforcing Governmental responsibility to Parliament. The first decisions of the Constitutional Council made it quite clear that, in the opinion of its members at the time, these were intended to be the sole ways in which Governments could henceforth be defeated.

First, the Assembly can defeat the Government either on its programme or on a declaration of general policy. The wording of this sentence (article 49) is ambiguous. It merely states that:

> After discussion in the Council of Ministers, the Prime Minister pledges the responsibility of his Government before the National Assembly, on his programme, or possibly on a declaration of general policy.

No special procedure is laid down. No occasion or time limit is mentioned. It has so far been generally understood that the submission of the Prime Minister's programme would take place at the beginning of the Government's period of office. The first two Prime Ministers did so submit their Government's programmes. If these precedents are followed, it means a return to the practice of the Third Republic, when newly appointed Prime Ministers asked for the confidence of the Chamber of Deputies, both in their programme

[1] *v.* Speech by M. Debré to the *Conseil d'Etat* on 27th August 1959: 'The draft Constitution, drawn up in the light of a long and costly experience, includes certain precise procedural mechanisms, which would be out of place in a document of this kind, were it not for our realization that they are necessary in order to change our habits. To break bad habits, strict rules are required.' (*Revue française de Science Politique*, March 1959, p. 14.)

and in the composition of their Governments.[1] If confidence is withheld, the Government resigns. Since no special procedure is mentioned, a majority of those voting is sufficient. A 'declaration of general policy' is generally assumed to be some kind of re-statement of the Government's programme which a Prime Minister might find it expedient to make, as, for instance, after a Government reshuffle. Such a declaration was made for the first time in October 1959.[2]

Second, the Assembly can defeat the Government by passing a vote of censure. A motion of censure must be signed by at least a tenth of the members of the National Assembly; the vote takes place not less than 48 hours after the motion has been tabled; and only the votes of those favourable to the motion are counted. The motion is carried only if it receives the votes of a majority of the effective membership of the Assembly. If it is defeated, the signatories cannot sign another motion of censure for the rest of the session.

Third, the Prime Minister (again after discussion in the Council of Ministers) may make an issue a matter of confidence. If he does so, confidence is presumed to have been accorded, and the proposal in question is presumed to have been carried without a vote being taken, if a motion of censure has not been tabled within 24 hours. A motion of censure is tabled, and voted on, in the same conditions as a motion of censure on the Government's general policy. If the motion is lost, the proposal is carried. There is no limit to the

[1] The essential difference between this procedure and that of the previous régime is that Prime Ministers under the Fourth Republic were designated (*désignés*) by the President of the Republic and their official appointment by him followed their *investiture* by a majority vote in the Assembly. (Up to 1954 an absolute majority of the effective membership was required). The Prime Minister presented himself alone, though, from 1954 onwards, the names of Ministers were communicated to the Assembly before the *investiture* debate.

[2] There was a request by some party spokesmen for a vote following the Foreign Minister's declaration at the end of April 1959. The Prime Minister was opposed to a vote, on the ground that the declaration was not one of general, but only of foreign policy. Following General de Gaulle's statement of France's Algerian policy on 16th September 1959, the Assembly, at the opening of the October session, debated a general declaration of the Government's Algerian and foreign policies. The procedure adopted was that, after the Prime Minister's speech, the President of the Assembly announced the Government's decision to pledge its responsibility on these issues. On 13th June 1962, 280 Deputies walked out of the Assembly and signed a manifesto in protest against the Government's refusal to allow a vote following the foreign affairs debate.

number of censure motions that may be presented by the same Deputies on matters which the Government has made questions of confidence.

RESPONSIBILITY IN THEORY AND IN PRACTICE

These provisions call for several comments. The idea that a strict rationing of motions of censure in each session is likely to decrease the frequency of Government defeats is implausible, and this was not the real purpose of the rule. It was intended rather to prevent the use of motions of censure by a small number of Deputies either for propaganda purposes or as part of a general tactic of obstruction.[1] Deputies have still considerable elbow room to defeat Governments, since there is no restriction on the number of censure motions relating to issues that the Government has made questions of confidence. What the procedure does put a stop to is the possibility that a Government may see its Bill defeated while it retains, constitutionally speaking, the confidence of the Assembly. Under the Fourth Republic this was possible, and sometimes happened, because only a majority of those voting was required to defeat a Bill, while a majority of the effective membership of the Assembly was required to defeat a Government, and it was often possible to achieve the first, but not the second.

This point may seem trivial to some British readers, since nothing, of course, obliged Prime Ministers of the Fourth Republic to stay in office in such a humiliating situation. But, as has already been pointed out, the resignation of a Prime Minister in the situation of Parliamentary deadlock that existed throughout most of the life of the Fourth Republic often achieved nothing, since his coalition, or one very like it, was often the only one to be able to command a positive majority in the Assembly. In such circumstances his resignation merely added to existing difficulties that of a long Governmental interregnum, at the end of which he might find himself

[1] The measure was probably partly inspired by the desire to prevent the kind of Communist obstruction that occurred regularly in the early years of the Fourth Republic. In the first Assembly of the present régime, the Communists numbered only 10 and so could not alone table a motion of censure, but at the time when the Constitution was drawn up it was generally estimated that they would number about 50, or somewhere in the region of a tenth of the Assembly.

back where he started from. The new procedure means that Governments are *obliged* to resign if the Assembly does not allow them to carry out their programme. The assumption now is that those who are not prepared to turn a Government out must let it get on with its job. And this is, indeed, what has happened, though for political rather than constitutional reasons.[1]

The rules are rigid, in the sense that Governments can be defeated only on a limited number of occasions and by a special procedure. It is therefore virtually impossible for such defeats to occur on snap votes, or as a result of a Parliamentary storm that blows up unexpectedly. But the rules are not rigid in the sense that they place any real obstacles in the way of an Assembly which has decided that it does want to get rid of a Government. They do not, however, affect what have been, since the war, the most frequent causes of Governmental instability. Of the twenty Governments of the Fourth Republic (leaving that headed by General de Gaulle out of account) only five resigned because they were constitutionally obliged to do so. Of the rest, eight resigned without being defeated at all, and seven resigned in circumstances in which, under the present Constitution (as under the last), Governments would be constitutionally entitled to remain in power.

Constitutions cannot impose unity and discipline, if none exists. Nor can they, with impunity, make too violent a break with tradition. It may be asked whether, if circumstances return to normal, Deputies will for long tolerate a system which allows a Bill to be passed without the Assembly's having voted on it at all.

PARLIAMENTARY CONTROL AND PARLIAMENTARY PRESSURE

Parliament carries out its work of supervising the Government in three main ways. During sessions, opportunity is provided for exchanges of opinion during debates, but the main method of supervision is during the first stage of legislative procedure, by the examination of Bills in Commission. All members of recognized Parliamentary groups are members of a Commission (though not of more than one). The permanent Commissions in France have been extremely powerful bodies, able to summon both Civil Servants

[1] *v. infra*, p. 155.

and Ministers before them to provide explanations and justification of measures being discussed in Commission. From 1956, to 1958, the powers of the Finance Commission, in particular, were extensive.

In addition to the permanent Commissions, there are special Commissions (each with not more than thirty members, of whom not more than fifteen may be drawn from the same permanent Commission) to which Bills may be sent instead of to one of the permanent Commissions. The Assembly may itself ask for this procedure to be adopted. There are also Commissions of Inquiry, equivalent to Select Committees of the House of Commons, and Supervisory Commissions (*Commissions de Contrôle*), which supervise the management and finances of nationalized industries and public services. When Parliament is not sitting, the permanent Commissions may meet only if convened by their President on the request of their *bureau.*

Information can also be obtained by individual Deputies by putting either written or oral questions to the relevant Minister. Questions on general policy are addressed to the Prime Minister. Written questions are printed in the *Journal Officiel.* Ministers are (theoretically) bound to reply within a month, and their replies are printed in the *Journal Officiel.* They may, however, delay their reply for one month, and sometimes two, and they may refuse to reply on the ground that to do so would be contrary to the public interest. If replies are unduly delayed, the President of the Assembly can ask the author whether he would prefer to put his question orally.

Oral questions may be with or without debate.[1] Ministers reply to them at a sitting reserved for this purpose once a week (in the Assembly, Friday afternoons). Questions without debate are called by the President and the questioner is allowed to speak for five minutes following the Minister's reply. The Minister may reply to this. No other speeches are allowed. Questions with debate are put by the questioner in a speech which may last up to half an hour. After the Minister's reply, the President may allow other members to speak for a period not exceeding fifteen minutes each. The Minister may give a final reply, if he so desires.

[1] Under the Fourth Republic, oral questions with debate existed only in the Senate, and then only from 1948 onwards.

Oral questions with debate formed the subject of the first major battle between Parliament and Government, because, as is evident from the foregoing brief description, they could have become an instrument of pressure on the Government if, as the Standing Orders originally provided, the debate had concluded with a resolution and a vote. The Constitution of 1958 attempts to draw a clear line between the search for information and the exercise of pressure. It does so in two ways, the first positive, by modifications of legislative procedure, the second, negative, by the refusal to allow a technique intended for the provision of information (oral questions with debate) to be used in effect as an instrument of pressure. As the Prime Minister, M. Debré, put it, the Government did not intend to be faced every Friday with an implicit vote of confidence. Votes on a resolution, whether or not it followed an oral question with debate, could not, of course, constitutionally, have defeated a Government. But such votes could have ended by weakening its authority.

The battle between Parliament and Government took place because the wording of the Constitution on this point, as on so many others, gives no clear guidance regarding the constitutionality of votes on resolutions and oral questions with debate. Assembly and Senate, therefore, at first included in their provisional Standing Orders articles permitting both.[1] The Constitutional Council, whose approval of Parliamentary Standing Orders must now be obtained, decided that votes on resolutions were unconstitutional.[2]

[1] The Assembly later withdrew its provisions for votes following oral questions with debate, after a long argument between Deputies and Government. Provisions for resolutions were retained. The Senate retained both procedures. Resolutions were voted in both Houses, before the procedure was declared unconstitutional. The Senate's case for retaining both procedures was that, since Governments are not responsible to the Senate, and the latter cannot, therefore, use the procedures laid down in article 49, to refuse it the right to criticize would be to reduce its status to that of a purely consultative organ without authority or prestige. This was also the view of the Senate under the Fourth Republic and it was M. Debré himself, as a Senator, who was responsible for the introduction, and extensive use, in the Senate of oral questions with debate. The constitutionality of the procedure was contested in some quarters, but it continued to be used by the Senate throughout the Fourth Republic.

[2] Resolutions are now in order only if they deal with matters concerning the organization of the House itself or if they are decisions to bring someone before the High Court of Justice, or to set up Commissions of Inquiry or supervision (*v. Règlement de l'Assemblée nationale*, September 1959, article 82).

The controversy was important because it indicated a possible weakness in the approach to the new institutions of certain of their supporters. It has been stated earlier that the purpose of the Constitution was to create a new relationship between Government and Parliament, closer to that which exists between Government and Opposition in Great Britain and, in the absence of a two-party system, to do so by laying down strict constitutional rules, limiting the capacity of Parliaments to make the lives of Ministers intolerable, even when they did not go so far as to defeat the Government. It has also been pointed out that French Constitutions have often been reactions against what was disliked in the previous régime. Both these points have affected relations between Government and Parliament under the Fifth Republic. It is true, as was pointed out in defence of the Government position, that British Members of Parliament do not feel the need to have a vote following Parliamentary questions. But there is no real analogy between British and French procedure on this point, because the party structures and Parliamentary habits of the two countries are fundamentally different. The fears of those who objected to a vote on a resolution following oral questions with debate arose from the possibility that the Government, though it could not be constitutionally defeated, could, nevertheless, receive a minority of the votes cast and so appear to the country to be going against the will of the Assembly. Such a situation would be unthinkable in the British Parliament, where the Government resigns if it is clear that it cannot count on a majority to see its policy through. British practice is not based on mechanical or arithmetical rules, but on political facts.

Some of those who defended the condemned procedures were, in fact, seeking not to weaken Governments, but to strengthen them, by providing a safety-valve permitting Deputies to criticize the Government on specific issues, when they did not necessarily want to challenge the Government's right to exist, and so did not want to propose a vote of censure. It may be that the vital difference between the French and British systems, namely, the absence in France of either a coherent majority or a coherent opposition, renders necessary certain safety-valves that are not required in a system which not only has both, but has, in addition, a basic unity of Parliamentary habits.[1] But to try to eliminate French divisions by acting as if they did not exist was to risk encouraging Deputies not to acquire the desired new Parliamentary habits, but rather to increase their ingenuity in exploiting old and familiar ones. It ought to have encouraged them to make more intelligent use of the Parliamentary question than they had hitherto done. But it did not. In the political circumstances in which they have so far been tried out, the new procedures have produced only frustration and rancour.

The changes in legislative procedure gave Governments constitutional authority to dominate in legislative debates in the Assembly. They have the right to priority for Government Bills in the Parliamentary time-table, the right to open the general debate on a Bill in either House, and also the right to propose Government amendments instead of having to resort to undignified subterfuges. This means that Deputies now hear the case for the Bill before they hear the criticisms of it contained in the report of the relevant Commission; and they now debate on the basis of the Government's Bill, instead of on the Bill as amended in Commission. Governments also now have power to restrict the exercise of certain rights possessed by Deputies. They can object to amendments from the floor, if these are put forward after the debate has begun – that is, without having been submitted to the Commission; they may ask the House to decide by a single vote on the whole Bill, or part of it, taking into consideration only their own amendments. or amendments approved by them. If there is disagreement between the two Houses on a Bill, Governments can help to see that their own views prevail. If they are in favour of a Bill they can enable the Assembly

[1] *v.* for instance, M. Guy Mollet's suggestion that a debate could be followed by a vote on a *motion d'orientation* (*Le Monde*, 5th June 1959), the *bureau* of the Assembly being authorized to decide whether its formulation was such as to make it in order. *v.* also speech by M. Legaret (*Indépendant*) on the debate of 26th May 1959 on the Standing Orders: 'To permit resolutions to be followed by a vote is to create an opportunity for an exchange of opinion. A refusal to allow them means that Parliament will be forced to reject the budget, or else, as it did in 1924, all Government proposals. It means substituting bad temper for frank explanations' (*Le Monde*, 28th May 1959). Cf. too the opinion of M. Brocas (Radical): 'It is essential that Parliament should be able to express its political opinions by a vote other than a vote of censure.' Even the *rapporteur* of the *Commission du Règlement*, a U.N.R. Deputy, expressed the hope that the Government would itself initiate debates on subjects of general interest in order to ensure that the opposition would be able to express its opinion freely, now that resolutions were out of order (*Le Monde*, 23rd July 1959).

to vote it in spite of the Senate's opposition; if they are opposed to it, they can, in effect, back the Senate against the Assembly, by refusing to intervene, thus ensuring that the Bill drops. What they cannot do, of course, is obtain the passage of a Bill voted by the Senate but rejected by the Assembly.

THE GOVERNMENT'S CONTROL OVER FINANCE

Under the Fifth Republic, the constitutional right of Deputies or Senators to propose measures involving an increase of expenditure is also severely curtailed. Similar, though less drastic restrictions had existed on paper during the previous régime, but under the Fifth Republic, Governments have more authority than they have had in the past to secure their enforcement in practice. It is perhaps worth while to recall briefly the methods by which the intentions expressed in the 1946 Constitution and in subsequent enactments were frustrated by Deputies.

Article 17 of the 1946 Constitution prohibited Deputies and Senators from proposing increased expenditure during budget debates. This provision, as well as those of what were known as *lois des maxima* governing certain aspects of budgetary procedure from 1949 onwards,[1] were evaded mainly in two ways. The Finance Commission was the judge of the admissibility of amendments to Finance Bills, and, since it was often at loggerheads with the Government, frequently took a lenient view of doubtful amendments. Moreover, a Deputy was in order in proposing amendments, if their adoption would not involve a *net* increase of expenditure, in other words, if he proposed to curtail expenditure elsewhere by an amount equivalent to the increase which the adoption of his amendment would involve. This second device proved a godsend to Deputies anxious to prove that they had their electors' interests at heart. Their amendments could propose real expenditure and theoretical – often highly problematical – economies, or expenditure to be accepted in principle, but incurred only at some future date, which absolved them from the responsibility of suggesting how the cost was to be met.

[1] The *loi des maxima* was an article inserted at the beginning of finance laws from 1949 onwards, reiterating in somewhat more detail and with more precision the prohibition of article 17 of the Constitution.

A '*décret organique*' of June 1956 tightened up financial procedure in a number of ways. Among other things, it debarred members of Parliament from proposing amendments to *any* Bill, if their adoption would result in an increase of expenditure. This reduced private members' financial initiative to the *introduction* of Bills, and these, of course, could often be killed in Commission. But the compensatory device was still used to evade the restrictions and members also had other weapons in their armoury.

Since the control of the purse is an essential principle of Parliamentary government, Parliament could, and still can, refuse to vote supplies. Under the Fourth Republic it could do this in two ways, by delaying the vote until certain conditions had been met, or by rejecting the budget altogether. The 1958 Constitution prevents delaying tactics by imposing a time-limit for budgetary debates, at the end of which, if Parliament has not voted on the proposals, the Government is authorized to introduce the provisions by decree.[1] Finance Ministers of the Fifth Republic do not, therefore, find themselves in the position of M. Edgar Faure at the beginning of 1952, when the Assembly had authorized the expenditure provided for in his budget, but had refused to vote on the articles providing for the revenue to meet it.

Parliament's second weapon remains. The threat to reject the budget altogether, failing certain concessions by the Government, can still place Ministers of the Fifth Republic in the position occupied by M. Faure in March 1955, when his request for special powers to apply certain tax reforms by decree was granted only on condition that he agreed to withdraw a highly unpopular (and highly effective) method of combating tax evasion.

Despite growing dissatisfaction with the Government, Parliament has not yet treated its right to reject the budget as a weapon. Here again, however, the reasons were political and had little or nothing to do with the efficacy of the new institutions. But the following three incidents may be indicative of some of the problems that Governments in different political circumstances from those of M. Debré will still have to face in their attempts to establish a new relationship between Government and Assembly in the field of financial legislation. One of the first measures proposed by a private member in the Assembly was that of an old Radical Deputy, with

[1] On the procedure for voting finance Bills *v. supra*, p. 97.

forty years' Parliamentary experience behind him, whose plan to restore certain ex-servicemen's pensions (the suppression of which by the provisional Government was generally unpopular) included the suggestion that the cost could be met by a simple transference of the necessary funds from the Ministry of Defence to the Ministry of Pensions! When doubts were expressed in the Finance Commission in July 1959 regarding the possibilities, under the new Constitution, of Parliamentary amendments to the Government's proposals for fiscal reform, the President, M. Paul Reynaud, another veteran Parliamentarian of the Fourth Republic, and a former Finance Minister as well as a former Prime Minister, reminded members that they still possessed the right of amendment 'on condition that any diminution of revenue is compensated for by a genuine corresponding increase elsewhere'.[1] In the budget debates at the end of 1959, the Prime Minister had to yield to pressure from the Assembly and agree to a partial restoration of ex-servicemen's pensions in 1960, and full restoration in 1961, if the financial circumstances made it possible. Even before the end of the first Parliamentary session, some of the Gaullist Deputies were discovering one of the essential facts of French Parliamentary life – the influence of the elector on the individual Deputy who is anxious to be re-elected. That this influence was not stronger was wholly due to the U.N.R.'s conviction that its future as a party depended on its support for General de Gaulle. But, as has already been pointed out, the party did discover another fact of Parliamentary life, namely, that a Parliamentary system needs a real Parliament as well as a strong Government.

[1] The *loi organique* of 2nd January 1959 governing the voting of Finance laws specifically states (article 42) that 'no additional article and no amendment to a Finance Bill is in order unless its purpose is to suppress or effectively to reduce an item of expenditure'. The wording is almost the same as that of article 58 of the *décret organique* of 19th June 1956.

The difficulty occurs also with Bills other than Finance Bills and is mainly one of interpretation. Strictly speaking, most proposals, if adopted, involve expenditure. M. Pleven pointed out that a resolution (if he had been speaking a few months later it would have had to be a Bill or an amendment) asking the Government to ratify a U.N. convention on the strengthening of measures to suppress prostitution had been ruled out of order on the ground that it would have involved increased expenditure on police. On this basis, he added, the Finance Commission could reject a resolution proposing the abolition of the death penalty on the ground that execution would be cheaper than imprisonment (quoted in *Le Monde*, 30th May 1959).

EXECUTIVE WEAPONS AGAINST THE ASSEMBLY

(*a*) **Incompatibility.** The consequences of the rule of 'incompatibility' between the functions of Minister and of Deputy have been discussed so far only in relation to the electoral system.[1] Its influence on the relations between Government and Parliament has been far-reaching. The inclusion of this rule in the Constitution was generally attributed to General de Gaulle, whose faith in the efficacity of the separation of powers is well known. Its supporters hoped that it would help to increase Governmental stability. They believed that Deputies might hesitate to turn Governments out in the hope of obtaining office, if the price was to be giving up their seat in the Assembly, and also, that Ministers would obtain a welcome relief from party pressure, both in the Assembly and in the constituencies for which they were elected.

Since Deputies are often also local Mayors and may retain this office if they become Ministers, since they are free to become candidates at the next general election when they have ceased to be Ministers, and since, while they are Ministers, they do not cease to be active party members, attending and speaking at party conferences, the second hope at least was doomed to be disappointed. On the other hand, when the Prime Minister looked outside the ranks of politicians for his colleagues, as the first Prime Minister of the Fifth Republic did, in the main,[2] fresh problems were

[1] *v. supra.* pp. 33 and 56.

The Member of Parliament who becomes a Minister must resign his seat within a month. During that month he may not vote. On leaving the Government, ex-Ministers formerly employed in one of the categories of the public service incompatible with Ministerial office receive their full salary for a period of six months, unless they find paid employment before then. They are not allowed during that period to take any post as director, or managing director of a nationalized concern, or as legal adviser to such a concern, nor may they take any such posts in concerns subsidized by the State, unless they had occupied such a post prior to becoming Ministers.

[2] In the first Government of the Fifth Republic, three important posts were, at first, held by politicians. They were Finance (M. Pinay), Justice (M. Michelet) and that of M. Soustelle, whose functions were less important than his personality. The portfolios of foreign affairs, the army, education, industry and commerce, public health, housing and the interior were all held by high civil servants, as was that of Delegate-General for Algeria. After a number of reshuffles, the Government included, at the beginning of 1962, rather more politicians, but none in a key role. Only two, the Minister of Agriculture, M. Pisani, and the newly appointed Minister of Finance, M. Giscard d'Estaing, had any standing in Parliament. M. Pompidou's Government did not present any significant changes, except for the inclusion of two leading M.R.P. politicians, MM. Schumann and Pflimlin, who resigned within a month, along with the three M.R.P. Ministers who had served in M. Debré's Government.

created. There was, for instance, the difficulty of maintaining the necessary contacts between Ministers and public opinion, and the danger of deterioration in the quality of both Ministers and the Civil Service if Ministers, as well as their private secretariats (*cabinets*), were to be generally recruited from the higher ranks of the administration. France is rightly proud of the quality of her higher Civil Servants. But if the ranks of these are regularly depleted, the Civil Service's loss will by no means necessarily be the Government's gain. Nothing in the conduct of affairs since June 1958 indicates that Civil Servants make particularly good Ministers. Indeed, more than one happening since then has borne out the contention that one of the most valuable functions of Ministers is the political one of telling Civil Servants what the public will not stand. There is also the danger that, after having been indifferent Ministers, Civil Servants may be less good Civil Servants. The problem of the 'politicization' of the Civil Service could be serious. For either the Minister goes back to his original job, in which case he will often be inescapably associated with the policy he has followed as a Minister, or else he will be moved elsewhere in order to avoid this result – to give him time to *se refaire une virginité administrative* – in which case the quality of the administration may suffer.

The incompatibility rule is mainly criticizable on the ground of the inevitable isolation of Governments from public opinion, if Ministers (whether politicians or technicians) are cut off from regular contact with opinion in the Assembly. It is true that the Assembly is itself often accused of being out of touch with public opinion. It has traditionally considered itself to be the authentic expression of popular sovereignty – *le pays légal*, as opposed to *le pays réel* – and, as such, it has been, on the one hand, too sensitive to certain aspects of public opinion, to pressure from local interests and pressure groups, for instance, and, on the other hand, often insensitive to general feeling in the country, because it constitutes a 'house without windows', a closed club, whose political controversies and values are not appreciated by the average citizen. It is nevertheless to the Assembly that Governments remain responsible and it is surely preferable that pressure groups should exert their influence there, through the normal channels of Parliamentary groups, rather than in the semi-secrecy of technocratic *cabinets* or in party meetings outside the Assembly. 'The worst Chamber will always be better than the best antechamber.'[1] For, though he ceases to be a member of the Assembly (or of the Senate), the Minister remains a member of his party. While Governments had a docile Parliamentary majority the disadvantages of 'incompatibility' were not fully apparent. When Government have again to fight for their majority, the relations between Ministers and Parliamentary groups could be vital.[2]

(*b*) **Dissolution.** Nor is the weapon of dissolution, henceforth to be used at the discretion of the President of the Republic,[3] likely to prove an effective substitute for good working relations between Government and Assembly. The only example of a dissolution during the present century was that of M. Faure in 1955. It was caused by Parliamentary deadlock over the electoral system. But the subsequent electoral campaign, in so far as it had any dominant theme at all, was concerned almost wholly with Algeria, on which the dissolved Parliament had had no coherent policy either. The result of the election was to produce an Assembly in which the balance of opinion on both these issues was virtually unchanged.

There is no reason to think that subsequent dissolutions would be more successful in obtaining from the electorate a clear expression of opinion, for the simple reason that neither French parties nor French elections are organized in such a way as to produce a clear choice for any coherent policy.[4] The elector votes for a party, or an electoral label, which often has no national organization behind it and whose relations with neighbouring parties or groups can vary from constituency to constituency. He has, therefore, no possibility of judging the relation between his choice of a candidate and the complexion of any future Government. This will be a coalition, whose programme, if it has one, is hammered out by hard bargaining between parties *after* the election.

[1] G. Morange, op. cit., p. 26.

[2] After the municipal elections in 1959, M. Debré announced that he was seeking to strengthen the contacts between the Government and the parties making up the Parliamentary majority. At the end of 1961, U.N.R. Deputies were still urging that this should be done. *v. supra*, p. 75. This problem became more acute, when M. Pompidou replaced M. Debré, since he was not even a member of the U.N.R. and had had no Parliamentary experience.

[3] *v. infra*, pp. 145 and 154, on the President's right to dissolve the Assembly.

[4] An election in which there was one dominating theme, say Algeria, might have constituted an exception to the general rule. President de Gaulle has, however, preferred to consult the electorate on Algeria by means of referenda.

A great deal of confusion has been created in French thinking about dissolution by fallacious comparisons with British practice. During the last years of the Fourth Republic a number of politicians and political scientists put forward proposals for a dissolution, sometimes automatic, sometimes semi-automatic, or at the discretion of the Prime Minister. In French writings on dissolution, the usual justification for it is the need for the Government to resolve a conflict with the Assembly by appealing to the nation, or by threatening to do so, which may in itself be sufficient to bring Deputies to heel. But this situation is in no way comparable to any conceivable one in which a British Government might ask for a dissolution. As has already been pointed out, the system of Cabinet government in a two-party system normally rules out a conflict between Government and Parliament. A dissolution would rarely constitute a threat to the Opposition; since the Government is already in power, it would usually stand to lose more than the Opposition. Nor is there any justification for assuming that a threat of dissolution might bring recalcitrant individual members to heel. They might all be holders of safe seats.

The truth is that in a multi-party system, as it exists in France, where parties are not in the habit of forming coalitions to fight elections on national programmes that are intended to be Governmental programmes, where the line between Government and Opposition is never wholly clear, and sometimes both unclear and inconsistent, a dissolution is bound to be a leap in the dark. It may thus become an instrument of political manœuvre. Before the Fifth Republic was six months old, certain Deputies were beginning to calculate the party advantages that might be derived from seeking to create circumstances in which the President might dissolve the Assembly. It would seem, therefore, that in circumstances more normal than those of the past four years, the threat of dissolution would always be something of a gamble and could not be counted on to strengthen a Government against the Assembly.

General de Gaulle implied at the beginning of the Parliament that there would be a dissolution if the Government were defeated, and M. Debré, at one moment, threatened to appeal to the country to settle the conflict over oral questions with debate. It was generally agreed that M. Debré had wanted a dissolution after the signature of the Algerian cease-fire agreement and the subsequent referendum ratifying it. General de Gaulle decided against a dissolution, however. If he had been correctly reported as saying to the members of the Government, on 9th January 1959: 'Gentlemen, this Government will remain in office throughout the Parliament,' he had, by 1962, changed his mind, for the Parliament had still almost a year to run when M. Pompidou's Government was formed. It was generally assumed that the President's decision was based on the calculation that a dissolution just then might well result in an Assembly more difficult to control than that elected in 1958.

(*c*) **The Referendum.** The objections to a dissolution as a means of strengthening the Government were not, in theory, applicable to a referendum. The President decides on a referendum, in theory, at the request of the Prime Minister or of Parliament, though he may refuse the request. It is easier for the electorate to give a clear answer to a specific question than it is for it to pronounce on the Government's policy as a whole, assuming that the question is properly worded. On the other hand, the use of the referendum under the Fifth Republic is limited to three types of measure – those concerning the organization of the public authorities, approving an agreement with the Community, or authorizing ratification of a Treaty which would affect the functioning of institutions. It was usually considered that the authors of the Constitution had in mind an issue such as that presented by the E.D.C. treaty of 1954, on which both Government and Assembly were divided. The Government of the day might well have preferred not to assume the responsibility for what was a difficult decision and one that, in the end, it never wholeheartedly took. A number of Deputies, too, would not have objected to handing over responsibility to the electorate.

THE BICEPHALOUS EXECUTIVE

It soon became evident that the referendum was regarded by General de Gaulle as a Presidential and not a Governmental instrument. Under the Fifth Republic, both institutions and Governments were serving Presidential purposes, and the relations between President and Prime Minister were largely the result of personal and exceptional factors, which made it impossible to predict how the same constitutional provisions might be expected to work with a different Prime Minister and a different President.

It was fashionable at first to regard M. Debré as an agent or a whipping-boy, to ask, even, as Professor Duverger did, whether he really existed.[1] Later, critics of the régime came to regard the Prime Minister as the real villain of the piece, both the king-pin of the régime and, sometimes, the saboteur, or would-be saboteur, of Presidential policies.

Wherever the truth lay, as the régime became increasingly unpopular, the conviction grew that, without M. Debré, the President could not exist. For it would be, surely, beyond the bounds of possibility to find another Prime Minister with his combination of intelligence, assiduity, conviction, even obsession, and masochistic devotion to the President.[2] Without him, the system could not have functioned at all. For the Government had no coherence, little co-ordination, and even less contact with public opinion, either inside or outside Parliament. In so far as it did function, this was owing to M. Debré's achievement in keeping his team (though only at the cost of numerous reshuffles of personnel[3]) with its toes firmly on the Presidential line.

By general admission, during these years, decisions in all vital fields were taken by the President and his use of some of the provisions of the Constitution discussed in this chapter was highly personal and totally unrelated to the principles or practice of Parliamentary government. He treated all his Ministers, including the Prime Minister, as Civil Servants, whether they were or not; he persistently ignored Parliament and parties, except to be rude about Parliamentary habits; and he left the Prime Minister to control Parliament with the procedural weapons at his disposal (mainly

[1] '*M. Debré, existe-t-il?*' (*La Nef*, July–August, 1959).

[2] *v.* M. Fauvet's anecdote no this point, in *La Fronde des Généraux* (Arthaud 1961) p. 21, '*Debré, dit de Gaulle, c'est saint Sébastien. Chaque fois qu'il reçoit une flèche, il souffre, mais ça lui fait plaisir.*'

M. Debré's methods, however, also contributed to the frustration of Ministers as did the President's effective control in certain fields. The Prime Minister was reported to be an indefatigable memorandum-writer, and to have a habit of stepping in and settling inter-Ministerial differences high-handedly, and sometimes without consulting or even informing the Minister concerned.

[3] *v.* M. Leenhardt's comment in the debate on the motion of censure on 15th December 1961:

'Under the Fourth Republic, the Prime Minister changed, but Ministers remained. Under the Fifth Republic, the Prime Minister remains and Ministers go. . . . We now have our third Minister of Information, our third Minister of the Interior, our third Minister of Agriculture and our fourth Minister of Education. In a word, this is not a Government. It is a sieve'.

articles 40, 41, 42, 44, 48 and 49), using for his own ends the referendum and the threat (or rumoured threat) of dissolution.

A Gaullist prediction in 1959 of how the 'bicephalous executive, might be expected to work had stated that Senate, President and Prime Minister would form 'a single bloc, the granite mass, the driving force and the principle of stability of the Fifth Republic'.[1] In fact, the Senate, like the Assembly, became increasingly hostile to both President and Prime Minister. These two did, indeed, form 'a single bloc', at least in public (though often only at the cost of some undignified and agile volte-face on the part of M. Debré). But they had only *one* head, that of the President, on whom the 'stability' of the Fifth Republic was wholly dependent. In April 1962, when M. Debré resigned, there was a good deal of speculation on the liklehood of the new Prime Minister's being able to control the Assembly as M. Debré had done. M. Debré was, at least, one of the leading members (though not the leader) of the majority party. He had had previous Parliamentary experience as a Senator, and had gained valuable experience in handling the Assembly, at a time when there was little risk of Deputies defeating the Government. M. Pompidou had none of these advantages and the general temper of the Assembly in 1962 was increasingly hostile to the President. The vote following his declaration of policy in the Assembly was, at best, a tepid welcome. It looked to many people as if M. Debré's indispensibility to the functioning of the Fifth Republic might yet have to be recognized.

[1] Marcel Prélot, *Pour comprendre la nouvelle Constitution* (Editions Le Centurion, 1958), p. 54.

CHAPTER VIII

The Presidency

THE PRESIDENTIAL TRADITION AND GENERAL DE GAULLE

The 16 Presidents of the Third and Fourth Republics had a certain family resemblance, because most of them were chosen to conform to a pattern. French members of Parliament have preferred to elect as President an elder statesman, generally respected by his fellow-members of Parliament, but neither an outstanding political leader nor a man of strong or extreme party views. All had been members of, and ten had been President of, one or other of the two Houses of Parliament. All but four were over 60 and two were over 70.

There are naturally a few exceptions to the general rule. Both Poincaré and Millerand had been Prime Ministers and M. Auriol had not merely been a prominent pre-war political leader, but was also the first and only Socialist to become President of the Republic. At the other extreme, one or two came near to possessing the qualifications recommended by Clemenceau, who advised his colleagues to 'vote for the most stupid', or those objected to by M. Herriot, when he accused the authors of the 1946 Constitution of trying to turn the President into a puppet. At the best, the qualities of Republican Presidents have been the kind of personal integrity and political wisdom possessed by M. Auriol, who did much to build up the prestige of the office in the early days of the Fourth Republic, or by his successor, M. Coty, who had the even more difficult task of helping to make possible a peaceful and legal transition to the Fifth.

Republican Presidents have not, as a rule, enjoyed peaceful periods of office. Some would have liked to play a more active role than the one allotted to them and were forced to choose one of the alternatives put before Marshal MacMahon – to give in or to get out (*se soumettre ou se démettre*). Indeed, three were forced to resign (though one of them had already by then been re-elected for a second term), two were murdered, one died in office, two resigned because of the collapse of the régime (though one had been re-elected for a second term) and three resigned for various reasons before the completion of their period of office. Only five completed their periods of office normally.

The first President of the Fifth Republic is an exception to most of the rules. He is the first regular-army officer to become President since Marshal MacMahon did so in 1873. He is the first President not to have been a member of Parliament. He was from 1940 to 1946 the acknowledged leader of the nation, first in exile and then at the head of the provisional Government, and he was, from 1947 to 1953, an outstanding political leader of the opposition to both the Constitution and the policies of the Fourth Republic. In normal circumstances, neither his personality nor his political opinions would have been considered by the majority of Frenchmen as recommendations for the post of President. Nor was the post one that would have recommended itself to him. The office of President has therefore, undergone a sea-change, which General de Gaulle was largely instrumental in bringing about. One result is that, for the first time since 1924, the President has become a subject of political controversy. The office, too, is under criticism. Among the many articles of the new Constitution that have been adversely commented on, those governing the functions of the President have been the most severely and the most generally criticized.

In one fundamentally important respect, both the new conception of the office and its first holder are, on paper at least, in line with both Republican and Presidential traditions. The Constitution provides for a President who is to be head of the State, but who in normal circumstances is not head of the Government. The functions of directing the Government and of determining its policy are specifically entrusted by the Constitution to the Prime Minister (article 20). A President can, and should, therefore, take a back seat, just as his predecessors did. General de Gaulle has indubitably occupied the driving seat in some fields and has intervened in most, but the circumstances in which he came to power make it impossible to predict the evolution of the office in normal conditions.

THE PRESIDENTIAL ELECTION

Presidents of the Fifth Republic are elected for seven years and presumably are indefinitely re-eligible, since the Constitution does not, as the 1946 Constitution did, specifically limit the number of terms of office. No qualifications for the office are mentioned either, the sole disqualification laid down in the 1946 Constitution – membership of a former reigning family of France – having been dropped. Election is by two ballots, unless a candidate obtains an absolute majority of the votes cast at the first. A simple majority only is required at the second. The Presidential electors include, along with Deputies and Senators, who elected the President under the two preceding régimes, an overwhelming majority of representatives of local authorities. With three exceptions, the Presidential electoral college is the same as that for the Senate. These exceptions are: (i) the inclusion of representatives of both the legislative and local Assemblies of the member-States of the Community, since the President of the Republic is also *ex-officio* President of the Community[1]; (ii) the choice as electors, in villages of up to 9,000 inhabitants, of Mayors and Councillors, instead of special delegates[2] elected by the Municipal Council; and (iii) a slightly less spectacular overweighting of the representation of small villages. The

[1] In subsequent Presidential elections, there may be only two exceptions, since all members of the Community have become independent. It is not yet known whether the six States remaining within the Community (of which the President of the Republic remains *ex officio* President) will continue to vote in Presidential elections. If so, the numbers of electors could be changed by bi-lateral agreements.

[2] For villages of up to 9,000 inhabitants, representatives are as follows:
Up to 1,000, the Mayor.
1,000–2,000: the Mayor and the first assistant Mayor.
2,001–2,500: the Mayor and the first assistant Mayor, and the Municipal Councillor with the highest number of votes at the previous Municipal election.
2,501–3,000: the Mayor and the first two assistants.
3,001–6,000: the Mayor and the first two assistants and the three Municipal Councillors with the highest number of votes.
6,001-9,000: the Mayor and the first two assistants and the six Municipal Councillors with the highest number of votes.

In 1958, in a college of 81,764 electors, 76,359 represented metropolitan France, and of these over half represented villages with populations of under 1,500. 286 represented Algeria and the Sahara, 1,262 the Overseas *départements*, and 214 the Overseas Territories of the Republic. 3,643 represented the member States of the Community. The last figure includes the electors of six States that subsequently left the Community on becoming independent.

representation of towns and villages with over 9,000 inhabitants is on exactly the same basis as for the Senatorial college.

The system is obviously open to criticisms similar to those made of the Senatorial college. In spite of the slightly different composition, the representatives of villages with under 1,500 inhabitants constitute a clear majority in both Presidential and Senatorial colleges (51 per cent, and 53 per cent respectively). In 1958, Paris, with a population of about 2,800,000, had 2,910 Presidential electors. According to Professor Duverger, *communes* with under 300 inhabitants, whose combined populations were only 2,850,000, had 16,312 electors. The President is, in reality, elected by village Mayors.

This system has been defended by, among others, M. Debré, whose argument was that France is a country of small villages. It has also been defended on the rather weak ground that both the previous system and election by universal suffrage had to be ruled out – the former as affording the President insufficient prestige (the 13 ballots required for the election of M. Coty in 1953 certainly did not provide a dignified spectacle) and the latter as giving him a too widely based authority. The disproportionality was justified on the ground that small communes had a right to their say, and that to give them a less disproportionate say would involve the special election of delegates, with the consequent risk of 'politicization'. It has been criticized by M. Duverger, on the ground that, like the Senatorial electoral system, it is an effort to restore a *régime des notables*, though whether, in this day and age, French village Mayors can still be legitimately regarded as 'notabilities' in the old sense is debatable. In the larger towns and in some villagas, local government elections are largely political, and even in the villages, the role of the *curé* and the *château* is not what it was. The Mayor is certainly an important personage and a genuine representative. But one must distinguish 'between those who are notabilities by virtue of their election and those who are elected because they are notabilities'.[1]

There are, however, other objections to the system. One is that, if there are more than two or three candidates, the President may be elected on a minority vote. This would defeat the ostensible

[1] Jean Rivero, *Regards sur les Institutions de la Ve République* (*Recueil Dalloz hebdomadaire*, 12th November 1958, p. 263.).

purpose of the system, which is to make the President at one and the same time a representative of the nation and one who cannot legitimately claim to be *as* representative as those chosen by universal suffrage. Provision is made for only two ballots. Electors vote in the administrative centre for the *département* (in the case of the electors of the States of the Community, in their own countries). It is likely to be extremely difficult for any agreement to be reached between electors between the two ballots in order to prevent a candidate from being elected on the second ballot by a minority vote.[1] Even under the previous system, when fewer than 1,000 electors were all under one roof and an unlimited number of ballots could be held until a candidate obtained an absolute majority, agreement on a candidate was often very difficult.

Another serious objection to the system is that it is more difficult to change than that governing elections to the Assembly or to the Senate, for, unlike the previous Presidential electoral system, that of the Fifth Republic has been included in the Constitution.[2]

The supervision of Presidential elections, including the investigation of alleged irregularities and the promulgation of the result, is entrusted to the Constitutional Council. The final stage of the count is held in public. In case of a Presidential vacancy, the President of the Senate replaces the President until elections can be held.

TRADITIONAL PRESIDENTIAL FUNCTIONS

A great many of the functions of the President are, in fact, those traditionally carried out by Republican Presidents. The President appoints the Prime Minister and accepts his resignation. He appoints and dismisses members of the Government at the request of the Prime Minister, presides at meetings of the Council of Ministers, of Councils and Committees of National Defence and of the Supreme Council of the Judiciary. He negotiates and ratifies treaties, accredits Ambassadors, appoints to some civil and military posts. He signs decrees in the Council of Ministers, promulgates laws (having the

[1] The second ballot is held a week after the first. No new candidate may stand at the second ballot unless presented by two candidates who agree to stand down for him (organic law of 7th November 1958).

[2] Some changes would not, of course, require constitutional revision, for instance, changes in the electorate of the member-States under article 6 or in the number of *communes*.

right to insist on a reconsideration of Bills by Parliament). He has the right of pardon.

In exercising these mainly formal functions, the President, like his predecessors, acts with the concurrence, and on the initiative, of the Prime Minister, whose counter-signature, together with that of any other relevant Ministers, is necessary. The most important exception is, of course, his appointment of the Prime Minister, for which, in the nature of the case, the resigning Government cannot take responsibility.

In a few respects, the Constitution gives the President of the Fifth Republic, even where these functions are concerned, a little more elbow room than his predecessors have had. For instance, the President now 'negotiates' Treaties (article 52), whereas under the previous Constitution he was merely 'kept informed' of the negotiations.[1] The list of offices to which he has the right of appointment is far longer than that contained in the 1946 Constitution. The President nominates the Prime Minister and the members of the Government proposed to him by the Prime Minister, without having to go through the intermediate stage of *désignation*.[2] In one respect, he seems to have somewhat less opportunity of independent action. To exercise the right of pardon he now requires a counter-signature, whereas the previous Constitution did not mention this requirement.[3]

Like his predecessors under the Third and Fourth Republics, the President is politically irresponsible for acts carried out by him in pursuance of his functions, except in the case of high treason, for which he can be tried before the High Court of Justice.[4] This provision is comprehensible in the case of a President who presides but does not govern, but less so in that of a President of the Fifth Republic who, even in normal circumstances, can exercise some degree of real power, and who, in an emergency, has the right to exercise almost unlimited power.

[1] But *v. infra*, pp. 137-8.

[2] *v. supra*, on *désignation*.

[3] It is worth remembering that the first President of the Fourth Republic, M. Auriol, though he sought advice on the matter of pardons, did not have a counter-signature. The constitutionality of this procedure was questioned by some.

[4] *v. supra*, pp. 39-40.

THE CONCEPT OF THE ARBITRATOR

The new powers possessed in normal circumstances by Presidents of the Fifth Republic really fall into two categories. First, the President can make a certain number of appointments without a counter-signature. It may, of course, be that Presidents will follow precedents in these cases and that the element of personal choice will be small, or in any case, that the choice will not be likely to give the President any significant additional powers. These are really powers exercised by virtue of the President's function, described in article 5, as guardian of the Constitution:

> The President of the Republic sees that the Constitution is respected, ensures by his arbitration the regular functioning of the organs of government and the continuity of the State.
>
> He is the protector (*le garant*) of national independence, of territorial integrity, and of respect for agreements within the Community and for treaties.

This concept, in itself, constitutes no break with Presidential tradition, though General de Gaulle has interpreted it very differently from the way in which his predecessors would have done. M. Auriol certainly considered that one of his functions was to ensure respect for the Constitution.[1] And, according to accounts, it was M. Coty who outlined to General de Gaulle the precise procedure which would reconcile his own conditions for a return to power with constitutional requirements.

The President's right to submit a treaty before ratification, or a law before promulgation, to the Constitutional Council, on the ground that it appears to be unconstitutional (articles 54 and 61) and his right to appoint three of the nine members of the Constitutional Council (article 56) seem clearly to be aspects of this function, differing only from other traditional Presidential functions in that there is no counter-signature.

General de Gaulle sees as falling within the scope of his functions as an arbitrator a second category of Presidential powers, which might be described as the right either to appeal or to refuse to appeal to the nation. The President has the right to have messages

[1] *v.* for instance, his speech of 15th November 1951: 'As I see my function, it is to defend the State, its Constitution, its institutions and also the permanent interests of France that this State represents.'

read in both Houses (article 18). He may decide either to accede to or to refuse a request submitted to him by the Prime Minister (during Parliamentary sessions) or by the two Houses conjointly, for a referendum on a Government Bill dealing with the organization of the public authorities, approving a Community agreement, or authorizing the ratification of a treaty which affects the functioning of institutions (article 11). And he may decide, after consulting the Prime Minister and the Presidents of the two Houses, to dissolve the National Assembly (article 12).

On a strict reading of the Constitution, none of these rights entitles the President to intervene directly in the processes of government. The referendum should be used only in the specific cases mentioned and the right of dissolution cannot be used more than once a year, since the Constitution prohibits a further dissolution within a year following a previous one.[1] Both referendum and dissolution explicitly hand over the right of decision to the electorate. Nevertheless, the choice of the circumstances in which these instruments are used could be a political choice. What has created disquiet is the constitutionalization of powers acceptable to Republican tradition only in abnormal circumstances, and for a limited time.

There are several ways in which the use of these three powers could involve a President in political controversy. It was evident, for instance, in May 1958, that M. Coty's Presidential message, threatening to resign if Parliament refused to accept General de Gaulle's candidature as Prime Minister, had a considerable influence on Deputies. This message was, of course, counter-signed by the Prime Minister, in conformity with the requirements of the 1946 Constitution. It is easy to imagine how, in a similarly tense situation, a President free to address both Houses on his own initiative and to express his own opinion rather than that of the Government might be able to influence the course of events. A Presidential decision to dissolve the Assembly could, in certain circumstances, enable a President to get rid of a Prime Minister, though the Constitution gives him no direct right to do this. For instance, in a case of conflict between President and Prime Minister, a well-timed dissolution

[1] If the President of the Senate is called on to act as *interim* President, he cannot use the powers of the President in relation to the referendum and the dissolution.

could result in the return of an Assembly favourable to the President's point of view, and so force the Government to resign. In the same circumstances, an ill-judged dissolution could place a President in the situation of President MacMahon in 1877, and so, perhaps, force him to resign. But the failure of an attempt by a President to produce an Assembly more amenable to the Government's point of view must surely bring the President into disrepute along with the Government. For, by voting against a Government supported by the President, the electorate would, in effect, be voting against the President too.

The Presidential right to refuse a request for a referendum is the right to decide not to submit to the electorate an issue that either the Government or Parliament considers ought to be so submitted. In deciding to exercise the right, a President would, therefore, either be siding with Parliament against the Government or with the Government against Parliament. In either case his position as an arbitrator would be weakened.

THE PRESIDENCY IN PRACTICE

Presidential functions have so far been discussed within the normal assumptions of French Parliamentary government. But, as has already been said, some of these assumptions were not valid during the first three years of the Presidency of General de Gaulle. In fields which he considered vital, the President ruled as well as reigned. Public interest was focused on him and not on the Prime Minister, and the President took great care to see that the spotlight remained on him.

At first, his prestige seemed to depend less on his interpretation of Presidential functions than on imponderables – on his personality, in contrast to that of the Prime Minister, who was from the start, and remained, unpopular with the politicians and unappreciated by the public. The President's exploitation of his personality – what came to be called 'the style' of the General – involved certain conceptions of the dignity of the office, a belief in Presidential pomp and ceremony, a visible occupancy of the chair of State, whether in his capacity as President of the Council of Ministers, as President of the Community, as the representative of his country on visits abroad, or as its chief spokesman in foreign affairs, either at home or abroad. Under his Presidency, the Council of Ministers became the real organ of decision, instead of, as it had been under the previous régimes, a body which normally ratified decisions taken in the Cabinet Council. Its communiqués became news, and news in which the most important personality was the President and not the Prime Minister. His visits to foreign heads of States, or theirs to him, were also front-page news, and there was no doubt that his past record, his physique, his obvious conviction of the importance of his role, his obstinate insistence on French prestige and French rights, his eloquence and, at times, too, his lack of it, all combined to keep before the public the qualities which were part of his conception of national leadership. The contrast with a Doumergue or a Lebrun was startling. And even M. Auriol and M. Coty, both excellent Republican Presidents, and much appreciated during their terms of office, seemed pale shadows in comparison. France not only had a President, she had also 'a State', as General de Gaulle had put it in his Press conference of May 1958, and she was seen by all to have both.

But there was much more to it than 'the style'. Decisions in the Council of Ministers were not always reached by and with the President. They were sometimes communicated to Ministers by him, if not imposed by him, and not always with their knowledge or consent. The declaration of 16th September 1959 on Algerian self-determination was made by the President in a televised broadcast, after the 'general outlines' of what he was to say had been 'communicated' to the Council of Ministers.[1] The articles of the Constitution authorizing the President to 'negotiate and ratify' treaties, and to be 'informed of the negotiation of treaties not requiring ratification', provisions almost identical with those contained in the Constitution of the Third Republic, had not been interpreted by Presidents of the Third Republic as entitling them to take over personal control of foreign policy. General de Gaulle did interpret them in this way. He held press conferences on both home and foreign affairs, outlining policies and answering questions – a procedure quite unprecedented for a President of the Republic. He was

[1] The words were those of an official communiqué. In his letter of resignation at the end of 1959 (*v. Le Monde* 10th January 1959), M. Guy Mollet stated that Ministers had not been given adequate opportunity to study the financial proposals.

personally responsible for determining France's attitude towards N.A.T.O., for a number of definitions of the basis of France's defence policy, for proposals on her role in European affairs and for statements on France's attitude to the Berlin problem.[1] The speeches in which the Prime Minister or the Minister of Foreign Affairs defended these policies in the Assembly or in the Senate took second place to (and, indeed, often followed) Presidential statements. The President sometimes implicitly (and occasionally explicitly) contradicted previous statements by his Prime Minister, who was obliged to eat his words.[2]

The tone of the President's announcements made it abundantly clear not only that he considered himself to be 'France's guide and head of the Republican State', but also that he intended to 'exercise supreme power to the full' and in the new spirit in which it had been entrusted to him.[3] He spoke of bearing on his shoulders the destiny of the country, of his mandate from the people, and of 'the legitimacy of which I have been the incarnation for twenty years'.[4] His

[1] For a discussion of the President's foreign policy, *v. infra*, chapter XI.

[2] The difference between the President's Algerian policy and that of M. Debré, as a Senator, is well known, and probably explains the often noticeable differences of tone and emphasis in statements by the President and M. Debré. But there were also more petty and frustrating kinds of volte-face often demanded of M. Debré. On 22nd November 1960, for instance, he informed Deputies that a referendum would be held in the second fortnight of January and that, until then, M. Delouvrier would remain in Algiers as Delegate-General for Algeria. The following day, the President informed the Council of Ministers that the referendum would be held during the first fortnight of January and that the Delegate-General was to be replaced immediately.

An example of a different form of Prime Ministerial humiliation is provided by the revelation by the President, at a garden party, of the essentials of a speech to be delivered the following day by the Prime Minister. As the *Manchester Guardian* Paris correspondent remarked of this occasion, 'this government by garden party has made an unfavourable impression. Nor is it a happy situation for M. Debré to have the President's next broadcast to the nation announced without (apparently) consultation with the Government, which had only just met'. (*Manchester Guardian* 30th June 1961.)

The importance of such examples lies less in their content than in the fact that they are typical of innumerable stories circulating in Paris, and presenting Ministers as often unaware of Presidential decisions concerning their departments. For instance, a communiqué of the Council of Ministers on 21st January 1962 confirmed the decision that troops would begin to be withdrawn in January, from Algeria, although the Minister of the Armed Forces had just informed the President of the Assembly Defence Commission that there would be a delay.

[3] Broadcast of 28th December 1958.

[4] Broadcast of 29th January 1960.

v. also similar statements in broadcast of 28th December 1958.

announcement on 16th September 1959 of the policy of Algerian self-determination made no mention of the Government, only of himself and the nation.

> 'I consider it necessary', he said, 'to proclaim here and now that there will be self-determination. In the name of France and of the Republic, and by virtue of the powers attributed to me by the Constitution to consult the citizens, I pledge myself, provided God grants me life and the people listen to me, to ask the Algerians on the one hand, in their twelve *départements*, to state definitely what they wish their future to be and the French, on the other hand, to approve this choice'.

As has already been pointed out, the Constitution does not authorize the President to hold a referendum, which is what he meant.[1] It merely authorizes him to refuse a Governmental (or Parliamentary) request for one. And article 20 specifically entrusts policy-making to the Prime Minister and his Government, not to the President.

Examples of this assumption of Presidential responsibility for decision-making are numerous. 'On my responsibility, and in full awareness of what is involved', he said, in his message to the army in Algeria, the following month, 'I have determined what our action must be in Algeria'. His concept of the hierarchical relationship of the different elements in the State in the process of decision-making was frequently expressed in the terms used by him in his broadcast to the army during the Algiers insurrection:

> 'In the name of France', he said, 'I have taken the following decision . . . self-determination is the only policy worthy of France, the only possible solution. It is the solution defined by the President of the Republic, decided by the Government, approved by Parliament and adopted by the nation'.[2]

A number of inter-Ministerial Committees were set up, in which, under General de Gaulle's Presidency, policy was formulated on

[1] The Constitution does, of course, entitle the President to 'consult the citizens' by way of a dissolution.

[2] Broadcast of 29th January 1960, c.f. also statement of M. Chaban-Delmas at a U.N.R. meeting in April 1960: '*L'U.N.R. appuira la politique inspirée par le chef de l'Etat définie et appliquée par le gouvernement . . .*'

c.f. also speech of 4th November 1960: '*Ayant repris la tête de la France, j'ai comme on le sait, décidé en son nom de suivre un chemin nouveau.*'

Algerian affairs, foreign affairs, and defence.[1] Ministers were frustrated by technical committees, by-passed by the President's personal advisers, confused by the duplication of Ministerial departments and others under the control of the Elysée or of the Hôtel Matignon, reduced to the status of executants of a policy in whose formulation they took less and less part. When in November 1960 M. Joxe was appointed Minister of State for Algerian Affairs, even the pretence of the Prime Ministerial control required by article 20 of the Constitution was dropped and M. Joxe was made directly responsible to the President.

In November 1959, the President of the Assembly, M. Chaban-Delmas, made his first contribution to the constitutional theory of the Fifth Republic, by attributing to the President, instead of to the Government, constitutional responsibility for policy within what he called the 'Presidential sector', covering foreign affairs, the Community, Algeria and defence. By this time, this picture so obviously corresponded to the *de facto* position that nobody attempted to deny it.[2] It was certainly not an accurate statement of the position as laid down in the Constitution. But as long as the Prime Minister was prepared to assume responsibility before Parliament for the President's decisions, to adapt his views to those of the President, even when he had only recently expressed different ideas, and to listen to Deputies quoting his past speeches against him, respect for the letter of constitutional regularity was ensured.

The political parties protested at times, but on the whole trusted the President far more than they did the Prime Minister. Paradoxically, it was sometimes left-wing politicians, opposed in principle to the Presidential system, who felt safer, in practice, in the President's hands, in spite of their strong objections to a number of his deci-

[1] On this 'government by committee' *v.* the complaint by M. Teitgen, for instance, at an M.R.P. departmental Congress in March 1960: 'Have we a Government? We have not. Ministers are not allowed to discuss the fundamental principles of policy. The Council of Ministers is short-circuited on all the essential questions by technical committees.'

[2] It was alleged by responsible political commentators that, as time went on, the 'Presidential sector' was more difficult to define. 'In practice', wrote M. Viansson-Ponté, for instance, 'any question, from the price of milk or sugar to negotiations on Algeria or European policy, can become part of the reserved domain one day and cease to be part of it the following day.' He went on to allege that Presidential interventions were sometimes on individual cases, and went into minute detail; that the President would sometimes take up a question and then drop it, and so on (*v. Le Monde* —November 1961).

sions. Thus, when the Assembly granted special powers to the Government in February 1960, following the Algiers insurrection, it was specified that the decrees must be signed by the President of the Republic.[1] The general public did not care a fig for constitutional niceties, being content to leave things to the President.

On two matters, however, Presidential interpretations of the Constitution, or what were assumed to be Presidential interpretations, were responsible for a general worsening of the relations between President and Parliament. The first related to articles 29 and 30, governing the holding of special sessions. These, according to article 29, are held 'at the request of the Prime Minister or of the majority of the members of the National Assembly' and must have 'a specified agenda'. In March 1960, such a request was made by 287 Deputies[2] (277 signatures were required) in order to discuss several Bills on agriculture that Deputies wished to introduce. In their view, the right to hold the session was then automatic, and no commentators up to this time had challenged this interpretation. The President held, however, that his duty, under article 30, to open and close such a session 'by decree of the President of the Republic' was not a pure formality. In his letter to the President of the Assembly he gave three reasons for refusing the request. First, the fact that pressure from agricultural interests had openly been brought to bear on Deputies constituted, in his view, an infringement of the Constitutional rule (article 27) forbidding 'specific instructions' (*le mandat impératif*) to members of Parliament from outside bodies; second, the private Member's Bills to be discussed involved expenditure and so would be ruled out of order (article 40); third, it was the President's duty, under article 5, to see that the Constitution was respected and, in his view, a special session was justified only by special circumstances. Moreover, the legislation proposed would not solve the agricultural problem which

[1] *v.*, also, M. Mollet's reply to the President in September 1961, when the latter complained that the Queen of England could speak personally to Parliament, whilst he could not deliver messages to Parliament, but had to have them read for him:

'*Vous savez aussi bien que moi que la reine y vient pour lire un discours préparé par le Premier Ministre et je préfère vos discours à ceux que fait Michel Debré.*' (Report in *le Populaire*, 28th September 1961, by René Schmitt, who was present.)

[2] Two special sessions had been held since the end of the previous regular session, but these had been requested by the Government.

demanded long-term measures and, therefore, in his capacity of '*arbitre*', he refused to sanction it.[1]

This was the first public controversy between President and Prime Minister on the one hand and Parliament on the other, and it drew from embittered Deputies and political commentators the inevitable protests that the executive was not 'bicephalous', but was headed in effect by a President of the Republic, acting, not as an '*arbitre*', but as head of a Presidential régime. There was even a threat that Senators would table a Bill to revise the Constitution in order to ensure the right of Parliament to hold special sessions, once the conditions laid down in article 29 had been complied with.[2]

The second constitutional difference of opinion was less technical. It concerned the President's general attitude to Parliament, as exemplified by his conception of the way in which the constitutional instruments of the referendum and the dissolution should be used. According to article 11, initiative in the matter of a referendum belongs to the Prime Minister or to Parliament. The decision to hold the referendum of 8th January 1961 was not only quite clearly a Presidential initiative, but was equally clearly taken to serve Presidential purposes, which were little if at all related to the specific legislative measure on which, in accordance with the requirements of article 11, the public was, in theory, expressing an opinion.

[1] For the text of the President's letter *v. l'Année Politique*, 1960, p. 640.

This letter raised, in fact, three Constitutional questions. (i) Had the President a right to discretion in the use of article 30, which required a counter-signature? (ii) Was it for the President to define what constituted a '*mandat impératif*'? Article 27 gives no guidance, but critics pointed out that the preparatory constitutional discussions had been concerned mainly with the quite different problem of outside pressure on Deputies to get them to vote in certain ways. (iii) Did the President's functions, under article 5, entitle him to interpret the Constitution? It was possible to argue, as M. Mollet did in a subsequent constitutional controversy, that it did not confer on the President any rights, but imposed on him an obligation, namely, to ensure the application of rules already laid down. This, of course, left the question open as to who was to decide, in cases of doubt, what precisely these rules were.

There was also a great deal of juridical argument based on the precise significance of the present tense used in article 29 – not '*peut être réuni*', but '*est réuni*', which was interpreted by critics as being mandatory; on comparisons with interpretations of the provisions of the 1875 and 1946 Constitutions on this matter, and on the use in both these texts of tenses that were clearly mandatory – '*devra*' (1875) and '*doit*' (1946, article 12). M. Debré was even quoted against himself. In his speech to the *Conseil d'Etat,* in August 1958, he had said: '*Des sessions extraordinaires peuvent être décidées à la volonté du Gouvernement ou de la majorité du Parlement*'.

[2] In fact nothing further was heard of this.

In fact, over a year later, this measure had not even begun to be applied.

During the campaign, press and political comment, as well as the tone of the President's two broadcasts, all assumed that this was a general vote of confidence in the President's Algerian policy, and an even more general reaffirmation of the public's confidence in his leadership. The results were, indeed, described as 'a blank cheque' for the President. He himself left no doubt on this score.

> 'Frenchmen and Frenchwomen', he said, 'you know that the reply you are to give is to me. For twenty years, events have made me the country's guide in the serious crises through which we have lived. Now, once again, my duty and my office have led me to choose our road. And, because it is a hard road, in order to succeed, I need the support of the nation. . . . That is why I appeal to you over the head of all intermediaries. In reality, as everyone knows, this is a matter between each of you and myself. . . .'[1]

This personal appeal, with its 'overtones of Bonapartism', was highly displeasing to the majority of members of Parliament, who, in accordance with Republican tradition, regarded themselves – 'the intermediaries' – as the legitimate representatives of, and spokesmen for, the nation.

If the referendum of January 1961 was more than a simple vote in favour of, or against, the Bill to set up a provisional executive in Algeria, that of April 1962 was more than a Bill incorporating the provisions of the Evian agreements. The first had 'tacked' on a general vote of confidence (or rather, the Bill was, in reality, tacked on to the vote of confidence!). The second tacked on a grant of extensive special powers to the President, who was empowered to conclude all agreements to implement the Evian agreements and, pending the assumption of power by an Algerian Government, to take the necessary measures either by ordinances or by decrees in the Council of Ministers.

Though the device of 'tacking' is contrary to the theoretical purpose of a referendum (which is to ascertain the opinion of the electorate on a specific issue), the danger of the O.A.S. and the continued threat of disaffection in the army could, perhaps, have

[1] Broadcast of 6th January 1961.

been held to justify its use in exceptional circumstances. It was certainly preferable in the eyes of politicians to a second period of rule by special powers under article 16. And the President, too, may be assumed to have preferred this method, because his power to dissolve the Assembly is suspended during the application of article 16. Moreover, in the actual circumstances of April 1962, it would have been difficult to justify recourse to article 16, in view of the conditions laid down in the article. But this was not the only alternative. Nothing prevented the Government from requesting the grant of special powers under article 38 to do what the referendum empowered the President to do – nothing, that is, except the President's desire to handle the Algerian problem himself and his openly expressed preference for the use of the referendum as an instrument of Government.

The most disquieting feature of the campaign to many Frenchmen was the President's notification to the public that the use of the referendum was to become a normal feature of government under the Fifth Republic.

> 'The referendum,' he said, just before the poll, 'is the clearest, the most honest and democratic of methods. The Constitution provides for its use and it is, therefore, becoming part of our habits, thus adding something essential to the legislative work of Parliament.'

This was the exact opposite of the truth. Many Frenchmen publicly explained that their vote meant 'Yes alas!', or 'Yes to peace and No to de Gaulle,' because the referendum provided no means of answering two distinct questions by one affirmative or negative. And far from adding anything to Parliament's work, the use of the referendum specifically removed from Parliament the right to legislate in fields regarded by the Constitution as belonging to the legislative field. In other words, the President chose to legislate by referendum, instead of leaving Parliament to legislate. Nothing in his behaviour indicated that he regarded Parliament as other than, at best, a subordinate machine, and, at worst, a nuisance.

> 'In reality', wrote M. Fauvret, 'General de Gaulle is interested neither in parties nor in Parliament; he is interested only in the nation. . . . His aim is to create and maintain a current of confidence between himself and the country. Repeated referenda,

televised broadcasts and appeals to the people from Town Hall platforms are his main weapons'.[1]

The facts bear out this view. During the three years ending in December 1961, General de Gaulle carried out 15 tours of the French provinces, visiting 59 *départements*, making 'whistle-stop' speeches in innumerable small hamlets, as well as in large towns, and meeting local notabilities. During 1961 alone, he gave six broadcasts and two press conferences, together with two important speeches on defence policy to army officers. Yet he seemed to attach little importance – and this was a major grievance of organized political opinion – to contact or co-operation with the political forces whose support in the Assembly and in the country was vital to the success of his policies. During the insurrections of January 1960 and April 1961, left-wing parties and Trade Unions gave massive support to the legally constituted authorities. But, as political commentators did not fail to point out, this support was never acknowledged.

> 'It would have been possible', wrote one eminent constitutional lawyer, 'for the head of the State to have looked to the political and social forces which had so decisively supported him in "the crisis of the barricades". He chose a different method, that of a solitude peopled with the crowds which look so well in processions and give so little real strength to régimes. History will doubtless point out the seriousness of his mistake in relying on public applause instead of on public opinion, on folklore rather than on folk.'[2]

All through this period, the President's references to his power to dissolve the National Assembly, conferred on him by article 12, were no less personal than his attitude to the referendum. And the effectiveness of his hints that he might use the power had nothing to do with the theoretical arguments on the purposes of dissolution. Parliamentary supporters of the dissolution had seen it as an instrument designed to strengthen the Government as against the Assembly, in particular, to prevent deadlock or Governmental instability. In the hands of the first President of the Fifth Republic, the threat (or the implied threat) of dissolution was effective solely

[1] *L'Avenir de la Cinquième*. II, (*Le Monde*, 3rd January 1962.)

[2] Professor G. Vedel in *Le Monde*, 1st November 1960.

because the survival of the régime depended on the President's remaining in office, and he left Deputies with the impression that if he felt obliged to dissolve, the complexion of the new Assembly might lead him to resign. In his first Presidential message to Parliament he had warned Deputies that the consequences of indulging in sectional quarrels would be an institutional crisis. The result was that though, at the end of three years, M. Debré was still in office, he had, during those three years, been obliged to have major or minor reshuffles,[1] involving the departure of eleven of the original team of 27 Ministers. The President saw, or affected to see, in the survival of M. Debré, evidence of a stability 'encouraged by the spirit and letter of the new institutions', which were in accordance with 'the will of the country'.[2] The majority of Deputies saw it as evidence of the political indispensability of the President. Nothing showed this up more clearly than the period during which the President assumed full powers.

EMERGENCY POWERS

From the first, the article of the Constitution which had aroused more criticism than all the others put together was that defining the President's power in abnormal circumstances. It is worth while, therefore, quoting its provisions in full.

> In a situation in which there is an immediate and serious threat to Republican institutions, national independence, territorial integrity or the application of international agreements, and in which the regular functioning of the constitutional public authorities is interrupted, the President of the Republic, after officially consulting the Prime Minister, the Presidents of the Assemblies and the Constitutional Council, takes the measures called for by the circumstances.
>
> He informs the nation by a message.
>
> These measures, on which the Constitutional Council is con-

[1] *v.* statement by M. Pascal Arrighi on 15th December 1961 (*Journal Officiel* 16th January 1961, p. 5683), who calculated that there had been 10 Governmental changes since January 1959.

[2] Broadcast of 29th December 1961.

> sulted, must be inspired by the will to enable the constitutional public authorities to fulfil their mission with the minimum of delay.
>
> Parliament meets as of right. The National Assembly cannot be dissolved during the period of exercise of the exceptional powers.

According to statements attributed to General de Gaulle, this article was intended to be precise and limited. It was intended to be used solely as a reserve power, in the event of a national disaster such as the defeat of 1940, or to enable the necessary instructions to be given if the political and administrative organs were to be disorganized by, say, an atomic war. The principle of the need to ensure the continuity of the State has not been contested. What has been generally contested, outside Gaullist circles, is that the method chosen would achieve its purpose. Even if M. Lebrun had possessed these powers in 1940, the situation would have been unchanged. It was not, in actual fact, the weakness of Presidential authority that was responsible for the capitulation and for the handing over of political powers to Marshal Pétain, but a regular vote of the two Houses of Parliament.

In 1958, the main objection of critics of the article was that its provisions could be deliberately abused by a President seeking personal power, and could even serve as technically legal cover for a *coup d'état*. The President alone is entitled to decide when an emergency, as defined by the Constitution, exists, and what measures should be taken. His obligations are merely to *consult* the Presidents of the two Houses and the Constitutional Council and to *inform* the nation. Neither the provision that Parliament meets as of right and cannot be dissolved during the emergency, nor that requiring the Constitutional Council to publish (with reasons) its opinions regarding the existence of an emergency, provides any real safeguard against Presidential unconstitutionality, since the President has the right to assume full powers. Supporters of the Constitution dismissed these objections, on the ground that the measures were designed to deal with some remote and improbable contingency, for which, in any case, detailed provisions would be impossible.

There were, as well as fears of misuse of the article, a number of uncertainties regarding the meaning of some of its provisions. For instance, if the emergency were such as to prevent the President from carrying out his obligation to consult the Constitutional Council, or to prevent Parliament from meeting, would he be able constitutionally to bring it into force? If Parliament did meet, what could it do? Were the President's powers unlimited? Could he, for instance, suspend the application of any parts of the Constitution, or even revise it? Would he be expected, or feel obliged, to inform Parliament of whatever decisions he was taking? And when normality had been restored, must he constitutionally cease to exercise the special powers?

The only occasion on which the President did assume full powers under article 16 was following the outbreak, on 22nd April 1961, of the military insurrection in Algeria, and the events of the following five months of emergency rule helped to clear up some of these constitutional ambiguities. The President announced in a broadcast on 23rd April that he was assuming full powers. Parliament met on 25th April (the date of the opening of the normal Spring session) and, in a message read to both Houses, the President stated that he expected Parliament to carry out its normal legislative functions, in so far as these were unrelated to the emergency. Eighteen Presidential 'decisions' were subsequently taken to deal with this, the last two bringing the period to an end. On 20th September, the President announced that article 16 would cease to be applied at the end of the month, but that a number of the security measures taken would remain in force for as long as Parliament considered this to be necessary.[1] Among those that, in the President's view, should continue to be applied were the decisions declaring a state of urgency, authorizing administrative internment and the holding of suspects for 15 days without a charge being preferred, banning the publication of certain material, and setting up special military Courts to try those charged with committing or abetting crimes against the security of the State.[2] These Courts,

[1] In some cases, 'decisions' had not mentioned a time-limit, in others a time-limit had been mentioned, unrelated to the duration of the emergency. In the first case, decisions were to cease to operate on 15th July 1962, unless Parliament decided otherwise, but Parliament was free to end the application of all of them by law.

[2] It should be perhaps noted, however, that a number of Deputies did announce their intention at the beginning of October to introduce a Bill to abrogate all decisions taken between 23rd April and 29th September, by virtue of article 16, on the ground that the last two decisions, taken on 29th September were contradictory: (*footnote continued p. 149, bottom*)

somewhat modified in composition, were to deal with charges brought after the end of the emergency period as well as with those relating to the insurrection. They were abolished in May, following the verdict of the High Military Court in the Salan case.[1]

This first experience of the application of article 16 was in many ways reassuring. There was general approval both of the President's assumption of full powers and of most of the 18 decisions taken. Only one aroused the fears of misuse of the article that had previously been expressed. By the time that the President announced his decision to bring the period of emergency to an end, there had been growing pressure for some weeks among left-wing parties for this to be done, but there was little or no criticism of the prolongation beyond the emergency period of certain security measures. The President's expressed desire, at the opening of the Parliamentary session, for Parliament to carry out its normal functions had been received with satisfaction. A number of useful precedents had

[1] The Government's decision to abolish the High Military Court followed the latter's pronouncement of the sentence of criminal detention for life on ex-General Salan. Ex-General Jouhaud had been tried by the same Court (presided over by the same man and, with one exception, composed of the same judges) on the same charges and had been condemned to death. The refusal of the Court to recognize extenuating circumstances in the case of General Jouhaud, who was General Salan's Deputy, and, moreover Algerian-born, while it did recognize extenuating circumstances in the case of the self-acknowledged head of the O.A.S. movement, aroused great indignation in the Government and in France generally.

'The exceptional powers conferred on the President by article 16', they said, 'can be exercised only so long as the regular functioning of institutions is in fact interrupted. They allow him to take only exceptional and provisional measures, with the sole purpose of re-establishing this regular functioning.

'Once this has been achieved, the exceptional powers disappear, as the second decision of 29th September recognizes. Given the provisional nature of these powers, it would be irregular for the application of measures taken under them to be prolonged beyond the period of application of the article itself.'

The Deputies in question (MM. Bidault, André Marie, Legaret, Legendre and Baylot, were all right-wing opponents of the President (For text of the *exposé des motifs*, v. *Le Monde* 5th October 1961.)

For a discussion of this point, *v.* Léo Hamon, *A propos de l'article* 16: *quelques questions juridiques*, in *l'Actualite Juridique*, 20th December 1961. In actual fact, the point was academic, since Parliament was free to abrogate any of the decisions which it did not wish to be prolonged. But on the general question of the constitutionality of prolongation there does not seem to be a clear answer. The point cannot be tested before the *Conseil d'Etat*, which regards '*décisions*' as belonging to the field of legislation and, therefore, outside its jurisdiction.

also been established – for instance, that the 'measures called for by the circumstances' should take the form of 'decisions', published in the *Journal Officiel*; that it was for the President alone to decide when his mission was completed, to announce this decision to the Council of Ministers, and to inform the nation in a final 'decision'; that Parliamentary sessions and political activities could, if the President so decided, be carried on normally; that it was for Parliament to decide by law when to end the period of application of such 'decisions' as continued to be applied with the ending of the emergency, if it disagreed with the date fixed. Certain questions still remained necessarily unanswered. The emergency had not been of a kind to prevent the President from fulfilling the initial formalities under article 16, or to prevent Parliament or the Government from functioning. But some doubt was expressed as to whether other obligations had, in fact, actually been fulfilled. For instance, was the declaration of the emergency in itself constitutional? There was no doubt that both parties and public approved of the decision and felt it to be politically necessary. And as the President's only constitutional obligation was to 'consult' the Constitutional Council on the matter, he was clearly technically in order, since nothing in the Constitution binds him to accept any assessment of the situation other than his own. But some constitutional lawyers found it difficult to justify the decision as being in strict accordance with the principles of article 16.[1] Two conditions are laid down. On the first, there was no disagreement. The insurrection quite clearly constituted 'an immediate and serious threat to Republican institutions, national independence . . .' etc. It was less clear how, on 23rd April, it had interrupted 'the regular functioning of the constitutional organs of government'. President, Government and Parliament were able to carry out their functions without let or hindrance. And though it could be argued that the authorities in Algeria could not

[1] *v.* for instance: Georges Vedel, quoted by Jean Lamarque in *Revue du Droit Public*, May–June 1961, p. 610.

It was also argued that the application of article 16 was unnecessary since most of the measures taken under it could have been taken under the special powers (voted in March 1955 and still in force). These powers would not, however, have allowed him to strip the rebel generals of their rank so quickly nor to transfer judges from Algeria. *v.* report of General de Gaulle's statement on this to the delegation of the Socialist Parliamentary group, on 26th September 1961. '*Quant à l'article* 16, *vous savez bien qu'il m'était nécessaire, pour faire condamner Challe et coffrer les gens de l'O.A.S., avec la police que vous connaissez, la magistrature qui est ce qu'elle est, et l'armée telle qu'elle se trouve.*' (*France-Soir*, 27th September 1961) (the delegate-general M. Morin was even arrested), these were not 'constitutional' organs, but authorities subordinate to the constitutional organs.

This problem provides another example of the bad drafting of parts of the 1958 Constitution. For to wait until the *threat* to 'the regular functioning of the constitutional public authorities' had actually materialized before taking steps to meet it (which, in the nature of the case might by then be impossible) makes political nonsense, even if it may be held to make constitutional sense. And that was obviously how the nation regarded it.

The question of what Parliament could actually do during an emergency as defined by article 16, when, although it could sit 'as of right' and could not constitutionally be dissolved, all powers were in the hands of the President, did arise as a result of this first application of article 16, and led to a major constitutional controversy.

The difficulty arose at the end of August, when Parliament decided to hold a special session to introduce a Bill dealing with the causes of the agricultural discontent which had led to farmers' demonstrations in a number of *départements* from June onwards. Although constitutionally entitled to sit throughout the emergency, Parliament had decided that the circumstances were normal enough to justify its going into recess on 22nd July, that is, at the end of the regular session. Deputies discovered that, on the President's interpretation of their functions during a special session held 'as of right' (that is under article 16, and not under articles 29 and 30), they were constitutionally entitled to discuss only questions relating to the emergency, which was the *raison d'être* of their right to sit. Consequently, they would not be entitled to introduce private members' Bills, which was precisely what they were intending to do. As the President put it in a letter to the Prime Minister:

> 'Except in circumstances involving immediate danger to the country and to the Republic, circumstances in which the Head of the State and the Government would certainly take the initiative, legislation outside the sessions would be unjustified.'

By 'the sessions', the President meant the normal sessions, as laid down in article 28, not special sessions as provided for under article 16. He went on to define what he saw as the functions of Parliament during such special sessions:

'In the presence of dangerous and tragic events, the nation's representatives must be able to make their voices heard, and the President of the Republic and the Government must be able to call on their support, as a matter of urgency.'

Since the President was constitutionally entitled to take all 'measures called for by the circumstances', members of Parliament could hardly have objected to a ban on private members' Bills dealing with the emergency, whether introduced in regular or in special sessions. But their proposed Bill was not related to the emergency.[1] The President's views, therefore, raised two constitutional issues. The first was the constitutional accuracy of the President's distinction between Parliament's rights in normal and in special sessions on the one hand, and in special sessions held by virtue of article 16 on the other. The second, was that of the President's authority to interpret the Constitution.

The answer to the first question depended on the answer to the second. The President of the Assembly gave his own answer to the second question when he ruled out of order a motion of censure that Deputies had decided to table during their special session, in protest against the restriction of their right to introduce Bills during it. This raised the further constitutional issue of the right of the President of the Assembly to interpret the Constitution. The President of the Republic contracted neatly out of the discussion by publicly repudiating all responsibility for the interpretation given by the President of the Assembly.[2]

The latter based his ruling, first, on the right of the President to interpret the Constitution, and second, on what he deduced to be the President's views. In his view, the President's exercise of full powers (article 16), together with his general responsibility (article 5) for ensuring respect for the Constitution, meant that it was for the President alone to determine, during an emergency, how the

[1] The proposed legislation was, in actual fact, ruled out of order on other grounds. In the Senate on 5th September, the President held that one Bill was out of order under article 40, and the Constitutional Council, appealed to by the Prime Minister, ruled another out of order under article 41. (*Journal Officiel*, 9th September 1961, p. 8427). On 12th September the proposed legislation was similarly ruled out of order in the Assembly.

[2] *v.* report of the President's meeting with the delegation of the Socialist Parliamentary group on 26th September 1961 in *France Soir*, 27th September 1961, '*Mais moi je ne l'ai jamais dit. C'est le Président de votre Assemblée Nationale qui l'a dit*', and in *Journal Officiel* 16th December 1961, p. 5676.

different organs of Government were to function. This meant that the answer to the first and second questions was that, during the application of the emergency, the President had full authority to decide *how* to apply the provisions of the Constitution; that is, to interpret them, if necessary.

Unfortunately, this did not dispose of the matter. There remained the third question. What authority had an interpretation made by the President of the Assembly, on the strength of his deduction of what the Presidential interpretation would be, based on a letter written by General de Gaulle to the Prime Minister and a statement made by him to Parliament on the opening of the normal sessions?[1] If there was no certainty that the President accepted this interpretation – and since he later repudiated responsibility for it, though without dissociating himself explicitly from it, what certainty could there be? – then it was difficult to claim that this was beyond all reasonable doubt a Presidental interpretation.

Nevertheless, it was clear that someone must decide what the constitutional position was. The Constitutional Council declared itself incompetent, as did the *bureau* of the Assembly and so, on the basis of these two Presidential pronouncements, the President of the Assembly concluded that, since the President had held that private members' Bills were ruled out during a special session held during the application of article 16, motions of censure must also be ruled out. For, of the two constitutional mechanisms for ensuring the responsibility of the Government to Parliament (article 49) namely, the 'pledging of Governmental responsibility on a Bill' and the tabling of a motion of censure by Deputies, the first was necessarily ruled out, if no Bill could be introduced. The second, he said, must logically be ruled out too,[2] in order to ensure 'a fundamental equilibrium of power'.

[1] The President's letter of 31st August was reproduced in *Le Monde* 2nd September 1961. For the text of his message to Parliament, *v. Journal officiel* (A.N.) 26th April 1961, p. 510.

[2] The logic of this argument is not evident to English minds and was not to many French ones. First, the Government's responsibility can be pledged on a declaration of general policy as well as on a Bill; second, nothing ruled out a Government Bill, unless the President disallowed it; and third, the Constitution cannot reasonably be interpreted to mean that one of the two methods is to be employed only if the other is not ruled out. The President of the Assembly considered them to be concomitant 'in order to ensure a fundamental equilibrium of power', a requirement nowhere laid down in the Constitution for the application of any part of article 49.

The constitutional issues were, in the event, clouded by a great deal of political controversy not always directly relevant. For instance, the President's opinion that the special session, though constitutionally in order, was politically unnecessary, since the proposed legislation could be introduced a few weeks later during the regular autumn session, was used by his critics as evidence to justify a demand for the ending of the period of emergency.[1] Some argued that the real reason for the denial to Deputies of the right to move a motion of censure was the fact that the President could not dissolve the Assembly during the application of article 16, and the President of the Assembly had, indeed, suggested in his communication to the signatories of the motion of censure that the right of dissolution was a concomitant of the right to defeat the Government.[2] Some disagreed with the President of the Assembly that the President of the Republic had authority to interpret the Constitution, on the ground that his obligation, under article 5, to see that constitutional rules were respected, gave him no right to decide what they were.[3] Many politicians regarded the distinction between Parliament's rights during 'normal' and 'special' sessions as being constitutionally invalid. They also regarded it as additional evidence of the desire of both President and Prime Minister to restrict Parliament's powers wherever possible.

[1] Though politically valid, in the circumstances, this argument was not necessarily constitutionally valid, for there could be circumstances in which Parliament could function normally, but some other constitutional organ could not.

[2] It is difficult to accept this view, either. There are, in fact, occasions when the two are *not* concomitant Thus, for instance, a second dissolution cannot occur within 12 months of the first, but nothing in the Constitution forbids a Government defeat during that time. And the President can dissolve the Assembly, under article 12, when the Government has not been defeated.

Two suggestions put forward during the controversy are perhaps worth a mention. The first was that, since the President's acts under article 16 are not countersigned, the Government cannot be held responsible (*v. François Piétri* in *Revue Politique et Parlementaire,* October 1961) and so the President of the Assembly could have ruled out the motion of censure more simply on this ground.

The second was that the real reason for the rejection of the motion of censure was not that it was out of order, but that the President of the Republic did not want it to be moved while he had no power to dissolve the Assembly, and left it to M. Chaban-Delmas to find a way of preventing it.

[3] *v.,* in particular, M. Guy Mollet's statement in *Démocratie* 61, 21st September 1961, '*L'article 5, en effet, ne donne aucun droit au président pour fixer des règles de fonctionnement mais lui impose, au contraire, le devoir de veiller à leur application*'.

INSTITUTIONS AND POLICIES

Politicians were exasperated, and increasingly so as time went on, on political as well as on constitutional grounds. As these constitutional wrangles showed, they resented what many of them saw as the deliberate use by the Government of the decisions of a politically subservient Constitutional Council, and of *ad hoc* interpretations of the Constitution, whether by the President, the Prime Minister, or the President of the Assembly, in order to enable the Executive to give dubious constitutional legality to specific political manœuvres. They believed that the letter as well as the spirit of the Constitution was being flouted by those responsible for it, who were said to approve of it, and who were able to behave in this way with impunity only because the political circumstances ruled out the use by Deputies of the constitutional mechanisms which would otherwise have enabled them to resist what they regarded as executive encroachments on their domain.

For the truth was, and everybody knew it, that, whether or not the emergency required the application of article 16, the *raison d'être* of the Fifth Republic and of its institutions was the existence of the continuing political emergency caused by the Algerian problem. Since this proved incapable of a rapid solution by some miraculous sleight of hand, a prolonged Algerian stalemate enabled the President to make the Constitution an instrument of his policy. Parliament would have made short work of Presidential constitutional interpretations, if the President had been anyone else, holding office at any other time. And it would have defeated some Presidential and Governmental policies if they, too, had not been regarded as part of the price that had to be paid for the continuance of the President in office.

In these circumstances, it is irrelevant to speculate on the possible evolution of the office of the Presidency or indeed of other institutions of the Fifth Republic, in more normal circumstances.

The how and when of a return to normality will themselves help to determine the future of the institutions. But, however the régime evolves, or even if it succumbs, the consequences of the President's policies in different fields will have to be reckoned with by any future President or régime. Part of the heritage will certainly be the bad feeling caused by what it is impossible to regard as other than unconvincing and politically inspired constitutional interpretations. No doubt any Constitution drawn up in the circumstances of 1958 could have worked only with difficulty. Where divisions cut too deep for the necessary elasticity and give and take between Government and Opposition, institutions reflect the divisions, but cannot provide a remedy. The 1958 Constitution, badly drafted as it was, invited the kind of constitutional and political wrangles that have consumed so much of the time of Parliaments since the war. The Government was justified, on the basis of experience, in concluding that the Opposition would obstruct where it could. But it, too, invited attempts to obstruct by failing to provide adequate safety-valves for the expression of criticism and opposition. The result was that the institutions themselves became one of the main sources of political controversy.

PART III

The Politics of the Fifth Republic

CHAPTER IX

The Presidential Sector

(i) The Community

Future historians will no doubt praise or blame the President primarily for his action in the fields of colonial and Algerian policy. Where the Community is concerned, the judgement is likely to be almost wholly favourable. France's policy of 'decolonization' was carried out with spectacular speed and smoothness and in a general atmosphere of co-operative comprehension.

Some credit for this must go to the Governments of the Fourth Republic and, in particular, to that of M. Mollet. His Government was responsible for the outline-law of 1956 which provided, and only just in time, for the basic administrative infrastructure on which effective independence could be built. The French Union had substituted for the pre-war Empire a system based on universal citizenship and the representation of all overseas dependencies in the French Parliament, on the provision of some degree of autonomy, mainly financial, in the 18 Overseas Territories of the Republic, and on the attempt, which failed, to create a semi-federal relationship between France and the three former Protectorates of Indo-China, Morocco and Tunisia, re-named Associated States. By 1956, all three had become independent and most of the Overseas Territories were already pressing for something nearer to real self-government.

This the outline-law of 1956 provided. It consisted essentially of four reforms: (i) the establishment in the Overseas Territories of Governmental Councils elected by the Territorial Assemblies which, though not at first *de jure* responsible, could, and did, shortly become responsible to the popularly elected body; (ii) the extension of the powers of Territorial Assemblies in matters of predominantly local concern; (iii) provisions for the Africanization of the administration,[1] and (iv) universal suffrage and the institution of the common electoral roll in the few remaining Territories (Madagascar and Equatorial Africa) where it did not already exist by 1956.

This meant the end of the tradition of direct French rule, except for the reserved subjects, admittedly constituting a long and important list. For France remained responsible for the essential services, – foreign affairs, defence, justice, the maintenance of individual liberties, communications, finance and foreign exchange and higher education – in all some 32 different services, headed by the President of the Governmental Council, a French official responsible to the relevant Ministry in Paris.

This reform, like the subsequent experiment of the Community, was already out of date before it had been fully put into application. But it was important in that it provided for some advance without involving constitutional reform, which, during the last years of the Fourth Republic, had become politically impossible, and also in that it provided a structure that could be easily adapted to the new needs of the Community.

THE COMMUNITY

The Fifth Republic's concept of 'the Community' replaced that of the French Union. It was never clearly defined, the Constitution merely referring to the fact that it was 'based on equality and the solidarity of its member peoples' and that its institutions were founded on 'the common ideal of liberty, equality and fraternity' and were designed 'to permit of democratic evolution' (article 1 and Preamble). Member States had the right to

> 'self-administration and the free and democratic management of their affairs'. (article 77).

All citizens were, moreover, to be equal in law, whatever their origin, race or religion, and to have the same duties.

The Community consisted on the one hand of the French Republic, and on the other of the 12 former Overseas Territories which voted 'Yes' in the constitutional referendum of September 1958.

[1] It was intended that eventually some 50 per cent of the students of the *Ecole Nationale d'Administration* should come from Overseas Territories.

The French Republic then consisted of metropolitan France, Algeria (including the two Saharan *départements* formed in 1957), the four Overseas *départements* of Guadeloupe, Martinique, Réunion and Guiana, and five small Overseas Territories (St, Pierre-et-Miquelon, the Comoro Archipelago, French Somaliland, Polynesia and New Caledonia), which voted in 1958 to retain this status. All of them elected representatives to the National Assembly and to the Senate. The administration of the Overseas *départements* has been completely assimilated to that of France (at their own request) since 1946 and they retain this status under the Fifth Republic. It would seem that the Constitution does not provide for any evolution towards independence, though article 73 provides for any 'adaptations' of their legislative régime or administrative organization that may be necessitated by their particular situation. The Overseas Territories also retain the status that they had under the Fourth Republic, though they can, of course, avail themselves of the possibilities for partial self-administration offered by the 'outline-law' of 1956. They are all small, poor, and economically dependent on France, and, so far, (with the possible exception of French Somaliland) seem unlikely to seek independence in any immediately foreseeable future. They can, in any case, avail themelves of the possibilities offered, under article 74, of such modifications of their status as would be needed to take into account 'their special interests within the general interests of the Republic', without any need for a revision of the Constitution.[1]

The 12 member States comprised Madagascar and eleven of the 12 former African Overseas Territories. Their choice of the new status consisted, first, of an affirmative vote in the constitutional referendum of September 1958. The twelfth, Guinea, voted *No* and so became immediately independent. The choice of the 11 and of Madagascar was then ratified by a decision of each Territorial Assembly the following autumn. The names by which each State wished to be known were announced, Constitutions were drawn up and submitted for the approval of the Territorial Assemblies, and representatives were elected during the following months to legislative Assemblies in each State.

[1] Since there is no longer a Minister for Overseas Territories, their affairs come within the purview of a Minister of State who is also responsible for the four Overseas *départements*.

FROM COMMUNITY STATUS TO INDEPENDENCE

By the time these formalities had been completed and the organs of the Community – Executive Council, Senate and Court of Arbitration[1] – had been set up, and even before the administrative reorganization necessitated by the creation of the Community could be completed, there were already signs that some of the new States wanted immediate independence. In September 1959, the federation of Mali (comprising since January of that year the States of Senegal and Soudan) decided to become independent. In December, Madagascar followed suit. In 1960, one after another, all eleven acceded to independence. The Community, as originally conceived, had ended almost as soon as it had begun.

INDEPENDENCE IN CO-OPERATION WITH FRANCE

In spite of the fact that the Constitution had provided (article 86) for changes in status, including accession to independence, to be made by agreement, it proved necessary to revise the Constitution to make independence compatible with membership of the Community. Article 86 of the Constitution was therefore revised in order both to enable a State to remain within the Community after independence and to enable any other independent State to become a member of the Community without thereby ceasing to be independent. In both cases, a simple agreement only is now required. This agreement, or subsequent ones, could determine the position of the State within the Community. Article 85 was also revised in order to make it possible to revise all the articles of Title XII (dealing with the Community) simply by agreement between the member States.[2]

[1] The composition and functions of these organs were provided for by organic laws.

[2] It was at first suggested that the procedure under article 78 should be used, rather than that under article 85. The former provides that matters dealt with by the Community can be transferred to the competence of individual States by agreement. Mali proposed that all affairs should be so transferred. A State would thus become *de facto* independent without the obligation of secession from the Community, which, under the first version of article 86 necessarily accompanied accession to independence. In the event, this somewhat devious procedure was abandoned and the simplified procedure under article 85 was used, which requires only that a law shall be passed in the same terms by the Parliament of the Republic and the Senate of the Community. (*footnote continued p. 163, bottom*)

All twelve States signed agreements providing for close co-operation with France in a number of fields, but only six – Senegal,[1] Madagascar and the four States of the former Equatorial Africa federation – decided to remain within the Community. This '*Communauté rénovée*' of seven States including the French Republic, is no longer, however, a federation. Its members are all juridically sovereign States, with the right to their own representation abroad, with their own armies and their own currency (though all have remained within the franc zone). All had become members of the United Nations by June 1961.

The agreements of co-operation follow similar lines, whether relating to States inside or to those outside the Community. The States agree to co-operate with France in the fields of foreign policy, economic and financial policy, and of higher education. All but Upper Volta have also agreed to co-operation in the field of defence, relying on French help to train their armies, and in some cases

[1] In August 1960, the Mali federation broke up. Soudan retained the name of Mali, but decided that the agreements providing for her continued membership of the Community were no longer valid. Fresh negotiations were opened in January 1962. Though, in the intervening period, Mali has remained within the franc zone and continued to receive French economic aid, she has joined the 'Casablanca group' (including Guinea, Ghana and Morocco) and has signed agreements with States behind the Iron Curtain, including the U.S.S.R. from which she received a large loan in 1961.

The use of this simplified procedure was criticized, however, by a number of Deputies as being unconstitutional, on the ground that article 85 specifies that the procedure is to be used for revision of 'the provisions of the present Title concerning the functioning of the common institutions of the Community', and that the proposed revision dealt not with the *functioning* but with the *nature* of the institutions. The *Conseil d'Etat* agreed with this interpretation, but the Government ignored its opinion.

The Government was in some difficulty. The procedures which the critics believed to be constitutional were either a revision of article 89 (which deals with revision) in order to constitutionalize the proposed method of revision, or else its use to carry out the revision. Both these would have required unilateral action by the French Parliament, which was not acceptable to the other States of the Community. Moreover, if the referendum procedure under article 89 had been employed, it would, as was pointed out, have created an odd situation, to say the least, for Moslems in Algeria fighting a war for independence to be required to vote on the desirability of giving independence to Mali! The Government decided that this obstacle, due essentially to bad drafting, could be surmounted only by giving political necessity priority over constitutional requirements.

granting France the use of certain military bases.[1] All States (including Mali) receive generous economic, financial and technical assistance from France.[2] They also obtain preference for their exports in French markets and accord French exports preference in their own markets. They have decided, too, to negotiate together a fresh agreement with the Six, in order to remain within the Common Market, after the expiry of the five-year Convention provided for under the Treaty of Rome. Co-operation in the field of education includes recognition by the States of French University qualifications and the organization, with French help, of Universities and other establishments of higher education. A number of technical committees have been set up – including committees on health and education – to study, in co-operation with French Ministers or officials, the practical problems of co-operation and the best methods of providing aid. In general, the French aim is to restrict French personnel as far as possible to expert advisers, mainly technicians, doctors and teachers, and to concentrate on training African personnel as quickly as possible. They wish, too, to avoid as far as possible aid in the form of block grants or budgetary subsidies, in order to ensure that funds are spent on the most urgent priorities.

Apart from the fact that the six States remaining within the Community continue to recognize the President of the Republic as President of the Community, it is at present difficult to define what membership of the Community actually involves. For while the institutions provided for in the Constitution and organic laws have lapsed, they had still not been replaced by the middle of 1962. Co-operation between the seven members is to be achieved by periodic meetings of heads of States, presided over, as were meetings of the Executive of the Community, by the President of the Community. This vaguely described and so far theoretical 'Commonwealth Conference' type of contact appears to be the only remaining

[1] Upper Volta is the only State which has refused to sign a defence agreement. Mali, which at the beginning of 1962 was negotiating an agreement of co-operation with France, will also refuse to allow French bases on her soil. There are French bases in Senegal, Mauritania and Madagascar.

[2] In 1959, France was contributing more economic aid for Africa than were the U.S.A., the United Kingdom or the Soviet Union. Total aid amounted to between 5 per cent and 6 per cent of the Budget, or 1·2 per cent of national production.

institutional link, though an 'advisory inter-Parliamentary Senate' is apparently to be set up as the successor of the former Senate of the Community.[1] It has also been stated that differences between members of the Community will be settled by conciliation and, if necessary, by a Court of arbitration.

THE FUTURE

No doubt the economic and technical needs of the new States greatly influenced their decision to remain either in the Community or in close association with France. But the association is nevertheless much more than one of self-interest. Political bonds remain strong. For instance, the Constitutions of the new States are in many ways modelled on the 1958 French Constitution, and the systems of local government, too, follow the French pattern. French remains the official language and French cultural influence remains strong. Indeed, the plans for the rapid Africanization of *cadres* in all the States of French-speaking Africa would be impossible of achievement without large numbers of French teachers,[2] and without the provision in French Universities of places for African students.[3]

How French-speaking Africa will evolve is still unclear. There are, as there were before independence, differences between the States as to what ought to be their relations with each other. M. Houphouet-Boigny, President of the Ivory Coast, has always rejected the view of M. Senghor, President of Senegal, that African States should form federations, on the ground that 'a union of

[1] Throughout 1962 the Community was in a curious state of constitutional no-man's-land. The provisions of articles 82, 83 and 84 and those of the organic laws dealing with the organs of the Community were clearly no longer applicable, yet had not been revised. The Executive had not met since March 1960 and States had been 'notified' early in 1961 that the Senate of the Community which had met only twice, on 15th and 30th July 1959, was to be considered as dissolved. What precise constitutional validity such a notification can have, even coming from the President, is not clear, but as long as all concerned accept it, it is effective.

[2] In 1960, there were 3,000 French teachers in Africa south of the Sahara, mostly in primary schools, but nearly 1,200 more were wanted in 1961. As secondary education develops, and as Universities or establishments for higher education are set up in the States, the demand will increase. The University of Antanarivo, opened in 1961, is financed and staffed by France.

[3] Even Guinea, during the years following secession in 1958, continued to send students to France, and 480 were there in 1961.

poverties will not produce abundance'.[1] The abortive federation of Mali is an indication of the difficulties of federation, and M. Senghor himself recognized that he had tried to move too fast. There have been, however, several associations of States aiming at closer economic co-ordination. The four States of the *Entente* (Ivory Coast, Dahomey, Niger and Upper Volta) formed such a Union in 1959 and the four States of the former Equatorial Africa federation (which are still members of the Community) formed a Customs Union in 1959. In 1961, 12 French-speaking African States (that is, all the former French Territories, excepting Mali and Guinea, but including also the Cameroons), following conferences at Brazzaville, Dakar and Yaoundé, formed the *Union africaine et malgache*, with the aim of concerting both foreign and economic policy on a basis of equality. They all oppose interference in the domestic affairs of other States, and especially interference by non-Africans in African affairs (as, for instance, in the former Belgian Congo). They stand, too, for the principle of national self-determination. In economic affairs they want increased co-operation and co-ordination, seeking also to negotiate as a unit their future relationship with the European Economic Community. In June, 1962, the group had 19 members, of whom 14 were French-speaking.

The Brazzaville, or Monrovia, group is intended to be a moderate, non-exclusive, African grouping, in contrast to the Casablanca group, set up in January 1961, by Guinea, Mali, Morocco, Ghana and the United Arab Republic, an organization described as 'revolutionary Africa *vis-à-vis* reformist Africa'.

It remains to be seen whether these tendencies will become permanent, or whether new groupings will emerge, cutting across the linguistic frontiers more than at present.[2] So far the French-speaking States of the Brazzaville tendency show every intention of remain-

[1] The twelve States of the former Community have a total population smaller than that of Nigeria. The population of Mauritania, the last of them to become independent, is approximately that of Manchester. Its area is twice that of France, most of it desert.

[2] The Cameroons have incorporated the Southern part of the former British Cameroons. The Union between Ghana, Guinea and Mali, set up at the end of 1960, was, in theory, not only to promote a common economic and monetary policy, but also to set up a common Parliament for Ghana and Mali. No concrete steps have been taken to carry out these plans, which actual geographical, monetary and economic conditions in the different States render highly unrealistic.

ing on good terms with both France and the West in general. In the United Nations they have been moderate and conciliatory, friendly towards the West, but (unlike the Casablanca group) have avoided becoming closely associated with either Western or Asian 'blocs'. In their foreign relations, they have deliberately sought to maintain good relations with France and their heads of State have paid official visits to France. President Senghor, who has worked hard for African independence, African co-operation and good Franco-African relations, has summed up succinctly what is at the moment the general attitude of French-speaking Africa to France:

> 'Educated in your schools', he said, during his visit in April 1961, 'we have become a little like you . . . France has rediscovered her vocation for liberating, enlightening and helping others. France spends most per head of her population on helping underdeveloped peoples. Senegal is witness that this help is disinterested. In spite of this effort of unprecedented solidarity, it is France that, of all the great Powers, exercises least pressure on us.'

CHAPTER X

The Presidential Sector
(ii) Algeria

It took General de Gaulle almost four years to achieve a cease-fire in Algeria. By that time, Algerian independence was accepted by most of public opinion in France as inevitable. The constitutional relationship between Algeria and France, however, remained what it had been under the Fourth Republic until independence was declared on 3rd July 1962, following the referendum on self-determination.

THE ALGERIAN STALEMATE

The 1958 Constitution, in fact, makes no mention of Algeria. Nor did that of 1946. Both refer only to 'Overseas *départements*', without specifying any by name. Algeria remained, therefore, a group of Overseas *départements*,[1] but, in practice, from 1956 onwards, was administered under a series of emergency regulations and even, for a time following the rebellion of 13th May 1958, came under military rule.

During the years following the outbreak of the rebellion in November 1954, a number of administrative changes had been made and a new Statute agreed to by Parliament, though it was never applied. These, like the provisions of the Algerian Statute voted

[1] The only official definitions of Algeria's pre-independence status are contained; (i) in an *avis* of the *Conseil d'État* of 27th March 1947, which classed Algeria as Overseas *départements*; (ii) in the Algerian Statute of 1947, which describes Algeria as: '. . . a group of *départements* enjoying corporate personality, financial autonomy and a special organization'; and (iii) in replies given in June 1959 by the Prime Minister to a series of questions (*v. Journal Officiel* 14th August 1959).

during the first years of the Fourth Republic and never fully applied, were always several steps behind the leaders of Algerian opinion, even those who, until some time after the outbreak of the rebellion, had still hoped for a settlement that would enable Algeria to remain within the framework of the Republic. It is now pointless to speculate on whether or not it might have been possible to avoid the rebellion altogether if the 1947 Statute had been applied in a more liberal spirit. By the time the 1958 framework law had been voted[1] – a law in some ways even less satisfactory to nationalist opinion than the Statute that it replaced – it was already far too late. In 1956, even the moderate nationalist movement led by M. Ferhat Abbas, the *Union démocratique du manifeste algérien* (U.D.M.A.), had gone over to the rebel *Front de la libération nationale* (F.L.N.), which had published in 1956 a programme based on complete independence. By September 1958, M. Ferhat Abbas was Prime Minister of the Algerian provisional Government, the *Gouvernement provisoire de la République algérienne,* or G.P.R.A.

If the Algerian background when General de Gaulle returned to power had changed irrevocably since the outbreak of the rebellion, that of France had changed very little. And, except for a small section of opinion on the non-Communist Left (including some Socialists, a few Radicals and some members of the M.R.P.), what change there had been had increased the gulf between Moslem and French opinion. General de Gaulle's greatest obstacle was that no section of public opinion, either in France or among the Europeans in Algeria, was prepared to contemplate the policy that either was or was to become his, namely, the creation of an independent Algeria.[2] M. Mendès-France who, as seems sometimes to be for-

[1] For a brief description of Algerian administration under the Fourth Republic, *v.* the author's *France: the Fourth Republic,* (Methuen, 1958).

[2] General de Gaulle's pronouncements on Algeria have not always been wholly consistent. It is probable that he started from a purely pragmatic position. As he said in December 1958, in his instructions to the newly appointed Delegate-General for Algeria, 'The Algerian problem is a matter between the entire French nation and Algeria as she really is. . . .' 'I do not make up my mind in advance about the political future of Algeria', he said in a speech shortly afterwards. Even though the facts convinced him, either from the first or very soon, that independence was inevitable, he would probably have liked to avoid this choice if it had seemed possible to do so. See, for instance, his comment on 29th January, 1960 on the option of '*francisation*': ' . . . *si un jour les Musulmans décidaient librement et formellement que l'Algérie de demain doit être unie étroitement à la France rien ne causerait plus de joie à la patrie et à de Gaulle que de les voir choisir, entre*

gotten, was in power when the Algerian rebellion broke out, never considered a negotiated peace, nor did the five following Prime Ministers. M. Mollet, who carried out some very useful administrative reforms, never abandoned the claim that any negotiation must be with valid spokesmen (*des interlocuteurs valables*) and not only with the F.L.N., a condition that effectively ruled out negotiation altogether, while the military stalemate made it impossible to hold elections. M. Mollet also stated that any solution reached as the result of negotiations must retain the 'indissoluble links' binding Algeria to France, a condition which made negotiations useless from the Algerian point of view, even if they could have taken place. Nor must it be forgotten that an Assembly in which Left and left-centre opinion was strong had, in 1958, defeated M. Gaillard and led M. Pflimlin to resign, for merely suggesting the possibility of negotiations, or of Moroccan and Tunisian 'good offices' in facilitating them.

The revolution of 13th May had revealed that to the political and military stalemate there must be added an executive stalemate. Some Ministers had been aware for years that Algiers had been dictating to Paris. Others were made aware of this in October 1956, when the Prime Minister accepted responsibility for the arrest in Algiers of five F.L.N. leaders, including M. Ben Bella, an arrest which had been carried out without authority from Paris and even without the Government's knowledge. The events of 13th May made clear to all that the French State could no longer rely on either its officials, its police or its army to carry out the Government's instructions.

This was obviously a situation in which, as General de Gaulle is said to have remarked, there *was* no possible solution to the Algerian problem.[1] He had added, however, that a solution must nevertheless be found. British and American critics of General de Gaulle's

[1] *v.* remark quoted by Rémy Roure in *Le Figaro*, 10th January 1961.

---

telle ou telle solution, celle qui serait la plus française.' But from March onwards he stated more and more frequently that he believed that the Algerians would not choose this option.

It is also probable that, to begin with, he under-estimated both the difficulty of convincing his fellow countrymen that a French Algeria was no longer possible and the extent to which army loyalty and discipline had been undermined in Algeria. It could, therefore, be that his statements often reflected what he thought it safe to say at the time and to the particular audience, rather than what he really believed, or intended to do.

foreign policy who believe its grandiose aims to be unrealistic might perhaps reflect more often on what they owe to precisely the same type of unrealism in his Algerian policy. Of the seven men who, since 1954, have been responsible for France's Algerian policy,[1] he alone refused to let the impossible defeat him. He simply set out methodically, and with guile as well as superb confidence – possibly at first over-confidence – to reduce the impossible, *via* the improbable, to the possible. It took him a great deal longer than he intended. But after three and a half years, he had at least achieved a solution on paper. Whatever the difficulties of Franco-Algerian co-operation, the old Algerian problem no longer existed.

In fairness to Governments of the Fourth Republic it must also be stated that President de Gaulle did not have to face two obstacles that only too often defeated his predecessors. First, they were harassed and overburdened by too many urgent problems at once, some of which – Franco-German relations, Indo-China, Tunisia, Morocco, economic recovery and modernization – had either been settled, or were well on the way to solution, when he came to power. The good they did is too often buried with them. And second, none of them had General de Gaulle's personal prestige with the nation, nor did they have, as he had, a docile Parliament. On the contrary, a large part of their energies had to be devoted, often unsuccessfully, to maintaining themselves in power.

When the final balance-sheet is drawn up, however, General de Gaulle will still have a great many items on the credit side that his predecessors did not have. To begin with, he had a policy. It was not always clearly discernible at the time, but, as one looks back, there are identifiable patterns of intention, disturbed here and there by his pragmatic adjustments, not always successful, to new factors as they arose.

THE PREPARATORY STAGE

His Algerian policy really falls into three distinct stages, each with its own 'insoluble' problems. The first was the stage in which it was necessary to obtain the tools for the job. He had to restore the

[1] MM. Mendès-France, Edgar Faure, Guy Mollet, Bourgès-Maunoury, Felix Gaillard, Pierre Pflimlin – all Prime Ministers representing Left or left-centre opinion.

authority of the State over both its military and its civilian agents; and he had to prepare Algeria for self-administration, if not for self-government. M. Mollet had already begun to prepare the ground for the second of these tasks, as he had done for the Overseas Territories by his 1956 outline-law. From 1956 onwards, partly in spite of the rebellion and partly because of it, administrative reforms had been carried out. They involved the re-organization of local government so as to make all Councils fully elective and to enable Moslems to participate on a much larger scale. Moslems would henceforth constitute a majority in Councils which had hitherto reserved three-fifths of the seats for Europeans. Pending the holding of elections, seats had been provisionally filled by nominated Councillors, many of them Moslems. The number of *départements* had also been increased, and by 1958, 12 of the proposed 15 Algerian *départements* had already been set up.

In spite of the continuation of the war, President de Gaulle decided, not only that the constitutional referendum and Presidential elections should be held on Algeria, but also that general elections to the Assembly (which had not been held since 1951) and to the Senate, and also local elections, should also be held there. The general elections did not produce the 'valid spokesmen' with whom alone French Governments had declared themselves ready to negotiate. Neither then nor subsequently was the 'third force' of moderate Algerian nationalists, hoped for in Governmental circles, revealed to exist. There was undoubted pressure on some Moslem voters, varying in extent from region to region, by French army authorities entrusted with the organization of the elections, to persuade them, by propaganda or by more direct methods, to vote for the Constitution and for *Algérie française* candidates. The candidates ranged, in the words of one commentator, 'from Conservative to Fascist', and virtually all represented the policy of integration.

Nevertheless, the elections were a valuable preparation for the future. In 1959, Municipal elections were held in 85 per cent of the 1485 *communes*; 60 per cent of the electors voted, and of over 14,000 Councillors elected, some 11,000 were Moslems. Moslem women, who had never voted until 1958, got used to voting. Some of the Moslem representatives in Paris, who began as supporters of *Algérie française*, changed their camp, once General de Gaulle had come out openly in favour of Algerian self-determination. And as time went on, the F.L.N. leaders themselves recognized how valuable Moslem experience of administration and local government would be to them when Algeria became independent, and approved of their supporters' acceptance of local and administrative responsibilities. The Constantine plan, announced by General de Gaulle on 3rd October 1958, provided for a five-year plan of economic and social development, including the provision of land for farmers, housing, employment, increased education, and also training for future Moslem administrators. One tenth of the posts in the public services in France and Algeria were to be reserved for Moslems.

It is not pretended that this plan did more than scratch the surface of Moslem poverty and economic and political backwardness. But it at least laid the necessary foundations for the training of Moslem personnel, the appalling lack of whom would otherwise have made any hope of real independence in the near future impossible. It was also important as an earnest of France's intentions to carry out the promise made by General de Gaulle that Moslems should henceforth have the status of first-class Frenchmen (*des Français à part entière*).

The authority of the State was, however, not fully restored either then or during the following years. After an intensive but discreet purge of officers implicated in, or in sympathy with, the revolution of 13th May, and a gradual restoration of civilian control in Algeria, General de Gaulle announced his plan for Algerian self-determination, almost fifteen months after his return to power. The offer was carefully phrased. Three choices were to be put to the Algerians: secession, '*francisation*' – that is integration – and what the President himself hoped for, namely, independence in association with France. Association was conceived of along the lines characterizing the relationship between France and the other present and former members of the Community.

Up to this point, it had been possible, though increasingly difficult, for those who had supported General de Gaulle in the belief that he would ensure that Algeria remained French, to persuade themselves that his 'ambiguous' statements on Algeria were consistent with this objective. From 16th September, 1959, this self-deception was no longer possible. But General de Gaulle's success in consolidating his position in France had not been accompanied by a similar success in Algeria. There is nothing surprising about this. It has been claimed that

> 'from the time that the first soldiers landed on the Algerian coast right up to the present difficulties, no régime and no Government has been able to impose a general policy on Algeria without the assent of the European population'.[1]

Even under the Third and Fourth Republics, neither of which had had to face the problem of an army so deeply discouraged, embittered, and affected by subversive influences as was the French army under the Fifth Republic, it was Algiers that gave orders to Paris, where Algeria was concerned. The result of the announcement of self-determination was, therefore, the outbreak in Algeria of a second insurrection on 24th January, 1960, the so-called 'revolt of the barricades'.

It was brought to an end within a week, with very little bloodshed. But if this reinforced the President's position by providing a striking demonstration of the support of the mass of the civilian population in France, it also made plain the persistence of wavering as well as insurrectionary elements in the army.

SETBACKS AND NEW PREPARATIONS

This meant that a second stage of consolidation and preparation was necessary before the policy of self-determination could be implemented. During this period, the President sought to do three things: to convince the army, and those civilians who still clung to the idea of *Algérie française*, that this policy was no longer possible in the twentieth century; to agree with the F.L.N. on a cease-fire, without which the Algerians could not be consulted on self-determination; and to continue to eliminate unreliable elements from both army and administration.

To those who approved of the President's policy, this period was discouraging, because France seemed to be marking time, or even taking steps backward. The President's attempts to win over the army led him, at times, to make placatory statements implying more sympathy with the point of view of the *Algérie française* supporters

[1] Georges Berlia, *Chronique constitutionnelle et parlementaire* (*Revue du Droit public*, Nov.–Dec 1961) p. 1159.

than he probably had.[1] The breakdown of the first official meeting between emissaries of the F.L.N. and the French Government, which took place at Melun in June 1960, seems to have been due to French as well as to F.L.N. intransigence. The year that elapsed between these abortive pre-negotiations and the official conversations on Governmental level, which took place at Evian and at Lugrin from May to July 1961, seemed to his supporters to be so much valuable time lost, and disappointment was all the greater when the Algerians, this time, broke off negotiations in July, and when months followed without any open attempt to resume them.

But though the attempt to achieve a cease-fire had failed for the time being, progress was being made in the other two fields. The purge of unreliable elements went on, necessarily unobtrusively.[2] And the President continued to prepare the way for the third and now, in his view, final stage of the Franco-Algerian problem. In his tours of the provinces he continually spoke of 'an Algerian Algeria', of an 'Algerian State', which would be responsible for its own affairs.[3]

On 16th November, 1960, the Government announced that a referendum would be held on the organization of a provisional executive in Algeria pending the vote of self-determination. The Bill providing for this contained also a first article affirming, in accordance with the promise of September 1959, that the vote on

[1] The most striking of these were during the so-called '*tournée des popotes*' in Algeria, shortly after the insurrection of January, 1960. If he was correctly reported, during these semi-private talks with officers, he insisted on the need for a military victory in Algeria as well as for the continued presence of the army in Algeria, and described independence as '*à la fois, une catastrophe, une sottise, une monstruosité*'. He added, however, that he believed that the Algerians would choose 'an Algerian Algeria linked to France.' It is necessary to distinguish between the President's use of the word independence in this sense, and in the sense (often described as secession) of independence without links with France. The 'catastrophe' to which he was referring applied to independence in the second sense.

[2] There were a number of purges and army postings after both insurrections, as well as dismissals or retirements of police officers and officials suspected of sympathies with the O.A.S. towards the end of 1961.

[3] *v.* for instance, the communiqué of 9th March 1960 and the speech at Rouen of 9th July where the phrase *Algérie algérienne* is used; 4th November, 1960, '*une Algérie qui . . . aura son gouvernement, ses institutions et ses lois*' and similar remarks on 20th and 31st December, 1960; at Verdun, 28th June, 1961, '*un Etat souverain et indépendant*'.

self-determination would take place as soon as conditions permitted, and that the decisions taken as a result of the vote would be ratified by the French people.

There seems no doubt that one of General de Gaulle's main intentions was to demonstrate by this referendum that he had the mass of opinion behind him. In this he succeeded, for 75 per cent of the voters in France approved of the Bill,[1] thus giving a convincing demonstration, to Frenchmen, European Algerians and the world, of the nation's backing for the policy of self-determination. In his speeches to army officers,[2] and in several of his broadcasts, he now began to emphasize that the army had other tasks than those it had been carrying out in Algeria. On 29th December he announced categorically that by the beginning of 1962, army and air-force units would be withdrawn from Algeria, that more would follow, and that, whatever happened in Algeria, the major part of the French army would be withdrawn to Europe and modernized. A Bill was passed, providing for the re-settlement of Europeans from all three North African territories formerly under French rule, but clearly intended to prepare for some European Algerians to leave an independent Algeria.

THE ACHIEVEMENT OF A CEASE-FIRE

The most hopeful signs that a fresh advance towards a solution was imminent were the resumption of negotiations in the autumn of 1961, though this time in secret, and the conciliatory statements made publicly by both the President and the new Algerian Prime Minister, M. Ben Khedda.[3]

[1] The referendum was held on 8th January 1961. The F.L.N. ordered Moslems to boycott the referendum and many obviously obeyed, as 40 per cent of the electorate abstained in Algeria. Of Algerians who did vote, 69 per cent voted in favour.

[2] On 14th November 1961 at the *Centre des Hautes études militaires* and on 23rd November at Strasbourg.

[3] At the end of October M. Ben Khedda expressed Moslem willingness to re-open negotiations, agreed to accept the basis of self-determination as laid down in the referendum of January, and, in putting forward G.P.R.A. terms, agreed to co-operate with France during the transitional period, to discuss the problem of 'leasing' bases to France, and grant certain guarantees to Europeans. General de Gaulle's broadcast of 5th September had already conceded Algerian sovereignty over the Sahara. That of 2nd October had conceded the right of the Algerians to organize local forces to assist the 'provisional executive' to keep order during the transition period.

There was, however, by then a new debit side to the balance-sheet. By the autumn of 1961, the political climate, both in France and Algeria, had worsened considerably. If the 'revolt of the barricades' had on the whole strengthened the President's position, the long-drawn-out trial of the leading figures in it, which lasted from October 1960 to the beginning of the following March, had the opposite effect. It was used by numbers of witnesses as a means of propaganda in favour of *Algérie française* and also to excuse, or even approve, those responsible for sedition.[1] The third Algiers insurrection, in April 1961, was led, not by extremist nonentities such as MM. Ortiz and Lagaillarde, but by four retired Generals, three of them among the most respected of the French army, and two of them former Commanders-in-Chief in Algeria, and it involved several of France's crack regiments stationed in Algeria. Though it collapsed after four days and two of the Generals were speedily brought to trial, this trial, too, revealed sympathies for the offenders in high places. An increasingly articulate and vociferous (though probably not numerically large) section of the French population was either openly supporting the policy of *Algérie française*, in meetings held under the aegis of the *Comité de Vincennes*,[2] or secretly working for it by terrorist methods such as the F.L.N. had used first in Algeria and then in France.

From the spring of 1961, France, as well as Algeria, suffered increasingly from terrorist attacks from both sides – attacks on policemen or on fellow-Moslems by the F.L.N. and plastic-bomb attacks by supporters of the O.A.S., led by General Salan, who had escaped capture after the April insurrection. What was loosely called the O.A.S. included a number of more or less independent and sometimes hostile conspiracies, and the agents themselves included a number of students, even some schoolboys, and a few army deserters and professional thugs.

The autumn of 1961 represented the lowest ebb of public confidence in General de Gaulle's ability to solve the problem, since his

[1] Witnesses sympathetic to the insurgents included Marshal Juin, General Weygand, General Massu and other officers. The trial constituted, in fact, a running debate on *Algérie française*, in which the patriotism of the insurgents was continually emphasized, and the Government blamed for having, by its policy, 'provoked' the people of Algiers.

[2] *v. supra*, p. 72. M. Soustelle took no part in these meetings. M. Bidault, who was the President, did, as did a number of other Deputies on the extreme Right.

return to power over three years earlier. Critics did not fail to point out that he had by then wrestled with it for as long as all the Prime Ministers of the Fourth Republic put together, without any more visible signs of success. The régime whose supporters had claimed to restore the authority of the State now appeared unable to control even its own officials, as witnessed by police brutality, when Moslems working in Paris carried out a large-scale demonstration on 17th October, and when left-wing parties and Trade-Union organizations demonstrated against the O.A.S. on 19th December.[1] In the Assembly, Socialists and Radicals proposed a motion of censure against the Government at the end of the autumn session, and in the debate, critics from Right to Left criticized the Government for its inability to suppress the O.A.S. The number of bomb incidents was increasing, and in Algeria, by the end of the year, the authorities were obviously unable to control the European population, most of whom sympathized with the O.A.S. Moslem terrorism, anti-Moslem 'rat hunts' and lynchings, mainly by European hooligans, including schoolboys, bombs and murders, O.A.S. broadcasts from clandestine transmitters – all these combined to produce a situation in which rumours of a new *putsch*, current since the end of the summer, became more and more insistent.

Two new dangers were thus added to the existing ones. For the first time, there seemed to be developing in Algeria a real race hatred, which, if not checked, would render the co-existence in Algeria of Europeans and Moslems impossible, whatever concessions might be finally negotiated on paper. And in France, the more spectacular exploits of the O.A.S. – the raiding of army bases, the kidnapping of a U.N.R. Deputy, for instance, and the exploding of a bomb in the courtyard of the Quai d'Orsay – these, along with many more commonplace bombings, were creating a real danger that public confidence would be undermined. Even during the April insurrection, it had been noted that some army officers and some officials had been non-committal, waiting to see which way things would go. By the end of the year, the increasingly anarchical

[1] Even more serious incidents occurred in February 1962 during a similar demonstration. It must be admitted that both demonstrations were illegal (as all demonstrations were banned), and that Communist elements were accused by Government spokesmen of provocation at both, though no convincing evidence was produced in support of the accusations. Eye-witnesses agreed in considering that, if such provocation existed, it was not a justification of police brutality.

situation, together with the intimidation carried out by O.A.S. agents, had led to incidents such as the refusal of a jury to serve at a trial[1] of O.A.S. '*plastiqueurs*' and to the acquittal by a Military Court of officers accused of torturing a Moslem woman, an acquittal which so shocked public opinion that it was rumoured that the Minister of the Armed Forces was himself contemplating an appeal to the *Cour de cassation*.

Some Government spokesmen maintained that all this constituted a last throw by the O.A.S. in the attempt to prevent a Franco-Algerian agreement and that, once the agreement had become a fact, it would rapidly die down. Certainly, with the renewal of secret negotiations, the Franco-Algerian problem had entered on the final stage. For General de Gaulle made clear in several statements that if this time the two sides failed to reach an agreement, he intended to 'regroup' the European population, which meant partitioning Algeria at least temporarily, pending the repatriation of European Algerians to France. By the middle of February, 1962, final negotiations were announced to be taking place somewhere in the Jura and an agreement was confidently predicted by the end of the month.

THE AGREEMENT

After delays of some weeks, during which the toll of murders in Algeria by both sides steadily rose, the agreement was announced on 19th March. After seven and a half years of war, the only question in most people's minds was, 'Is it after all, too late?' Could the O.A.S. still prevent the application of the agreement, by provoking Moslems into mass riots, thus presenting the French troops with the agonizing choice between obeying orders while their compatriots were being murdered, or siding with the O.A.S. in prolonging a hopeless war?

The terms of the agreement were such that it was to the interests of both sides to make every effort to apply it. Indeed, it seemed probable that it could never have been reached, had it not been for the threat of the O.A.S. to the creation of an independent Algeria, and the fear of the F.L.N. leaders that, if they delayed any longer, they would not be able to count on French help to deal with it.

[1] At Nîmes, on 25th January 1962.

For the evacuation of French troops from Algeria, announced by General de Gaulle in his broadcast of December 1961, had already begun. Time was no longer on the side of the Moslems.

From the point of view of both sides this agreement ought to have been regarded as bringing peace with honour. France was to retain the use of the base at Mer-el-Kebir for 15 years; until independence became a fact, the tricolour would fly in Algeria, and French and Algerian administrators would share in administering the country. European Algerians would remain French citizens and have the right to stay in Algeria for three years, with full civil and political rights, before finally opting for Algerian citizenship, or deciding to remain French citizens. France recognized Algerian sovereignty over the whole of Algeria, including the Sahara, and guaranteed French aid, under the Constantine plan, during the first three difficult years of independence, and perhaps for a further three years. Oil interests were to be shared and French prospectors to have priority.

Even on the most optimistic assumptions, it was obvious that after all the violence and bitterness, it would be incredibly difficult, and perhaps impossible, to carry out the terms of the agreement. For months, the situation would be critical, and for years precarious. But the essential first step had to be taken before the task of trying to solve the real problems of Algeria could begin. General de Gaulle perhaps derived some ironic satisfaction from the realization that, if the agreement did succeed in bringing a real cease-fire and the beginnings of co-operation between the two communities, the O.A.S. would have had their share in the achievement of what had looked like an impossibility for so many years, and what they had so nearly made impossible when success was at last in sight.

What lay ahead were, indeed, whole series of preliminary steps, each with its own problems and difficulties. After the cease-fire, the referendum; then general elections and the formation of a Government; the reorganization of normal life in towns and villages from which Moslems had been uprooted in order to be 'regrouped' by the French army; the formation of parties and Trade-Unions; the transfer of local administration from French to Moslem forms. For, if it was true that Algerian nationhood had been forged in the war for independence, it was also true that Algeria had known up to then only

French forms of government, French parties and French ways. The Algerian nation was an idea. It had yet to be translated into fact.

During the three months separating the cease-fire from the referendum on self-determination, it looked at times as if the cost of translating it into fact might still involve inter-racial bloodshed in Algeria and opposition in France on a scale that General de Gaulle, like his predecessors, had always struggled to avoid, sometimes at the cost of jeopardizing the achievement of the cease-fire agreement. Even the arrest of numbers of O.A.S. leaders and the trial in Paris of the head of the movement, ex-General Salan, and his Deputy, ex-General Jouhaud failed to reduce the daily quota of terrorist attacks and murders of Moslems, designed to provoke them into retaliation, and so start up the war again. The F.L.N. remained surprisingly disciplined, and cases of Moslem reprisals were relatively few, but, as weeks passed, the provisional Executive found it more and more difficult to withstand the desire of more extremist Moslem elements to bring back the A.L.N. troops from Morocco and Tunisia in order to deal with the O.A.S.

At the end of May, the decision of the special High Military Court not to condemn ex-General Salan to death, on the ground of 'extenuating circumstances' (undefined), gave fresh encouragement to the O.A.S., at a time when it appeared to be at last beginning to weaken. It seemed as if O.A.S. and European Algerians were actually seeking to invite an appalling slaughter of the European community, as well as to endanger the French State itself. The campaign collapsed, however, in June, and agreements between the provisional Executive and O.A.S. leaders in Algiers and Oran enabled the referendum to be held without incidents. Over 91% of the electorate voted for independence in co-operation with France. A declaration by the President of the Republic proclaimed Algeria independent on 3rd July, and sovereignty was transferred to the Algerian provisional Executive.

THE BALANCE-SHEET

What is the balance-sheet of the President's Algerian policy?

As far back as 1959, M. Raymond Aron said of General de Gaulle's progress towards a solution of the Algerian problem that

> 'Where Algeria is concerned the General has disappointed everybody, yet driven nobody to despair.'[1]

In the war- and bomb-weary mood of 1962, most people at first would have welcomed with relief *any* settlement that seemed likely to bring peace. But relief wears off, and with the resumption of the normal political battles, most probably centring on the Presidency and the President, the first part of M. Aron's statement may well sum up the final attitude of the general public and of those left-wing and centre elements that, on the whole, supported the President's Algerian policy. Gratitude is rare in politics and the President has used his indispensability in this field to get his way in others where his policies are far less acceptable to most of his fellow-countrymen. In 1962, the second part was no longer true. From April to July, O.A.S. activities and the queues of European Algerians fleeing to France before Algerian independence became a fact, provided ample evidence of that.

Whatever results the President achieved must, therefore, bring widespread discontent. Where Algeria was concerned, the French had been demanding not merely the impossible, but incompatible impossibles, leaving it to the President to find a way of doing what none of his predecessors could do, while they nursed their divisions, pending the hoped-for return to normality. However much of a miracle his success in ending the war and bringing Algerian independence really was, those who supported him at first, because they wanted to keep Algeria French, were bound to feel that they had been cheated, while those who wanted an independent Algeria felt that they had been made to pay an exorbitant price in foreign affairs and in political and constitutional matters.

But there were also specific criticisms of the President's methods in the field of Algerian policy, and especially two, coming from his supporters. The first was that the pace was slower than it need have been because French concessions were made too grudgingly and too late and so encouraged Moslem intransigence and violence, by making them appear to be paying propositions. For instance, from October 1958 to April 1960, the French maintained that negotiations must not be with the F.L.N. alone but with 'all tendencies'. Yet

[1] In *Preuves*, November 1958, p. 10.

when negotiations did take place they were with the F.L.N. alone.[1] All along, the President refused to accord the G.P.R.A. – the Algerian provisional Government – the status of a Government, referring to it usually as '*l'organisation extérieure de la rébellion*'. Yet when the first Evian conversations took place in 1961, they were clearly between Governments, and clearly dealt with the future of Algeria, on which the French had always maintained that the G.P.R.A. could have no authority to take decisions. It was generally understood that these negotiations broke down owing to disagreements regarding the Sahara and, in particular, regarding the inclusion of the Sahara in a future Algerian State.[2] Yet a month or so later, in a press conference, General de Gaulle specifically conceded Algerian sovereignty over the Sahara. The President stated more than once that no negotiations could take place without a cease-fire. This had been M. Mollet's position, too. Yet they took place, not only without a cease-fire, but in an atmosphere of heightened tension, owing to an actual increase of terrorist attacks. It was not until October 1961 that the President conceded the Algerian demand that Algerian and not French forces should be mainly responsible for maintaining order during the interim period between the cease-fire and the referendum on self-determination.

These belated concessions helped to confirm the F.L.N. in the view that time was on their side, that intransigence paid. It took the threat of the O.A.S., both to the régime in France and to the possibility of enforcing a cease-fire, to make the F.L.N. realize that time had ceased to be on anybody's side and to bring from their leaders an offer to co-operate in the effort to get rid of the O.A.S. danger.[3]

Some of the French rigidities were doubtless due to French divisions. Not all the President's officials believed in '*Algérie*

[1] An announcement by the Minister for Algerian Affairs, M. Joxe, that he intended to consult the rival nationalist movement, led by M. Messali Hadj, was so resented by the G.P.R.A. that there was for a time a risk that the Evian talks would not even open. Even in September 1960, after the Melun talks with F.L.N. leaders had already taken place, General de Gaulle repeated that France would not '*traiter avec les seuls insurgés, avec la seule organisation extérieure de la rébellion*'.

[2] General de Gaulle stated in September, however, that this had not been the reason for the breakdown. (*v.* report of General de Gaulle's discussion with the delegation of the Socialist Parliamentary Group. (*France-Soir* 27th September 1961).

[3] *v.* G.P.R.A. communiqué of 10th January 1962.

algérienne.' But the second criticism of the President was that his methods in themselves led to the mishandling of problems and the distortion of orders. His aloofness, his remoteness from ordinary mortals, his contempt for politics and politicians, the insistence with which he regarded himself as the Captain and everyone else, supporters and opponents alike, as passengers[1] increased the risks of misunderstanding, or even of sabotage, between the giving of an order and its execution.

Whether this was wholly a personal failing, or whether it is partly accounted for by his military training is a fascinating though probably fruitless speculation. But it is perhaps worth noting in this context President Truman's feelings about President Eisenhower when he was waiting for the latter to succeed him in office.

> 'He'll sit here,' said President Truman, 'and he'll say, "Do this! Do that!" *And nothing will happen*. Poor Ike – it won't be a bit like the Army.'[2]

The French complaint was not that when General de Gaulle said 'Do this!' nothing happened, but that the relationship of what did happen to the order was often obscure. As a French politician who had worked closely with General de Gaulle put it: 'The General tends to feel that when he has given an order, it has been carried out.'

There is a third criticism, but of the Government, rather than of the President. It is that, in spite of its claims to have restored the authority of the State, the French Government has been either unable or unwilling to take steps to prevent the high moral cost of the Algerian war. Large sections of the French population have felt ashamed and humiliated by the revelations of the regular use of torture by some sections of the French army, by the use of violence against civilians by the French police, and by the evidence of the corruption of young Europeans in Algeria, who have been encouraged to regard racial violence and 'rat hunts' as permissible and normal.

[1] *v.*, for instance, his failure to pay any tribute to the support of parties, trade unions and other organizations during the two insurrections – an omission which was commented on unfavourably – and his broadcast of 5th February 1962 in which he actually used the word 'passengers' relating to the public.

[2] Quoted in *Presidential Power*, by Richard Neustadt. (John Wiley & Sons. Inc. New York, 1960), p. 9.

The President himself is reported to have replied, when questioned regarding police violence: 'It is inexcusable but not of primary importance'.[1] What, then, was the primary objective of the President?

There is little doubt that the Algerian problem itself was, in his eyes, and increasingly so, a secondary matter. Whether or not he had all along regarded Algerian independence as inevitable, or merely understood the facts before most of his compatriots, by the end of 1959 he was not merely convinced that Algeria must be independent, but also that until she was, the Algerian problem would continue, as he put it in January 1960, to 'block all roads'.

By the autumn of 1961, he was ready, if necessary, to cut his losses, to partition Algeria, to accept secession, which would leave an essentially non-viable, economically and politically backward and traditionally anarchic country to wrestle as best it could with the enormous problems of premature independence. But he still hoped for an association, for which he was prepared to pay a high price in economic, technical and cultural aid, partly because he sincerely believes in France's mission to help her former dependencies, but also because his primary objective is, as it has been all his life, a strong France, with a strong army, able to lead Europe and stand up to both East and West. The main road that Algeria blocked was that leading to a more important role for France as a great power.

[1] This is one of the many apocryphal stories about General de Gaulle. It has also been quoted as applying to torture.

CHAPTER XI

The Presidential Sector (iii) Defence and Foreign Affairs

The heritage of the Fifth Republic in the field of foreign affairs presented the President with fewer intractable problems than did the Algerian situation. After the years of deadlock over the European Defence Community, Governments of the Fourth Republic had succeeded in settling the problem of the Saar and in putting Franco-German relations on what looked like a secure basis for both political and economic co-operation. France's self-confidence in the economic field was steadily increasing and the apparent success of the first year's experience of the working of the European Economic Community was creating an image of economic stability and dynamism that compensated to some extent for the political instability and the failure in Algeria, so widely criticized both inside and outside France.

THE EVOLUTION OF FRENCH ATTITUDES

General de Gaulle's personal interventions in the field of foreign affairs were at first welcomed by his compatriots, while statements by the Foreign Minister, M. Couve de Murville, reaffirming France's loyalty to the Atlantic alliance, her intention to play her part in N.A.T.O. and her readiness to agree to nuclear disarmament within the framework of a general disarmament programme, helped to reassure France's allies.

General de Gaulle succeeded, indeed, in his first months of office in killing two birds with one stone. He increased France's prestige abroad, and used this prestige to strengthen his authority at home in preparation for the difficult task of dealing with the Algerian imbroglio. The rapid improvement of Franco–Tunisian relations, badly strained since the Sakhiet bombing in February 1958, the confidential memorandum to President Eisenhower and Mr Macmillan in September 1958, generally assumed to be a claim by France to membership of a tri-partite directorate of N.A.T.O., the President's emphasis on good Franco–German relations, and the publicity and prestige which France derived from the continuous series of Presidential visits to foreign heads of States and from theirs to him[1] – all these helped to convince the man in the street that France now had a head of State who would insist that France be treated as a great power. If, in 1953, Mr Dulles could threaten 'agonizing reappraisals' of America's relations with France; if, in 1954, the *Manchester Guardian* could describe France as 'the weakest link in the Western alliance'; if Sir Winston Churchill could complain, in 1955, of the 'empty chair' that ought to have been occupied at international conferences by France,[2] but so often was not, owing to frequent Government changes – then, at least, from 1959 onwards, France was once again a power to be reckoned with. The Government remained in office. The President was not merely visibly filling the chair, in his television broadcasts and press conferences at home, or in his visits abroad, he was also making his personality increasingly felt in Europe and in N.A.T.O.

To a general public still suffering from the effects of the post-war inferiority complex caused by France's weakness during the immediate post-war years of struggle, first for recognition and then for great power status, tired of being regarded as 'the sick man of Europe',[3] and of fending off hostile resolutions on her North

[1] For instance, in 1958, the visit of Chancellor Adenauer and General de Gaulle's visit to the Chancellor; in 1959, visits to Italy and Great Britain and the visit of President Eisenhower; in 1960, visits to America, Canada and Great Britain, and the visits of Mr Kruschev and of Chancellor Adenauer to France; in 1961, the visits of Chancellor Adenauer, President Kennedy, President Lübke to France and General de Gaulle's visits to Bonn and Great Britain; in the first six months of 1962, Mr Macmillan's visit to President de Gaulle and Chancellor Adenauer's State visit to France.

[2] In a letter of 12th January to M. Pierre Mendès-France.

[3] On the post-war psychological atmosphere, *v.* the author's *French Politics: the first years of the Fourth Republic* (Royal Institute of International Affairs, 1953), Chapters 12 and 13.

African policies in the General Assembly of the United Nations year after year, the President's tone and 'style' continued to give satisfaction. In particular, his criticisms of the United Nations[1] were extremely popular, and many Frenchmen shared his view that France ought not to occupy a subordinate position in N.A.T.O. His acts, however, soon ceased to give satisfaction to large sections of more informed opinion in France, and by 1961 were causing despondency both at home and abroad. France was being described by correspondents as 'the despair of her friends'[2] and General de Gaulle was accused of having created 'an atmosphere of quiet desperation'[3] among those in Washington who wanted to negotiate promptly with the Soviet Government over Berlin. His address to army officers in Strasbourg, on 23rd November 1961, and the Prime Minister's speech in the Senate called forth from a Radical Deputy the following protest: 'Such a tone of intransigent nationalism has rarely been heard. It has caused consternation among many of us in France and among how many of our friends outside!'[4] His press conference of 15th May 1962 produced widespread consternation both at home and abroad.

NATIONAL DEFENCE AND RELATIONS WITH N.A.T.O.

The most important of France's grievances within the Atlantic alliance were, first, the absence of a combined strategy and of any pooling of atomic secrets, and second, inequality between the three theoretically equal partners represented on the Standing Group. Both the American Strategic Air Command and British Bomber Command, equipped with thermo-nuclear bombs, remained under national control. It followed that, in the last resort, the decision whether or not to use these weapons lay with these two, and General de Gaulle felt that France was thus placed in a position of subordination to Great Britain, being called on to undertake equality of risks, without equality of responsibilities. France also complained

[1] *v.* for instance, his press conference of 5th September 1960 where he talked of '*les nations dites unies*', and his references to '*le machin*'. As *The Times* commented on 4th October 1960, the United Nations had become 'the main Aunt Sally of the Gaullist régime'.

[2] *Le Monde*, 4th October 1961.

[3] *The Times*, 29th August 1961.

[4] *Journal Officiel*, 16th December, 1961, p. 5678.

that Great Britain also occupied a favourable position in that she held more, and more important, commands than France.[1]

On this factual basis, French opinion had built up a resentment amounting to a belief in the existence of a virtual Anglo-Saxon directorate within N.A.T.O. Failing a favourable reply to the memorandum of September 1958, France must, therefore, in the President's view, take steps to ensure that she possessed an effective national defence, including the possession of a nuclear deterrent. And until such time as something nearer to equality existed within N.A.T.O., the principle of the integration of defence would be replaced by that of co-operation.

This view was expressed most clearly by the President in the address he gave on 3rd November, 1959 to the *Centre des Hautes etudes militaires*:

> '. . . If a country like France makes war, it must be her war and her war effort. . . . Naturally, in such an event, French defence would be co-ordinated with that of other countries. That goes without saying. But it is indispensable that it should be ours, that

[1] France's specific grievances were:

(i) The fact that in the North Atlantic command she had no essential responsibilities (two sub-sector commands only) and that the British predominated in the sector commands of the Channel committee.

(ii) Great Britain's position was more important than that of France in the European Command.

- (a) The Deputy Supreme Commander at Shape was British, and the French naval Deputy at Shape was of 'symbolic importance' only.
- (b) Though the French held the Central European command, they had no sector command of land forces, and only one naval command – the Western Mediterranean. The British not only held the Mediterranean command, but also three sector commands (North Europe, Gibraltar and South-Eastern Mediterranean), and also the air-force Command in Central Europe.

(iii) The French language was progressively being displaced by English within the administration of Shape.

(iv) Under article 6 of the North Atlantic Treaty, Algerian defence is guaranteed by N.A.T.O. The French, and in particular, M. Debré, frequently maintained that France was undertaking this defence and had a right to expect solidarity from her allies in N.A.T.O. Several members of N.A.T.O. in fact have voted against France in the United Nations on resolutions regarding Algeria, and the United States has abstained.

M. Debré never appeared to consider that his claim that Algeria was a French affair and no concern of the United Nations effectively contradicted the above point of view and that, if France's policy in Algeria were, in reality, a N.A.T.O. policy, it could not be unilaterally determined. In fact, this was an expression of resentment rather than a serious argument.

France should defend herself with her own arms, for her own ends and in her own way....

'It follows, evidently, that we must produce in the coming years what is described as a "striking force", capable of use anywhere and at any time. And it goes without saying that it must be a force equipped with atomic weapons which – whether we produce or buy them – will belong to us. In circumstances in which France risks destruction from any part of the world we must have a defence which can act anywhere in the world.'

Steps to implement this policy had by then already been taken. France refused to participate in a Tactical Air Force pool, and also to have rocket sites and stocks of atomic weapons on her soil, unless she had control over their use.[1] The two hundred or so American fighter-bombers, stationed in France, and intended in case of war to be equipped with tactical atomic weapons, were, therefore, evacuated from France during 1959.

In March 1959, the French Government also informed the N.A.T.O. Council that French ships of the Western Mediterranean sector, which were intended in case of war to form part of a pool under N.A.T.O. command, must remain under French command. But in accordance with the doctrine of co-operation rather than integration, they were to be allowed to accept N.A.T.O. missions, by agreement.[2]

Was this policy merely a demonstration of French pique? Was the President prepared to risk weakening the Atlantic alliance in order to obtain what he regarded as France's rights? And did this policy bring dividends?

Certainly, it did not bring, at least during the following two years, the reorganization of N.A.T.O. that the President wanted, nor was there any hard evidence that his desire for information on

[1] The French resented the fact that the command of Central European air forces was held by an Englishman and that Fighter Command units placed at the disposal of Shape would in practice be defending the defence zone constituted by Great Britain

[2] National control of the French Mediterranean fleet was held to be important, since it covered the route to North Africa, and, in his press conference of 25th March, 1959, the President stressed the point that France might be called on to defend regions south of the Mediterranean. But no doubt the fact that a considerable part of the American and British fleets remained outside N.A.T.O. weighed with him as well.

atomic developments in America was likely to be granted. There was, however, some increase in consultation, particularly between heads of States, mainly as a result of the increasing dangers of the general international situation. There was no apparent response to the President's suggestion, in his press conference of 5th September, 1960, and again in April the following year, that N.A.T.O. should be reorganized so as to enable it to undertake extra-European activities.[1] But *de facto* co-operation in the field of defence was improved during 1960, by an agreement between France and the N.A.T.O. Council for a unified early warning system and for unified command and operational control of West-European air defences in the forward area either side of the Franco-German frontier. France agreed, too, to accept German supply and training bases on French soil. In 1961, a further agreement was reached permitting the training of French troops in nuclear weapons (though not in France, for the President did not give way on the principle that while the warheads remained in American hands they could not be stocked on French soil). Some United States air-force units also returned to France, though without their nuclear equipment.

But if the policy failed to achieve its main objective, it did, at first, achieve the secondary one, already mentioned, of increasing the President's prestige at home. It was when it came to 'going it alone' in atomic policy, and carrying out atomic tests while other great powers had suspended theirs, that he succeeded in uniting against him the European-minded Right and Left, and right-wing opponents of 'Europeanism' who believed that a French deterrent was an expensive luxury, or even a myth, together with much of African opinion which wanted disarmament and the end of atomic weapons.

Between February 1960 and April 1961, the French carried out four atomic tests at Reggane in the Sahara, and, in the autumn of 1960, a Bill was introduced in the Assembly to provide for a French atomic striking force (*la force de frappe*). It was responsible for three votes of censure and met with criticism on all sides, in party conferences as well as in Parliament. The project was described, for instance, by M. Maurice Faure (who became President of the

[1] The phrase used was as follows: '*. . . nous considérons que, tout au moins entre les Puissances mondiales de l'Ouest il faudrait qu'il y ait quelque chose d'organisé au point de vue de l'Alliance, quant à leur comportement politique et éventuellement stratégique, ailleurs qu'en Europe, et particulièrement au Moyen Orient et en Afrique, où ces trois Puissances sont continuellement impliquées.*'

Radical party the following year) as a deterrent which 'will not deter our enemies from attacking us but will deter our friends from coming to our help'.[1] by M. Dorey (M.R.P.) as 'a game of poker', and by M. Schmitt (Socialist) as 'a form of megalomania which should cease'.[2]

There were four main objections. The first was miltary and technical and amounted to the argument that since the only real strategic defence was American, the possession by France of atomic weapons would merely increase the danger of the use of atomic weapons against her, without significantly increasing her defence potential, the proposed striking force being out of date before even going into production, and in any case not available before 1970. The second and third objections were political. It was argued on the one hand, in particular by the 'Europeans', that, if the proposed striking force were necessary, it should be European, not French, and for financial and military reasons as well as for the political reasons; that a French deterrent would risk being regarded by the uncommitted nations as a manifestation of French imperialism, and by France's European partners as a threat to European unity. On the other hand, it was argued that since Europe's real defence against atomic war was the stalemate created by the Russian and American deterrents, France's only real contribution to defence was the improvement of conventional defence within N.A.T.O. The fourth objection was economic. The project would cost too much and would risk so overburdening the budget that the result might be the reduction of expenditure on defence in other fields.

In its defence, the Government insisted on the need for France to have an up-to-date national defence, both on military grounds and in order to fulfil her commitments to the Community, and also in order to improve France's position in relation to her allies. As General de Gaulle put it, France must have it, if she did not wish to be merely 'an integrated satellite'.[3] And as the Minister for the Armed Forces put it:

'We are in no way refusing to integrate our atomic arms in the

[1] Speech at the Radical Party conference in October 1960.

[2] Debate in the Assembly, 18th October 1960.

[3] Speech at Albertville in October 1960.

system of the North Atlantic Treaty. Our sole condition is that our American and British allies shall do the same.'[1]

One cannot help feeling that the last was perhaps the determining reason and that much of French opinion thought so too.[2]

This was the first major controversy of the régime in the field of foreign affairs. The Bill was twice defeated in the Senate, where, except for the U.N.R., only a handful of Senators supported the Government. And though all three motions of censure in the Assembly were defeated, over two hundred Deputies voted against the Government on each of them.

EUROPEAN POLICY

During the first years of the régime, the President made two proposals to meet what he saw as the need for increased political and military co-operation between the partners in the Common Market. The first proposals were couched only in very vague terms. They comprised: regular consultations between heads of Governments; the setting-up under the control of Governments of a number of specialized organs, whose task would be to co-ordinate policy on a less technical level than that on which the policies of the Six were co-ordinated within the European Economic Community; the setting-up of a European Assembly made up of delegates from national Parliaments – a somewhat puzzling suggestion, since it would appear, on the surface, merely to duplicate the existing Common Assembly.[3] He also proposed a European referendum, designed to give popular support – presumably for the European 'idea', though the President's words, 'so as to give this European starting-point the support and participation of the people which is indispensable' (*de manière à donner à ce départ de l'Europe le caractère d'adhésion, d'intervention populaire qui lui est indispensable*), gave no clear picture of its utility, except as a vague, plebiscitary demonstration.

[1] Debate in the Senate in November 1960.

[2] Press comment on atomic policy frequently stressed the point of French inferiority, *vis-à-vis* her allies. For instance, the first explosion at Reggane was hailed as evidence that France now qualified as a member of the 'atomic club' – *v.*, for instance, articles in *Le Monde*, 17th February 1960 and 1st March 1960.

[3] In his press conference of 15th May 1962 he made it clear that he was not thinking in terms of an additional European Assembly.

The sting lay in the President's remarks in introducing the proposals – his statement that Europe could be built only on States, which were the sole realities; that the 'more or less supra-national' organs of Europe were technically useful, but could have 'no political efficacity or authority', that only States could take vital decisions, that such decisions could be taken 'only by co-operation'; and that only at some future date would bonds be forged and habits formed, making possible a speedier progress towards European unity.

Insistence on inter-governmental institutions also marked the Fouchet Plans, put forward at the end of 1961. These did little more than clothe the President's general proposals of 1960 in a somewhat more precise institutional framework. The draft treaty proposed, it is true, an 'indissoluble' Union, with a Council, composed of Heads of States or of Governments meeting periodically, a European Parliamentary Assembly and a European Political Commission. But Council decisions were to be unanimous; the European 'Parliament' was merely to make 'recommendations' to the Council or ask questions; and the Political Commission was merely to carry out Council decisions. Though drafted by a Committee of the Six and submitted to the Commission of the European Economic Community, this plan was generally understood to be of French inspiration. It was certainly in harmony with the President's views. Not unnaturally, however, some members of the Six wanted to revise the draft in order to create closer political ties than these.

The hard core of resistance came from Benelux, on the ground that if Great Britain were about to enter the Common Market, she ought to be represented during the negotiations on closer political unity. France's objection to this, in spite of the known British preference for *l'Europe des Etats* seemed to point either to French fears of British rivalry to her leadership in Europe, or to French coolness towards British membership of the European Economic Community, possibly for the same reason. Though the President was reported to have been discouraging regarding British hopes of associating the Commonwealth – '*cette immense escorte*' as he is reported to have called it – with the Common Market, on Great Britain's application for membership of the European Economic Community he remained in public non-committal. At his press conference of September 1961 he merely remarked in reply to a question that the Six had always hoped that

> 'others, and in particular Great Britain, would sign the Treaty of Rome, subscribing to the obligations and, it is assumed, receiving the advantages therefrom.'

In his press conference of May 1962 he did not refer to the question of British membership at all. He seemed, however, determined to alienate his five partners in E.E.C., since he attacked the supranational approach with more venom than he had ever done before – with the immediate result that all five M.R.P. Ministers resigned in a bloc from M. Pompidou's recently constituted Government. At this time, the French Government was also claiming that the right to negotiate with new candidates for membership of the Coal-Steel Pool belonged to States and not to the Council, which France's European partners interpreted as yet another attempt to strengthen Governmental at the expense of supranational organisations.

All this, together with the President's sustained refusal to participate either in disarmament negotiations or in talks on Berlin, and his policy of an independent French deterrent, led to the increasing isolation of France and to increasing criticism of the President, both at home and abroad.

CRITICISMS OF THE PRESIDENT'S FOREIGN POLICY

In France there was much criticism among the 'European' Left and also among some right-wing Deputies. In the debate on the motion of censure in December 1961, M. Jean Legendre (Independent) exclaimed:

> 'I am for the integration of Algeria in the Republic. I am for the integration of France in Europe. I am for the integration of Europe in N.A.T.O. And you (i.e. the Prime Minister) have done exactly the opposite. Your policy is not integration, it is disintegration – disintegration of Algeria, disintegration of Europe, disintegration of N.A.T.O."[1]

[1] M. Legendre added that condemnation of the Government implied condemnation of General de Gaulle's policy (*v. Journal Officiel*, 16th December 1961, p. 5679). The President is constitutionally irresponsible and should not, therefore, be criticized in the Assembly – a provision constantly ignored in Parliament under the Fifth Republic.

How far is this true?

Supporters of the régime can argue convincingly that in the fields of defence, in particular of atomic defence, of Europe, of disarmament and of his attitude to the United Nations, the President was merely continuing to carry out the policies of his predecessors and that the differences were mainly of emphasis and 'style'. The assumption of personal responsibility, the use of the first person singular, the refusal to acknowledge the contributions of others,[1] all tended to obscure the very real degree of continuity. France's atomic policy was decided as far back as 1951, and every Prime Minister since then has had his share of responsibility for it. The decision to abandon the purely peaceful uses of atomic energy and to manufacture an atomic bomb was taken by M. Mollet's Government, in July 1956.[2] In the field of disarmament France has had the same representative on the United Nations Disarmament Committee for the past ten years. When France's Algerian policy was criticized by the United Nations in 1959, this was for the fifth year in succession. And whatever General de Gaulle said about the possibility or desirability of European integration at some time in the future, France had, up to the middle of 1962, fulfilled the obligations of the Treaty of Rome. With the help of the well-known French Parliamentary devices for making time stand still, even the difficult compromise on agricultural policy was achieved in time for the Community to enter on its second stage.

Even the tone of some of the General's remarks can be explained away. Since an Algerian settlement was his first objective in time, he had to use what cards he had in order to achieve it. His obstinacy, the refusal to accept subordinate status, the appeal to patriotism, the emphasis on French greatness – these had served him well in the past. Putting the United Nations in its place and stressing France's economic recovery helped him in his campaign to restore civilian

[1] *v.* the reply attributed to General de Gaulle in reply to an objection by General Valluy: '*Je n'ai pas de prédécesseurs*' (quoted in Fauvet, op, cit. p. 41 N.). This failing has led the President at times to some odd claims to paternity, as, for instance, in his press conference of May 1958, when he took the credit for a social and economic policy drawn up in France during the resistance, and which was only half carried out when he resigned in January, 1946. It is true that he had approved of it in 1945.

[2] The vote on the Bill (11th July, 1956) showed virtually only the Communists as opposed, except for 27 Radicals, whose reasons had nothing to do with atomic policy.

self-confidence. The emphasis on France's need for strong and up-to-date national defence, including atomic weapons, was designed to turn the thoughts of army officers away from Algeria and towards Europe.[1]

When all this has been conceded, however, including, too, the President's reiterated statements on the need for French co-operation within the Atlantic defence system, his obviously genuine belief that the organization was militarily inadequate, and his partial mitigation, in practice, of the policy of refusal to integrate French forces under a N.A.T.O. command, there still remain three substantial criticisms of his foreign policy. The first is that in all countries, and in France more than many, political attitudes are important, and sometimes more important than deeds. Whatever the criticisms that can be made of the United Nations, and there are many, it still represents, for many of the President's compatriots no less than for other countries of the West, the only existing and functioning prototype for an eventual, hoped-for, effective international organization. British reactions to Lord Home's criticisms at the end of 1961, mild though these were in comparison with the French President's open scorn and contempt, are sufficient evidence of the truth of this. A Right-wing French elder statesman like M. Pinay resented the President's attitude to N.A.T.O. for reasons that were, *mutatis mutandis*, similar, and it was reported that more than anything else it was his opposition to the President's policy in this field that led to his departure from the Government in January 1960. The President sometimes played his admittedly poor hand badly, for he could not afford to drive too far into opposition those whose support he needed in the Assembly, in order to keep in power the Government on which he relied to carry out his policies, Yet, at times, he seemed to take a perverse pleasure in shocking. frustrating and annoying the non-Communist and moderate Left. In May 1961, M. Mollet came to the conclusion that, if 85 per cent of the French were for the President on Algeria, 80 per cent of the same Frenchmen were against him on everything else. It was, surely, a needlessly short-sighted policy to alienate so many of his compatriots.

[1] The fact that the President addressed army officers twice on this theme during November 1961, when he had finally decided to end the Algerian war, in one way or another, within the next few weeks or months is an indication of the fact that the attitude of the army was still a major problem, and therefore a major obstacle to the achievement of his foreign-policy objectives.

The second criticism is one of method. The allegations of rigidity, of concessions made too late to produce the desired effect, have already been discussed in relation to the President's Algerian policy. In his N.A.T.O. policy, his handling of Franco-Tunisian relations in 1961 and his position on the Berlin crisis there was evidence at times either of excessive rigidity, or of a juridical formalism that tended to defeat its own ends, or of an obstinacy which was attributed by some to delusions of grandeur and by others to an outdated and unrealistic concept of France's position and potential in the modern world.

The Bizerta episode illustrates the extent to which French methods not only spoiled an excellent case, but also helped to increase French isolation. Tunisia's ultimatum to France in July 1961, demanding an immediate phased withdrawal from the base at Bizerta, and the attack by Tunisian troops on French planes, were both juridically unjustified and politically ill-timed, for France was expecting to have a difficult negotiation with the Algerians on French occupation of the base at Mers-el-Kebir. Whatever internal difficulties had led the usually moderate Tunisian President to take this step, the generally predicted result was the end of '*Bourguibisme*'. Instead, M. Bourguiba extricated himself from his dilemma with considerable political agility and agreed to return to the *status quo ante*. France, on the other hand, let her case go by default, owing to her decision, on juridical grounds, to boycott the special session of the General Assembly of the United Nations, and at the end of August she therefore found herself virtually without defenders and in an absent minority of one, for 66 nations voted for and none against an Afro-Asian resolution requesting immediate negotiations for the withdrawal of French troops from Tunisian territory. In his press conference the following month, the President held out no more than a frozen olive branch to President Bourguiba, who had benefited from a good deal of anti-colonialist sympathy in the United Nations. 'What is the use', said one commentator acidly 'of winning yourself an equal place in tripartite consultations if you then manœuvre yourself into the corner.'[1]

The third criticism of General de Gaulle's foreign policy is that it is essentially nationalist.

[1] Darsie Gillie in the *Spectator*, 1st September 1961.

'There is,' said M. Duverger, 'a world of difference between the generous and seignorial nationalism of the President of the Republic and the ranting, petty, legalistic nationalism of the Prime Minister.'[1]

That is true, but whether the objectives are long-term and large-scale, or petty or immediate, no reader of General de Gaulle's Memoirs can doubt that for him, at least, patriotism *is* enough. Since patriotism, rightly understood, must be the basis of all national foreign policies, the real question at issue is whether General de Gaulle's has not remained too 'seignorial' for the twentieth century.

THE PRESIDENT'S OBJECTIVES

For Anglo-Saxon critics, especially American, General de Gaulle's nationalism has a Maurrassian quality. 'France first', becomes in practice 'France alone', the pursuit of '*la grandeur*'.[2] There were times during and shortly after the war, when his 'pursuit of large-scale ideas with small-scale resources' did seem, at times, to indicate that he was suffering from delusions of grandeur. Looked at in retrospect, however, it now appears clear that, for most of the post-war period, French foreign policy was determined by the consciousness of weakness and the search for security. Up to 1954, security was conceived of, to the point of obsession, in terms of the prevention of German aggression. The methods were, first, to keep Germany weak and hold on to the economic union with the Saar, and second, when this proved impossible, to enmesh Germany firmly in a supra-national West-European organization. Following the decision to rearm Germany, this European organization was to have a Constitution and a supra-national army. When these plans, too, failed, the struggle for security was renewed in 1955 through direct Franco-German agreements and through the institution of a European Economic Community, part of the purpose of which was to come back, via the roads of technical and economic integration, to the original goal of political integration, the construction of a closely knit West-European super-State, within which Germany could be firmly held on the side of the West.

[1] *M. Debré existe-t-il?* in *La Nef*, July–August, 1959, p. 6.

[2] The American tendency to overplay this theme is visible in, for instance, E.L. Furniss's *France – Troubled Ally*. (New York, Harper), 1960.

From 1954 onwards there developed, with the loss of the former Protectorates and the outbreak of the Algerian rebellion, and with the rapid economic resurgence of the new Federal German Republic, a new sense of weakness. France was becoming 'de-colonized', and thus losing both status and man-power. She was also in a state of economic stagnation and political instability. 'French foreign policy', said M. Mendès-France at this time, 'means her national recovery.'

In his study of the foreign policy of the Fourth Republic, Alfred Grosser concluded that:

> 'In foreign policy all the questions of post-war France can be reduced to one: how can equality and dependence be reconciled? . . . France is no longer one of the very great powers. How can her desire to be treated as an equal be reconciled with her need of economic and military aid?'

'The Fourth Republic's answer to this question was', he says,

> '. . . the creation of a political structure within which equality is achieved through reciprocal and not unilateral dependence. This structure may be called Europe, the French Union or the Atlantic Community; it may represent a fact or a fiction; its purposes may be justified by the facts, or it may be an unattainable dream. But seen in the context of these two antithetical conditions, all régimes and all Governments had only one choice.'[1]

What General de Gaulle is seeking, and what the Gaullist movement sought, is strong government, a strong France able to play a leading role in Europe. It is a policy that goes back at least as far as Sully, and is essentially similar to M. Briand's proposal, put forward between the wars, for a United States of Europe. But it has continued, with modifications, the methods of the Fourth Republic. The 'political structures' of the Fifth Republic are called the Community, Franco–German co-operation, the Common Market, *l'Europe des Etats* and an Atlantic alliance based on national defence systems and international co-operation.

The main differences in the situation of the Fifth Republic have been, on the one hand, France's economic recovery, which made her

[1] *La IVe République et sa politique étrangère*, Paris, Armand Colin, 1961. pp. 397–8.

less 'dependent' than under the Fourth, and on the other, the war in Algeria and the disaffection of the army, which weakened her position within the Atlantic Alliance. On the necessity of economic recovery, General de Gaulle agrees with M. Mendès-France's diagnosis. The theme of '*rénovation nationale*' perpetually recurs in his broadcasts, and his economic policy of 1959 (*vérité et sévérité*) was intended to encourage further steps along the road to economic modernization and financial stability. But he has insisted also on the essential condition, for a strong France, of political stability, which the new Constitution and his leadership were designed to fulfil.

> 'The degradation of the State,' he said on 15th May, 1958, 'has as its inevitable consequence the alienation of the peoples associated with us, the confusion of the army in the field, the dislocation of the nation and the loss of independence.'

The alienation of the peoples associated with France, arrested by the President's policy of decolonization, could not be prevented until the Algerian problem was finally out of the way and the disaffection of the army overcome. With it all settled, France should be able to drive a hard bargain in the Atlantic alliance, for the French army would then be in a position to supply much-needed reinforcements to the European defence potential. Already the movement of French troops to Europe has begun, and the arguments in favour of *l'Europe des Etats* – the insistence that 'Men die for their country', the assurances of military modernization, have been brought to bear on French officers in order to help to convince them that their future role is in Europe, not in Algeria.

If this is, indeed, how General de Gaulle's mind is working, then, for him it is hard realism. It is he who has his feet on the ground and his 'European' opponents who are standing on their heads. What matters is what exists today, not the distant goal of European integration, just as what mattered in Algeria was the fact of twentieth-century nationalism, not the myth of *Algérie française*. And what matters in East–West relations is to drive the best bargain possible with the toughest of all negotiators.

This is the context in which General de Gaulle saw the Berlin crisis in 1961 and 1962. And if it was true that Mr Kruschev did not intend to risk a war, and that it was, therefore, safe to call his bluff, his argument was logical. His firmness was not unwillingness to negotiate, but unwillingness to waste time on fruitless negotiation. He likes to stick to facts – serious preparation, serious discussions, practical proposals – and he has no time for the diplomacy by propaganda, public meeting and invective, which have characterized summit meetings so far, and are more likely to characterize an 18-power than a 4-power meeting. The same argument applies to his attitude to disarmament. France is ready to put forward concrete plans for nuclear as well as conventional disarmament, and, indeed, France's representative on the Disarmament Committee, M. Jules Moch, has been doing just that, with patience and ingenuity, for the last ten years.

The argument may be logical, but it seems to contain at least two political weaknesses. If, as it often appears, General de Gaulle's ultimate objective is French leadership of a strong and united Western European alliance, a confederation, as he likes to call it, within the Atlantic alliance, yet constituting a powerful 'third force', then it is unlikely to be achieved by these methods, which all his would-be partners deplore. He is, indeed, an uncomfortable ally. His conviction of the logic of his case, his lofty isolation from other human beings, his rigidities, or those of his officials – all these make co-operation with him difficult. Nor is it probable that his European partners are as convinced as he is of the inevitable rightness of French leadership of Europe. It is not easy for his allies, whether inside or outside Europe, to distinguish between delusions of grandeur and what clearly appear to him to be no more than legitimate claims to France's rights.

His atomic policy is a case in point. To his European partners, it appears both unrealistic and undesirable. Nor is it likely, to judge by the experience of the past three years, to improve France's position in the Western alliance. But it could easily weaken France's position in the world. This is the second weakness. In spite of her improved economic position, France still remains, as she was under the Fourth Republic, in a situation of 'reciprocal dependence' – as, indeed, do all nations in the modern world, to a greater or lesser degree. The President is anxious to strengthen France's links with under-developed areas, particularly with French-speaking Africa. He has not only talked about the need to help under-developed areas, he has backed up his words with deeds. But economic aid is not enough. The President's scorn for the United Nations, his atomic policy, and his attitude of belligerence towards the West are likely, in the long, if not in the short run, to create difficulties with the French-speaking African nations, whose foreign policy must take into account the need for United Nations support, if possible with, but if necessary against, the Western nations. What is at present a great potential advantage to France in her relations with the African nations (even in spite of the repercussions of the Algerian problem), namely, her rapid decolonization of the former French-African possessions, could easily be lost by a tone and vocabulary more adapted to the colonialist than to the post-colonial era. In this field, as well as in that of European relations, the President's 'marriage with his century' still seems to be not yet satisfactorily consummated.

CHAPTER XII

The Personality of the Fifth Republic

In 1959, Raymond Aron wrote that 'the combination of an executive *à la Louis XIV*, and a Parliament disciplined *à l'anglaise* by the efforts of M. Debré is, in the long run, an impossibility'.[1] It still looked impossible in 1962. But what had the combination achieved in the interim?

Though *Le Canard enchaîné* likes to portray the President as Louis XIV, General de Gaulle's rule has, in fact, had little in common with the absolute monarchy of either Louis XIV or his successor. What it does have in common with absolute monarchy is the kind of political atmosphere that it engenders. It has been described as 'internal "depolitization" plus a foreign policy'.[2] It has something of what Chamfort meant when he described French government in the eighteenth century as 'an absolute monarchy tempered by songs', though for its first three years, while the Algerian problem overshadowed everything else, its atmosphere was more sombre. The Fifth Republic could, perhaps, best be described as having been during those years a semi-dictatorial Republic in which absolute boredom was mitigated by outbursts of bad temper.

REFORMING ZEAL IN A CLIMATE OF APATHY

The régime was certainly a Republic of a sort. The Parliamentary machine ticked over. In accordance with article 4 of the Constitution, parties carried on their normal activities. Party conferences were held regularly and long reports of their debates and resolutions appeared in a press, whose freedom to criticize the

[1] in *Preuves*, June 1959.

[2] by Pierre Viannson-Ponté in *Le Monde*, 22nd July 1959.

Government (and, indeed, the President) was in no way restricted. Parties were free to defeat the Government's Bills, turn the Government out, draw up party and coalition programmes, or even new Constitutions, since all except the U.N.R. disliked the existing one. The circumstances in which underground parties had drawn up new Constitutions during the Vichy régime and the German occupation had been infinitely more difficult.

Yet during these three years, parties were disunited and without clear objectives. Political leaders remained in the position of critical observers, apparently unable to think about, or prepare for, the succession to a régime that they were united – or almost – in deploring. By the autumn of 1961, the National Assembly was described as having 'dug itself into a state of rancour'.[1] The public's interest was focused on the President, one of whose chief merits was, in their eyes that: 'He, at least, doesn't play politics.'[2]

This 'depolitization', or political vacuum, characteristic of the first years of the régime, did not imply any absence of legislative activity. The Government spent the eight months from June 1958, during which it had special powers to draw up the Constitution and to rule by decree, in a frenzy of reforms. Over three hundred decrees were made, many of them providing useful frameworks for wholesale, and often overdue, reorganization in a number of fields. But these, like most of the legislation during the following years, were Governmental initiatives and, for the most part, they interested neither politicians nor public.

The reforms introduced during the period of provisional government fall into four main categories. First, there were politico-administrative reforms – the reform of the local electoral system, proportional representation being abandoned (except in large towns[3]), in favour of the traditional list system with two ballots; plans for the creation of a regional administration for Paris, for the

[1] Darsie Gillie in the *Guardian*, 23rd October, 1961.

[2] An admiring comment by a local Mayor, during the President's tour of the South-West at the beginning of November 1961, reported in *l'Express* 28th September 1961, a paper not noted for its admiration for the President. The general atmosphere of these Presidential tours is brilliantly caught in this article by Jean Cau.

[3] *Communes* with a population of 120,000 and over retained the proportional system, which was used previously in *communes* of 9,000 and over.

long-promised Charter of the *Radiodiffusion et Télévision française*;[1] the reorganization of the Law Courts in accordance with the existing distribution of the population; the reform of judicial procedure in order to speed it up and simplify it; and also the improvement of the working conditions of judges and public prosecutors.

The second category covered a wide range of social and economic reforms. These included: provisions to carry out the specifically Gaullist policy of 'Capital and Labour co-operation' by schemes for profit-sharing and participation in management; the reform of the educational system, providing for the raising of the school-leaving age from fourteen to sixteen by 1967, the improvement of the methods of selection of children for secondary schools at the ages of eleven or thirteen, the reorganization of the syllabus for the *baccalauréat*, the modernization of methods of teaching, and the provision of a new science faculty for the University of Paris. They also included plans for the reorganization of the Paris markets and water supply, the authorization of rent increases to enable long overdue repairs to property to be carried out, the encouragement of building, the improvement of hospitals, and the reorganization of the system of medical charges and reimbursements under the health service.

Thirdly, the defence system was reorganized with the intention of bringing it more into conformity with the needs of the atomic age. A new state of 'alert' (*la mise en garde*) was provided for, which can be declared by the Government, without recourse to Parliament, and which, in an emergency, could enable steps to be taken rapidly to protect the civilian population. Military service was increased from 18 to 24 months[2] and liability to serve in the civil defence services was extended for 10 years beyond the period of liability for ordinary call-up. Provision was made for the decentralization of commands, for the streamlining of military administration, and for the setting up of a new defence committee, including the Prime Minister and senior Ministers, and presided over by the President of the Republic. The main purpose of these provisions was the

[1] This provided for financial and administrative independence, but, as has been made only too clear, not for greater independence from political control by the Government.

[2] This was theoretical only. In practice, most conscripts were already serving for 27 months.

attempt to provide for speedy political as well as military action, by means of both co-ordinated and elastic procedures.

The fourth category included the Government's financial and economic measures announced at the end of 1958 – the so-called austerity programme (*vérité et austérité*). The main provisions were the devaluation of the franc by some 17 per cent and the introduction of the 'heavy' or new franc, worth 100 old francs, together with reductions in State expenditure (including some family allowances and ex-servicemen's pensions), increases in investment, the reduction of some subsidies (including some on foodstuffs and farm implements), the simplification of some purchase and local taxes, and the imposition of a number of new 'austerity' taxes. The last-mentioned created widespread dissatisfaction, owing to their uneven and sometimes illogical incidence,[1] as did the announcement at the beginning of 1959 of a number of price rises.

In spite of some gloomy predictions, France's economy proved buoyant enough to absorb these demands, without any new inflationary spiral set in motion by either wage or price increases. The primary aims of the measures, namely, to enable French producers and exporters to withstand the first impact of competition within the European Economic Community, and to increase French prestige in the world by a demonstration of her financial as well as her political stability, were largely achieved. The methods, however, provided an interesting example of the weaknesses of the new system. The reforms have been outlined at some length because the good intentions and achievements of the Fifth Republic are likely to be forgotten, as those of the Fourth have tended to be. No doubt the Government was led to make hay while the special powers lasted, partly because previous Governments had too often been unable to act owing to Parliamentary opposition. But these reforms did constitute a policy and not a patchwork as Governmental policies had so often had to be. Some of the injustices and anomalies which aroused public anger were, however, the result of replacing political by technocratic and bureaucratic control. Many of the measures were little more than outline schemes that had to be

[1] The tax on 'visible signs of wealth' was particularly resented for reasons sometimes good, sometimes bad. One example quoted was that of the taxpayer who, having been obliged in a period of acute housing shortage to rent a flat he could ill afford, then had to pay increased taxes on top of the rent, because his flat constituted 'a visible sign of wealth'.

completed by subsequent legislation and decrees.[1] The latter belonged to the Governmental and not to the Parliamentary sphere, and in any case politicians had no sense of participation, since the principles had already been laid down by the Government. What remained to members of Parliament was the Budget, which occupied most of each autumn session, and a handful of Government Bills in the spring session, most of them semi-technical and of little general interest. At the end of the first spring session, commentators pointed out the general poverty of the legislative programme. Laws or programme-laws on social, sanitary, school and general 'equipment', supplementary estimates, fiscal reform – this was virtually all. Few private Members' Bills were passed and none of any importance. There were no Parliamentary questions on other than individual or local matters, no resolutions, no interpellations, no successful motions of censure.

The drama had gone out of politics, and it continued to be absent except for what have been called the occasional bursts of bad temper. Full-scale debates were rare and all-night sittings non-existent. After the presentation of his Government and the ensuing vote of confidence in the middle of January 1959, M. Debré made no general declaration of policy on which a vote could be taken until October of that year. Speeches were often made to half-empty benches, which filled up in time for Deputies to record the votes on which part of their incomes now depended. Even the Budget debates were not the annual battle that they had usually been under the Fourth Republic. There was no need to resort to stopping the clock, or voting provisional monthly credits (*douzièmes provisoires*). Apart from the skirmish of 1959 on ex-servicemen's pensions, Ministers of Finance had an easy time, and all three Budgets were voted before the end of December, without recourse to the provisions of article 47, designed to prevent Parliamentary obstruction.

Some useful legislation was, in fact, voted during these years, in particular the laws to prevent alcoholism, including a measure for the gradual abolition of the privilege of home distillers (which M. Mendès-France had tried unsuccessfully to deal with), the setting up of the proposed administrative authority for the Paris region, reforms of local administration, the programme-law on agriculture.

[1] It was estimated that the military reorganization and the judicial reforms would take about six years to complete.

. . . But the political climate was one in which the familiar hostile collaboration between Government and Parliament characteristic of the previous régimes had become a ding-dong battle between M. Debré and Deputies, punctuated by occasional flare-ups.

GOVERNMENT VERSUS PARLIAMENT

Since the chief weakness of the régime was that nobody except the Gaullists liked it, it was natural that the new institutions should themselves be one of the chief causes of conflict. The passage of the new Standing Orders involved a six-months' battle, and Deputies on the Right as well as on the Left resented the Constitutional Council's decision ruling out of order the only remaining devices by which they could make the Government uncomfortable without actually defeating it. They were irritated, too, by U.N.R. references to 'the system' and 'renewal', and particularly by M. Debré's sermonizing manner, described as being 'like that of St Just dominating the Convention'. Relations between Government and Parliament included mild sniping by Deputies – one of the most popular shots being the quotation from M. Debré's speeches as a back-bench Senator of passages most likely to embarrass him as Prime Minister – and guerilla warfare, in which the main weapons used by both sides were interpretations or evasions of the Constitution and the Standing Orders. The Government evaded Parliamentary criticism by crowding out private Members' Bills from the agenda,[1] postponing replies to written Parliamentary questions and postponing or 'grouping' awkward Oral questions to suit Government needs.[2] Deputies retaliated by moving the previous question, by misusing points of order to make critical speeches, by protesting in debates against what they held to be violations or abuses of the Constitution, at least twice by walking out of the

[1] The figures are illustrative. By the end of July 1961, 900 private Members' Bills and 500 Government Bills had been introduced since the beginning of the Parliament. 199 Government Bills and 7 private Members' Bills had been passed. (cf. the figures quoted on p. 105.)

[2] *v.*, for instance, examples quoted in *Vie et droit parlementaire* by Léo Hamon and Claude Emeri (*Revue du Droit Public, Novembre–Décembre,* 1961), in particular, the following interchange: *M. le Président. . . . Le sujet que vous traitez, pourrait utilement faire l'objet d'une question, écrite ou orale, déposée dans les formes réglementaires. M. Ahmed Djèbbour : Nos questions ne sont jamais retenues'.*
The Deputy in question was using the 'point of order' to make a criticism.

Assembly,[1] and twice by tabling motions of censure on their own initiative. Both in 1960 and 1961, there were major battles over the constitutional rights of Deputies, involving the President as well as the Prime Minister. The constitutional implications of these have already been discussed, together with the problems created by the President's personal control of policy in the so-called 'Presidential sector.' The main political consequences of this permanent struggle between Prime Minister and Deputies was that the régime, together with its Constitution, steadily acquired in the minds of Deputies a discredit rivalling the discredit of politicians themselves in the minds of the public during the previous régime. Whatever the ostensible subject of debate – motion of censure on the Budget, or on the atomic striking force, the theme of Deputies was the régime and the abuses of the constitutional provisions by the Prime Minister. During the debate on the first motion of censure in November 1959, Deputies as far apart as M. Leenhardt (Socialist) and the late M. François Valentin (*Indépendant*) attacked the Prime Minister's use – or abuse – of constitutional provisions. 'The Government acts as if we had no Constitution' said the former. M. Georges Bonnet (*Entente démocratique*), in the debate on the second reading of the Budget in December, said: '. . . nothing is left of the Parliamentary régime, nor of the separation of powers, nor of the right so often discussed of the legislator to legislate.' A year later, in the debate on the second of the three motions of censure on the atomic striking force, M. François Valentin (*Indépendant*) asked:

> 'What is left of the lofty concepts of the Constitution, somewhat theoretical, but clear, and which a little confidence and warmth could have made living and durable? What is left of Parliament? Just enough to keep it as a scapegoat. . . . Sadly, I confess to a profound nostalgia for the Fifth Republic.'[2]

The complaint that 'the Constitution is being treated with contempt' (*la Constitution est bafouée*) became almost a slogan, when, to

[1] Over half the Deputies (most of them, except U.N.R. Deputies) walked out on 12th September, 1961. There had been a walk-out by some Algerian Deputies the previous 5th July, and 280 Deputies walked out on 13th June, 1962.

[2] Debate of 22nd November 1960.

the Prime Minister's alleged irregularities,[1] there were added those attributed to the President. The Socialist party's 'constructive opposition' had undergone such serious strain by the autumn of 1961 that the National Council held in September found the party nearer to unity than it had been for three years. One delegate even treated the conference to a lengthy commentary on Presidential as well as Prime Ministerial infringements of the Constitution.

THE FIFTH REPUBLIC VERSUS THE FOURTH

With the exception of the permanent war centred on interpretations of the Constitution and the debate on the atomic striking force, the only political issues that really aroused interest in Parliament during these first years were old and familiar. The first motion of censure of the régime was tabled by Deputies in response to a Governmental 'pledge of responsibility' during the debate on the Budget in November 1959. Though it was used in order to launch a general attack on the Government's economic and social policy, its attitude to Parliament and on the evolution of the régime towards personal rule, it was directly caused by the hostility of Deputies to the suppression in the plan for fiscal reform of ex-servicemen's pensions.

This was an old battleground between Government and Parliament. During M. Gaillard's Government, there had been a Governmental attempt to replace quarterly by annual payments. Parliamentary opposition was such that, at the opening of the session on 14th January 1958, the Prime Minister was obliged to make the acceptance of the agenda a vote of confidence, because the *conférence des Présidents* had insisted on a debate on the proposal, though it had been voted in principle. Successive devaluations had reduced the amount of the individual pensions to a sum barely sufficient to pay for a round of drinks, so that no hardship was

[1] Deputies were particularly incensed by the Prime Minister's use of articles 44 and 45, during the Budget debates in the autumn of 1959. The former was held by him to justify his insistence on a single vote on a Bill, including, along with articles already voted, others specifically 'reserved' by the Assembly. The latter was held by him to justify the addition of 15 Government amendments to the version of a Bill agreed on by a joint Commission of both Houses, before submitting it to the Assembly. Whether or not Deputies were right in their conviction that the Prime Minister's interpretation was in conflict with the spirit and intention of the Constitution, the actual wording of the articles does not indicate that the interpretation was contrary to the letter. As in so many articles, the precise meaning of the phrases in dispute is not clear beyond reasonable doubt.

involved in the change. The whole point of the operation was to enable Deputies to demonstrate to their constituents that their hands had been forced, and two days were wasted in order to achieve this.

Two years later, what was essentially the same battle was being fought all over again, and the 'system' won, as it had done on the previous occasion. M. Debré's Government conceded a partial restoration in 1960, to be followed by a full restoration in 1961, if the economic circumstances permitted.

The only subject that aroused public[1] as well as Parliamentary passions during the first year of the régime was the Education Bill, which revived the perennial anti-clerical quarrel, last exacerbated by the *loi Barangé* of 1951. The 1959 Bill sought to institute a contractual relationship between Catholic schools and the State system. Before it was voted, the Minister of Education[2] had resigned, as had over half the members of the Higher Educational Council, and M. Pierre-Olivier Lapie, a former Socialist Deputy who had presided over the Commission of Inquiry on whose findings the Bill was based, had been expelled from the party, merely for agreeing to preside over an impartial fact-finding Commission which had no powers.

The main provision of the Bill was the offer to Catholic schools of four options, each of which would ensure some degree of aid from State funds. First, they could remain in the situation resulting from the application of the *Barangé* law, which was the traditional position of complete independence from the State. Schools which chose this option would continue, for at least three years, to receive the small subsidy agreed to in 1951.[3] The second option was that of complete integration within the State system, which would, of course, have entailed the loss of the special privilege of including religious instruction in the school curriculum. The remaining two

[1] Prefectoral reports commented, as did many Deputies, on the strength of feeling on this issue throughout the country.

[2] The Minister, M. Boulloche, was a former official, but was known to have Socialist sympathies.

[3] In 1959, Catholic schools had received some five milliard francs out of a total subsidy of 33 milliards. The subsidy was used by State schools mainly to improve equipment, and by Catholic schools to supplement the inadequate salaries of Catholic teachers. Anti-clericals had refused to agree to any subsidy to Catholic schools unless the State schools also received one.

were compromises. Catholic schools could choose one of two forms of contractual relationship. The first, the *contrat d'association*, provided that the State would assume full financial responsibility where teaching standards and curricula conformed with those of the State system. Teachers could either be directly employed by the State or else choose a contractual relationship. The essential aim of the Bill was to ensure that the State controlled teaching standards and the qualifications of teachers, in return for aid. The second form of contract, *le contrat simple,* provided for a more flexible arrangement, mainly for elementary schools, in which approved teachers could receive payment from the State, based on their qualifications. The School had to undertake in return to meet certain requirements. Catholic schools accepting either form of contract were to be free to continue their existing practice of giving religious instruction.

The anti-clerical Left objected to the Bill because it broke with the principle of the separation of Church and State, laid down in 1905. For them, the only solution to the problem of Catholic schools was nationalization, that is integration in the State system, which, in their view, provided adequate facilities for extra-curricular religious instruction, sometimes on school premises.

The Bill had a difficult passage and left a heritage of bad feeling as had done the passage of the *Barangé* law. The alienation of the two important and organized left-wing movements, Socialist and M.R.P., from 1951 to 1956 and in the 1956 elections had significantly increased the difficulties of obtaining a stable majority in the National Assembly. There were signs towards the end of 1961 that Socialist demands for a repeal of this law might jeopardize Socialist and M.R.P. co-operation in the sixties as their demands for the repeal of the *Barangé* law had done in the fifties.

THE TWENTIETH CENTURY VERSUS THE NINETEENTH

The only two motions of censure tabled by Deputies on their own initiative were both concerned originally with the constitutional issue of Parliament's right to meet in special session.[1] The second had

[1] The first was debated on 5th May, 1960 and the second on 15th December. As finally tabled, however, the latter condemned the Government for the 'clumsiness, weakness and internal divisions, which had prevented it from dealing with the threats to the Republic,' and much of the debate was on the O.A.S.

originated in September 1961 but, having been ruled out of order, was not tabled until the middle of the regular session, and was voted on only at the end of the session. The original pretext had by then lost its importance, owing to the growing threat from right-wing terrorism.

The constitutional implications of the quarrels regarding Parliament's right to meet in special session have already been discussed. But the reasons why Parliament had wanted to meet have not. On both occasions, private Members' Bills were to be introduced to deal with discontent among farmers.

This, too, was a long-standing problem, inherited from the Fourth Republic, but actually exacerbated by the growing economic dynamism of the country. Modernization had not been carried out at the same rate in agriculture and in industry. France was still a country of 'Renaults among the Poujades', to quote M. Aron's phrase.[1] The Poujadist movement of small and uneconomic tradesmen seemed to have largely disappeared as an independent political force. The 'Poujades' of agriculture – the small farmers and the small wine-growers in the South – were victims of the new industrial revolution. They resented the Government's economic policy which, by keeping down food prices in order to prevent inflation, had, they felt, achieved industrial prosperity at their expense. They wanted the Government to prevent, instead of assisting, the import of cheap food, and to pay them a guaranteed price which would bring their standard of living up to that of other sectors of the economy.

This was not the only grievance, though it was the most immediate. There was also the fear that, with France's entry into the Common Market, the position of the small farmer was bound to worsen. Fear and resentment combined to produce the riots of 1960 (in which some Poujadist elements certainly played a part) and the more considerable disturbances of 1961 when, from June to August, farmers, mainly in Brittany and Central France, drove tractors, farm carts and lorries into market towns, blocked roads and attacked *Sous-Préfectures*.

The Government had already taken action in 1960 to deal with the basic long-term problem, which was that France had too many small and uneconomic farms, too many middlemen, and inadequate

[1] *France, immuable et changeante*. (Paris, Calmann-Lévy, 1959.)

marketing arrangements. The reorganization of agriculture, including the attempt to rationalize and regroup farms more economically, had been going on for years, but slowly, because French farmers are conservative, and because some sectors had established vested interests. The Government's programme for agricultural development, voted at the end of the July session of 1960, concentrated on this basic problem of modernization. The farmers' complaints were, first, that it was applied too slowly. They wanted better agricultural education and social security. The Breton farmers, particularly hard hit, wanted better storage facilities for surplus butter, modernized slaughter-houses, improved transport and aid in training surplus farmers for other work. But, second, they wanted some alleviation of the immediate problems of their standard of living, and the disposal of the current year's crops. The farmers' action proved an effective spur to Governmental action. A series of emergency measures was announced and the Prime Minister called several round-table conferences to consider future action.

The opposition did not fail to point out that action in response to pressure by violence and illegality could not fail to create the impression that only violence paid. There was, however, a strong argument against the position of the majority of the Deputies. In their way, the Fourth Republic's way, they were also responding to pressure. For what they were proposing to do was to use familiar palliatives that were not merely irrelevant, but might be positively harmful to France's future position in the Common Market. To pay farmers uneconomic prices in order to keep uneconomic farms in existence was not merely playing the politics of the Third and Fourth Republics.[1] It was siding with a sector of the economy which still had one foot in the nineteenth century, instead of concentrating on bringing it wholly into the twentieth.

THE REPUBLIC AGAINST TORTURE

As the Algerian war dragged on, in spite of the prevailing political apathy, increasing uneasiness developed into shame and humiliation, as numbers of French citizens came to realize its serious moral impact. This affected directly only the army, but in a democracy the

[1] They were also, in 1961, proposing to bring in a hurriedly concocted private member's Bill covering problems that the Government was known to be going to deal with by legislation on the opening of the session in a few weeks.

body politic is responsible for its army, and France has always held this view very strongly. The realization of the moral problems involved grew only slowly, too slowly in the view of some outside observers. When one looks at the situation as it appeared to French citizens, however, the slowness seems inevitable.

To begin with, people had got accustomed in the early years of the rebellion to stories of Moslem atrocities, the victims of which were more often other Moslems than Frenchmen. Moslem terrorism in the towns – bomb-throwing and murders – was also a familiar happening. There was, indeed, a mass of authentic evidence of burnt farms, murder[1] and often torture of innocent victims (the wiping out of whole families, for instance, including small children), torture and often savage mutilation of French soldiers, the intimidation of Moslems (in particular, of Moslem elected representatives to the Algerian Assembly), and extortion by the F.L.N., under threats, of financial contributions to the rebel movement.[2] This last-mentioned type of blackmail was extensively practised among the large population of Algerian workers in France, who were living on Moslem standards, but being paid at French rates.

There was evidence also that Moslem rebels, when arrested, automatically, and on F.L.N. instructions, complained to the *juge d'instruction* of beating and torture. The author of *La Question*, whose restrained and factual account of his own torture at the hands of French army officers carried conviction to tens of thousands of readers[3], was himself an admitted French Communist running a Communist organization engaged in helping the rebels. The most prominent of those who, at first, protested against the use of torture by the French army were either Communists or fellow-travellers, with their own anti-French axe to grind. And nobody in France is under any illusions regarding the credibility of Communist propaganda. In other words, self-deception was all too easy while

[1] According to the F.L.N. leader Belkacem Krim, '*L'attentat est le stage accompli par tout candidat à l'A.L.N.*' (quoted in *Revue jougoslave de politique internationale,* January 1960).

[2] A café proprietor said in evidence at the Jeanson Trial: 'There are times when, if you are asked to pay you must pay. You don't know what is in your visitor's pocket.'

There were, too, a number of authenticated massacres of Moslems. That at Melouza, for instance, involved barbaric mutilations.

[3] *La Question*, by Henri Alleg (*Editions de Minuit,* 1958) was at first banned but sold over 60,000 copies in a clandestine edition.

the case was being put mainly by Frenchmen and Frenchwomen whose loyalty to France was itself suspect, and whose political sympathies were with a party whose propaganda is systematically built on lies and half-truths.

Three factors helped to transform what was for a long time little more than a vague uneasiness into a widespread moral protest – widespread, that is, in politically active and in religious circles. The first was the gradual emergence not only of reputable but of irrefutable evidence of the truth of allegations of torture. Even in spite of its tainted source, *La Question* does have a ring of truth. But other books and other witnesses shouted truth aloud, especially at the trial, in 1960, of Francis Jeanson and members of his organization of active workers for the F.L.N., and of the Abbé Davezies in 1962. When a high French official, M. Paul Teitgen, could say in evidence that he had resigned his post as head of the Algerian police because of the practice of torture; when a former, highly respected M.R.P. Senator, M. Fonlupt-Esperaber, could come forward and say that torture by French officials had existed *before* the F.L.N. had made it a regular instrument of war, and that it had spread to the army as early as 1954; when he could cite a report of the former Delegate-General of Algeria, M. Delouvrier, in support of his evidence, then it was impossible for honest Frenchmen to go on behaving like ostriches.

Moreover, evidence was gradually but steadily seeping in from humbler sources. Conscripts returning from Algeria brought back stories of their own experiences; priests on duty with the troops, or who had heard soldiers in confession, became convinced of the seriousness of the problem;[1] some serving officers sent accounts of what they had seen to French newspapers and periodicals.[2]

[1] In his evidence at the trial of the Abbé Davezies, M. Teitgen quoted the thanks expressed to a Catholic padre in 1958 by 'a general commanding the 10th Parachute division', for the padre's 'rational and impartial' comments on the battle of Algiers and the methods by which it had been conducted. The wording had convinced him, said M. Teitgen, that torture was no longer regarded as 'an individual failing', that its use was being justified on moral grounds. No names were quoted. But everyone was aware that the General at the head of the 10th Parachute division and responsible for suppressing Moslem terrorism in Algiers at that time was General Massu.

M. Teitgen had also given evidence at the trial of Francis Jeanson.

[2] Some young officers refused to serve and, since France does not recognize the legitimacy of conscientious objection, were sentenced to periods of imprisonment. *v.*, for instance, the case of a young Catholic teacher, Jean le Macer, quoted in *Le Monde*, 5th August 1960.

The second factor was the growing number of protests by political and religious organizations and by intellectuals, together with the courage of editors of newspapers and periodicals in publishing reports of protests and demonstrations and the texts of manifestoes with their signatories. The third factor was the attitude of the authorities themselves. Articles or numbers of periodicals were sometimes confiscated for publishing stories about the use of torture by the French army. Some alleged victims of torture were unable to prove their case in a Court of law owing to obstruction by the army authorities. Two in particular, became symbols in the minds of French people of official complicity in injustice in order to cover awkward revelations regarding torture. The first was the case of Maurice Audin, a French Communist, who had disappeared[1] and was alleged by his widow to have been murdered, after having been tortured by army officers. The other was that of a Moslem girl, Djamila Boupacha, whose lawyers tried unsuccessfully for years to extract from the army authorities the necessary photographs to establish the identity of officers who, according to her (and to medical evidence supporting her case), had subjected her to peculiarly revolting forms of torture.[2]

The result of this accumulation of evidence was a gradual crescendo of protest, from Cardinals and Archbishops, Protestant pastors, political parties, intellectuals and left-wing organizations of different kinds. The most publicized of the protests, the so-called 'Manifesto of the 121', in 1960, did harm as well as good. It was signed by a number of intellectuals (ultimately by many more than the original 121), including Civil Servants, university professors and writers. It included, unfortunately, a specific incitement to young

[1] In his evidence in January 1962, M. Paul Teitgen said that during a year's service in Algiers he had personally established that 3,014 people had 'disappeared'. 'I denounced that', he said, 'and I went.'

[2] The inadequate facilities accorded to the Patin Commission (*la Commission de Sauvegarde*), set up to investigate alleged instances of torture, did not argue any marked enthusiasm on the part of the authorities for efficient inquiries. The President, for instance, had no expense allowance and was obliged for three years to pay his own fare to and from Algiers.

At the beginning of 1962, and in spite of honest attempts to get at the truth by a French *juge d'instruction* in the provinces, the case of Djamila Boupacha seemed no nearer to being heard. Certain serious papers continued to give steady publicity to the difficulties that Djamila Boupacha's lawyers were encountering. Eventually, both she and her alleged torturers were amnestied under the Evian agreements.

Frenchmen to mutiny or desert if called on to serve in Algeria. Its publication was, therefore, understandably, banned and some of the signatories who were in the employ of the State were suspended.[1]

How effective were these protests?

Their direct influence is impossible to assess. They certainly had an indirect influence in strengthening the movement for peace, even if it had to be at a high cost. But they were protests by a minority, and a minority predominantly of the Left. The majority of the public found the problem too difficult and left it to the President. Extreme right-wing opinion was, from April 1961 onwards, learning from Moslem terrorists how to retaliate even more effectively in kind.

What is important about the protests is the freedom with which they were made and with which they were reported in the Press. The occasional confiscations of newspapers and periodicals received publicity, and rightly so, but in spite of them, only the Manifesto of the 121 failed to obtain publication somehow. And it is possible that some attempts to suppress evidence actually secured a wider audience than would otherwise have been obtained. For each time an article was confiscated, or the sale of a book banned, the Press provided free publicity. It is permissible to wonder whether M. Alleg's book, for instance, would have had such a success, if it had not been banned. At first most of the books published were by small publishers, usually by the left-wing '*Editions de Minuit*'.[2] In February 1962, however, the house of Gallimard published the story of Djamila Boupacha, written by Simone de Beauvoir and with a cover design by Picasso. And at the anti-O.A.S. demonstrations which took place in all university towns on 6th February,[3] a statement was

[1] Like other confiscated or banned documents, this was obtainable and gradually became known to a wide public. The offending passage in it reads as follows:

> 'We respect and consider justified the refusal to take up arms against the Algerian people.'

This phrase shocked a great many French people and a number of protests against torture specifically repudiated the right of soldiers to refuse to serve – for example, the protest by Cardinals and Archbishops in October 1960 and the Protestant protest the following month.

[2] For instance, *L'Affaire Audin* (1958) by Pierre Vidal-Naquet, *La Gangrène* (1959), *Notre Guerre* (1960) by Francis Jeanson.

[3] The anniversary of the left-wing anti-Fascist demonstrations of 1934 which led to the Popular Front.

also read, condemning the tolerance of torture in Algeria. In Paris, its author, Professor Georges Vedel of the Paris Law Faculty, read it personally (not on university premises, however) to an audience of 4,000, together with some 10,000 university teachers, students and schoolchildren assembled outside.

> 'To tolerate torture,' said Professor Vedel, 'would be the defeat of all efforts for the slow conquest of human dignity, whether individual or collective. Where a country no longer has justice, it no longer has liberty.'[1]

THE REPUBLIC AGAINST THE O.A.S.

From about the middle of 1961 onwards, protests against torture and against the activities of European terrorist organizations, loosely referred to as the O.A.S., had become part of the same battle. More and more French citizens realized that they might have to fight for the body of the Republic as well as for its soul. By the beginning of 1962, the Press was including alongside the daily list of 'explosions of plastic bombs', a list of 'protests against the O.A.S.'

Singularly little reliable information is available about the O.A.S., its size or equipment, the relations between different terrorist organizations and their relation to General Salan, the extent of support for General Salan in the army, and the extent to which an attempted coup would have received support in France from Civil Servants or public.

Up to the insurrection of April 1961, there had been relatively few plastic-bomb incidents in Paris, most of them doing very little damage. Indeed, it sometimes appeared as if they were not intended to do damage or take life, except for the murder of the Mayor of Evian, who had received threatening letters accusing him of 'betraying his country' by agreeing to receive the Algerian delegation in Evian for the peace talks. During the summer, the movement was clearly spreading in Algeria. Wireless transmitters were put out of

[1] The full statement is reproduced in *Le Monde* 7th February, 1962. The references to torture were specific as well as general and the statement mentioned the recent acquittal by a Military Court of three officers accused of murder, which was described as 'more than a betrayal of national and human values.'

action and O.A.S. messages broadcast from clandestine transmitters by supporters of General Salan.

The first real evidence of a considerable O.A.S. network in France came with the arrest, at the beginning of September, of a group of '*activistes*' and the discovery of documents relating to an O.A.S. network in South-West France, apparently led by M. Ortiz, who had been condemned to death in his absence for his part in the insurrection of January 1960, and was then in Spain.[1] Most of the members appeared to be former Poujadistes,[2] members of banned extremist groups, such as *Jeune Nation*, or participants in the insurrections of 13th May, 1958 or 24th January, 1960. M. Lagaillarde, also sentenced in his absence for his part in the January insurrection, appeared to be running a network of his own, along with ex-Colonel Lacheroy, formerly the head of the *cinquième bureau* in Algiers, another fugitive. The two leaders appeared to be on bad terms with each other and there was no evidence, at least at that time, of any connection between these two movements and that believed to be directed by General Salan. The documents found included a series of code names for different leaders (Salan was apparently Jupiter and Soustelle Miaou). The whole set-up had a rather spurious and amateur cloak-and-dagger air about it.

On 8th September, however, there came the attempted assassination of General de Gaulle on the road, half-way between Paris and Colombey-les-deux-Eglises, and a few days later, a letter sent directly from General Salan to *Le Monde*, in which he attacked the President, suggested that the attempted assassination was a put-up job, and repudiated all responsibility for it.[3] He did, however, make it quite clear that he was, indeed, the leader of the O.A.S., but he

[1] M. Ortiz had also been connected with the 'bazooka' affair, that is the attempted assassination of General Salan in 1957, when the latter had been thought not to sympathize with the 'ultra' point of view.

[2] Among former Poujadiste Deputies known to be involved were MM. Demarquet and Bouyer.

[3] The letter was printed in *Le Monde* 20th September 1961. An O.A.S. document published by the *Délégation générale* a few days later contained references to plans to assassinate the President and also included a number of names of conspirators and their pseudonyms. In November, General Salan gave an interview to C.B.S. in which he said that his aim was to prevent a Communist Government from taking power in Algeria. A Government headed by M. Ben Khedda would be, he said, a Communist Popular Republic. (*v. Le Monde* 8th November 1961.

stated quite categorically that he had no intention of seeking power in France.

> 'There is a Constitution,' he said. 'There are Parliamentary Assemblies and there is a French people.'[1]

By the autumn, O.A.S. activities in Algeria had already taken on the forms that were to become characteristic daily items of news – the rampages of hate by European youths, the vicious circle of Moslem and European murders, funeral riots. Pirate broadcasts were becoming more frequent. In October, there were three of them within three days. O.A.S. orders appeared from time to time, ordering Europeans to wear O.A.S. emblems, fly flags, strike, or beat out *Algérie française* on pots and pans. Rumours of an impending *putsch* became more frequent. One rumour attributed to General Salan a plan to seize power in Algiers and Oran, proclaiming an autonomous French Republic in that area. He would then call on General de Gaulle to recognize the *de facto* partition of Algeria. According to this rumour also, General Salan had no intention of trying to seize power in France.[2] Other rumours claimed that the O.A.S. had no intention of launching a *coup d'etat* either in Algeria or in France, but was merely carrying out a terrorist campaign designed to prevent any negotiations between France and the G.P.R.A., presumably by convincing the G.P.R.A. that the French would be unable to implement any agreement.

In France, the plastic bombs continued and political support for the O.A.S. became more open. There was the vote in the Assembly of the so-called 'Salan amendment', in November.[3] A few days later a meeting organized by the *Comité de Vincennes* in Paris drew an

[1] An appeal purporting to come from the O.A.S. was distributed by M. Lagaillarde's organization, suggesting that this movement was thinking in terms of power, and of the imposition of some kind of corporatist Constitution. (*v. Le Monde* 23rd September 1961).

[2] It will be remembered that, at his trial, General Challe denied that he had ever had the intention of trying to seize power in France. This alleged Salan plan had its strong points – it could have been presented as a 'vote on self-determination', by the most pro-French areas, and might have appealed to some sectors of the army whose general state of mind at this time remained an unknown factor. (*v. l'Express* 16th November 1961.)

[3] *v. supra*, pp. 69–70.

audience of about 3,000 to listen to inflammatory speeches by right-wing Deputies.[1]

Public opinion was by now becoming seriously alarmed at the spread of lawlessness in France. There were stories of O.A.S. blackmailing levies on business firms (an F.L.N. technique) and much publicity was given to the attempt to blackmail Mlle. Brigitte Bardot.[2] The Mayor of Marseilles, the Socialist Senator, M. Defferre, said that the city was in the grip of O.A.S. racketeers; 151 Mayors in the Vaucluse said that they had received orders to resign, from sources claiming to be O.A.S. agents. In December, jurymen called to try a group of '*plastiqueurs*' at Riom refused to serve because they had been threatened by the O.A.S.

Anti-O.A.S. demonstrations began in provincial towns and spread later in Paris. When on 15th December the National Assembly debated the motion of censure condemning the Government for not taking effective steps to suppress the O.A.S., the Government had by then begun to act. On 6th December it was announced that all supporters of the O.A.S. would be liable to internment and that those proved to have contributed to O.A.S. funds, or journalists proved to have interviewed O.A.S. leaders, would be liable to be charged with complicity in the actions of a seditious organization. The *Comité de Vincennes* had already been dissolved in November. A decree of 6th December now dissolved all *de facto* organizations of the O.A.S.

From this time on, O.A.S. and anti-O.A.S. activities both increased. The O.A.S. went in for more and more spectacular operations – thefts of ammunition from army stores, kidnappings, bombs directed against progressive university professors and journalists[3]

[1] Among Deputies who spoke were MM. Bidault, Le Pen, Marçais and Delbecque – all well-known supporters of *l'Algérie française*, and the ex-Poujadist Deputy and former police commissioner Dides, who was arrested after the meeting for having accused the Head of the State of 'imposture and double-dealing'. This charge was later dropped but M. Dides was kept in administrative internment.

[2] *l'Express* published a copy of the threat and reported that a number of business firms had admitted to being blackmailed by the O.A.S.

[3] Among well-known personalities whose homes were '*plastiqués*' at the beginning of 1962 were professors Vedel, Pinto and Duverger; MM. Hubert Beuve-Méry, Fauvet and Planchais (*Le Monde*), Mme Françoise Giroud (*l'Express*) M. Malraux, Minister for Cultural Affairs, M. Alain Savary (former Deputy), M. Vigier (Senator), MM. Serge Bromberger, Michel Droit (*Figaro*) . . . and a number of others.

as well as against Deputies, and one in the courtyard of the Quai d'Orsay itself. Anti-O.A.S. demonstrations were held, involving clashes with the police, partly because all demonstrations were banned, partly (or so it was alleged by Government spokesmen) owing to Communist provocation. Anti-O.A.S. organizations were set up, there were meetings of 'defence groups', at least one of which threatened to reply to violence with violence.[1] A number of Councils of *départements* called for the intensification of action against the O.A.S., associating this demand with the desire to see negotiations with the F.L.N. Riot police were drafted to Paris and big towns; many people were questioned, or arrested, and cars were examined. The arrest, at the end of January of one of the leaders led to the discovery of documents showing that the O.A.S. was making extensive and systematic use of schoolchildren in their bomb attacks.[2]

The most important and impressive of these demonstrations was that of 13th February when some 200,000 people followed the funeral procession of the victims of police violence during the demonstration a few days earlier.[3]

All this had two main results. On the one hand, intimidation by the O.A.S. was generally admitted to be having some effect. For instance, at the end of January, another trial of alleged '*plastiqueurs*' – this time at Nîmes – was unable to proceed, owing to the impossibility of getting a jury to serve. On the other hand, public opinion was visibly shocked to discover that the police themselves could act as they had done at the anti-O.A.S. demonstrations. There was a growing feeling that the police were less enthusiastic about arresting O.A.S. suspects than about beating-up anti-O.A.S. defenders of law and order. Taken together with the evidence of police violence against Moslem demonstrators the previous October, these clashes with the police strengthened fears that the police force was itself not

[1] The *Comité de défense républicaine*, which was distributing pamphlets at the beginning of January 1962.

[2] This was Philippe Castille, arrested on 31st January. He was one of the men who had tried to murder General Salan in 1957, and had been sentenced to ten years' imprisonment, but had escaped. One of the complaints of anti-O.A.S. elements was the ease with which prisoners convicted of O.A.S. activities managed to escape.

[3] Six of the eight victims were, in fact, known Communists.

immune from infiltration by activist and pro-O.A.S. elements.[1] There was a fear both of the general spread of violence in France and of the unknown strength of support for the O.A.S. 'We are ashamed,' wrote François Mauriac, 'to be the only great modern State that is not properly policed.'[2]

MYTHS AND REALITIES

There are two things to note about the climate of this growing movement of protest. First, it was moral rather than political and was, like the 'ban the bomb' movement, essentially unrelated to party politics. It expressed itself in strikes – mainly, brief token demonstrations – and marches – in the main by Trade-Union movements, dissident Socialists and members of teaching and students Unions, but in which Communist Unions participated. By the end of 1961, after the clashes with the police, there was a more self-conscious sense of the need to defend Republican values. But it expressed itself in traditional reflexes and attitudes more appropriate to long past dangers than to future ones.

In the circumstances, marches, token strikes, and the mass demonstration on 8th February on the occasion of the funeral of the victims of clashes with the police two days earlier could even constitute a danger, as some Socialists were well aware. At the crucial moment, when the loyalty of the army to the State was likely to be put to the test any day, the non-Communist Left had nothing to gain by creating the impression in the minds either of the a-political public or of the army that the only serious opposition to the O.A.S. was Communist-dominated. In the event of an attempted *coup*, the slogan '*l'O.A.S. ou les Communistes*' could be as effective as was, in

[1] The police in Paris were, and had been for a long time, required to do an impossible job. They were a special target for Moslem attacks. According to the statement by M. Frey in the National Assembly on 31st October 1961, 47 policemen were killed in Paris between 1958 and the autumn of 1961 and 12 between May and October 1961 alone. They were called on to provide door-watchers to protect potential victims of the O.A.S. and also to keep order in conditions which in their view, called for military rather than police methods. They also had grievances about their pay. It was admitted, however, that there had been extremist infiltrations (though small and chiefly during the early fifties, when ex-Commissioner Dides was at the *Préfecture*) and that the special brigades formed at that time to deal with demonstrations were allowed to use violence. There has been an anti-Communist element since this time, and there has been a small 'activist' element composed of men repatriated from Algeria.

[2] *Le Monde* 6th January 1962.

1958, that of '*De Gaulle ou les paras*'. All demonstrations were banned. Yet the Communists pressed for joint demonstrations against the O.A.S., and, according to Government spokesmen, were responsible for deliberately provoking incidents with the police, thus whipping up fear of the Communists in some quarters, while they whipped up hostility to the police in others. The tone of the demonstrations was reminiscent of that of 1934, and Frenchmen have not forgotten that 1934 had led to the Popular Front of 1936.

A solemn and eloquent warning of the danger of this kind of opposition was given by the editor of *Le Monde*, under his pen-name, Sirius:

> 'The protestors,' he said, 'ought not to have any illusions about the meaning and scope of their action. Any battle against the forces of law and order, at least as long as these do not appear to have gone over to subversion, risks serving the interests of subversion.
>
> 'Trade-Union leaders ought to beware of myths, and especially of the myth of the general strike. A strike can be effective in getting rid of a specific and too flagrant injustice, or in improving working-class conditions, But repeated absences from work for political reasons will only increase disorder. They will not paralyse subversion but serve its purposes, as happened in Italy, where incessant strikes and finally a general strike helped instead of hindering the advent of Fascism.'[1]

This was M. Mollet's dilemma, and it was not always properly understood in Great Britain. On the one hand, since such demonstrations are traditional expressions of left-wing Republican opinion in France, he welcomed the evidence that they provided of the reawakening of the sense of political responsibility. On the other hand, he recognized that ephemeral gestures, recalling February 1934, without any effort to relate them to the needs of 1962, might do more harm than good.

The second thing to note about the political climate at the end of 1961 and the beginning of 1962 was that the parties themselves showed little sign of readiness to meet any political emergency, even after the warning that they had received on September 9th,

[1] *Le Monde* 15th January 1962.

when they had learned of the abortive attempt to assassinate General de Gaulle.

At the time of the referendum of January 1961, M. Fauvet had given the following description of the attitudes of French parties:

> 'Under the present régime,' he said, 'as under the previous one, all parties, even when in power, have had at least one foot, and sometimes both, in the opposition. All of them have had opportunities to propose clear policies and to make provision for an alternative Government, but not one of them has done so. Not one of them has disciplined itself, modernized itself, modified its views so as to harmonize them with those of like-minded parties, in order to end the atomization of French political life.'[1]

If this constitutes a harsh judgement, that of François Mauriac, writing almost exactly a year later, is even more severe.

> 'Are our parties moribund,' he asked, 'or will they revive? In any case, they have made little use of the respite that they owe to de Gaulle, whose régime is precisely what Pierre Mendès-France is demanding, namely, a transitional Government whose job is to deal with immediate problems. That is what de Gaulle has done and is still doing. We are living in a strange and contradictory régime – a liberal dictatorship, in which one man carries the whole burden of the State, yet cannot act as a dictator and impose his will by force, because he is a liberal and a Christian.
>
> 'Others, alas, have turned this contradiction to their own advantage but, you Socialists at least, cannot blame him for your own impotence.'[2]

It was not only Socialsts who deserved the reproach. Indeed, M. Mollet was one of the few who, in the autumn of 1961, did at least try to prepare for the situation that would be created by a Presidential vacancy, whenever and however it might occur. He proposed that the Socialist party should campaign for an understanding with 'groups or individuals whose principles are those of political democracy' (that is, excluding Communist organizations) on the immediate action necessary to enable France 'to be governed democratically, with or without de Gaulle'. He explained that this

[1] *Le Monde* 22nd – 23rd January 1961

[2] *Notre République* Jan. 1962.

meant, as a beginning, support for the strict application of constitutional provisions to fill a Presidential vacancy.[1] The minority within the party, led by MM. Gazier, Pineau, Dardel and others, wanted a more precise basis for concerted action, including an agreement to draft a Constitution 'ensuring full democracy and an effective and stable executive, so that past errors can be avoided', modifications of the electoral law designed to secure a more proportional representation, democratic planning for economic expansion and social progress and the 'nationalization of the educational system'.

Since the last proposal was quite obviously a declaration of war against the 1959 Act providing for State aid to Catholic schools, the chances of such a platform obtaining any significant support from the only important non-Socialist democratic forces on the Left, namely the M.R.P. and the associated Catholic Trade-Union Confederation, would obviously be nil. M. Mollet had been careful to avoid direct provocation of this kind. But his approach was no more pleasing to the only other outstanding left-wing leader, M. Mendès-France, who did not wish to commit himself as openly as M. Mollet had done to excluding co-operation with the Communist party.

M. Mendès-France's plan for ensuring a peaceful and constitutional transfer of power, announced in a press conference on 25th September, was at the same time more and less precise than that of M. Mollet. It was less precise because, while he insisted on the need for a wide popular appeal, he gave no clear indication of how this was to be obtained. It was more precise in that it proposed the formation of an interim Government whose specific tasks would be to end the Algerian war and draw up a new Constitution within two months. Since the last Constitution drawn up by a popular Assembly had taken over a year and involved two general elections, this objective in itself seemed unrealistic, for nothing indicated that the political parties were any more agreed than they had ever been on the question of a Constitution.

In any case, neither of these suggestions appeared to arouse any

[1] Article 7 of the Constitution provides that in the event of a Presidential vacancy, or incapacity duly certified, the functions of the President are carried out temporarily by the President of the Senate, who is not empowered to use articles 11 and 12. A Presidential vacancy or permanent incapacity must be followed by the election of a new President within from 20 to 50 days.

enthusiasm during the following months[1] and the parties entered the dangerous period of the Franco–Algerian cease-fire, with all its threats of anarchy, civil war, and *coup d'Etat*, without any clear idea of where they were going. Their achievement up to then had been, at best, to try to ring the alarm bell in face of threats to individual liberties and to the spirit of Republicanism.

PRESIDENT AND PARTIES

The failure of parties was due partly to the difficulties of the situation. The political atmosphere was one of uncertainty and impermanence. Three insurrections within three years, together with the threat of a fourth, the daily reminders that violence and perhaps anarchy were just round the corner, did not provide the kind of background against which constitution-making in advance seemed a profitable occupation. It was due partly to the political atmosphere of the age. France is not the only country to discover that economic affluence has encouraged political apathy. But the chief explanation is the combination of the discredit of party politics and of politicians under the Fourth Republic and the discredit which they continued to suffer from in the eyes of the President.

'A nation is not on the one hand a man and on the other millions of citizens who listen to him in silence,' wrote the Secretary-General of the M.R.P., M. Simonnet. 'A nation is a permanent dialogue between the people and those to whom they have entrusted the governance of the Republic.' In the Fifth French Republic, there was no dialogue, either between the man and the citizens, or between the man and those whom the citizens had elected to represent them. For three and a half years, they, or the majority of them, remained loyal to him, because not merely the governance, but also the survival of the Republic appeared to them to depend on him. But if the Republic could not live without the President, Republicans could not live with him. For this conception of national leadership is precisely that of a man who wants to speak for millions, whom he expects to listen in silence.

Whether or not such leadership can really incarnate the national

[1] M. Mendès-France's tour of the provinces during the following months did not provide any convincing evidence of significant support for his plan, even on the Left.

spirit and create unity in moments of grave crisis, except for a very short time, is doubtful. For as soon as the crisis is transformed into a prolonged emergency or a test of endurance, leadership is not enough. An efficient machine is required. In the army, a chain of command may suffice, but a democratic Republic needs the machinery of Parliamentary government. And the machinery of Parliamentary government needs parties. Sir Winston Churchill, who was a great House of Commons man, realized this during the war. He never failed to associate himself with Parliament and refused to agree to Parliament's leaving London. Léon Blum reminded General de Gaulle as far back as 1942 that there could be no democracy without parties. He meant responsible parties. The docile legislative and ratifying Assembly, looking on while all the vital decisions were taken in their absence, which is General de Gaulle's conception of Parliament, is completely foreign to French Republician tradition.

General de Gaulle is uninterested in political machinery and has no patience with the intrigues and the inefficiency that Parliamentary government often involves. During the first year of the régime, it looked as if the combination in the government of the Fifth Republic of a super-man President, ministerial technicians and a frustrated Parliament would lead to anarchy and deadlock. Instead, it led to a political vacuum and to the discouragement of the Parliamentary supporters of the President as well as of his opponents. A number of U.N.R. Deputies discovered by experience, and to their surprise, that the Parliamentary function which they had despised had something to be said for it after all, but that the leader whom they were committed to follow ignored them, while the Prime Minister read them lessons instead of working with them. Whether on the side of the Government or of the Opposition, Parliamentary groups found that idleness did not encourage a sense of responsibility, but led to boredom and internal quarrels. Deputies found their role as spectators increasingly irksome, but seemed unable to think positively about, or to prepare for, the future.

THE FUTURE

The circumstances were incredibly difficult for everybody concerned. Nevertheless, Parliamentary sessions need not have been used by Deputies quite as much as they were to let off steam, or to play the familiar game of politics which, in the past, had helped to convince the President that politicians were normally petty, and opposition politicians 'snarlers, grumblers and grousers'. Nor can the long Parliamentary vacations wholly excuse democratic parties for their share in creating a 'long vacation of democracy,'[1] which leaves them ill-prepared to meet whatever constitutional or political crises await them in the near future. For with the passage of the Algerian problem from the realm of principles and policies to that of application – however difficult application may turn out to be – the Fifth Republic entered on a new phase. If the threat of civil war becomes a fact, then the dreams of Deputies of a return to more familiar Republican and Parliamentary habits are doomed to disappointment. What M. Fauvet has called the 'man-Constitution' then becomes so in the fullest sense of the term, by the application of article 16 'to the fullest possible extent',[2] and the future, like that of all revolutions, becomes unpredictable.

If, on the contrary, the threat recedes, then the man may become expendable, and the Constitution a subject of renewed controversy. On the Left, some only too familiar views are already being aired. Reference has already been made to one.[3] The second is not dissimilar. At its Congress in December, 1961, the *Ligue des Droits de l'Homme* succeeded in convincing the delegates of the need to prepare for 'a modern, democratic régime'. Agreement was reached on two points: the need to repeal the 'clerical laws' and to restore the right of dissolution in a form very similar to that included in the 1946 Constitution.

Since the latter failed to achieve its purpose and succeeded, instead, in achieving others, wholly regrettable, this constitutional début by the Left is not promising. But neither Right nor Left has so far given any sign of unity, purpose or leadership, either on constitutional or on political problems. The divisions of 1958 remain intact, with the possible exception of those concerning

[1] For the development of this theme *v.* François Fontaine, *La Démocratie en Vacances* (Paris, Julliard, 1959), and P. Viannson-Ponté *Risques et Chances de la Vᵉᵐᵉ République*, Paris, Julliard, 1959.

[2] The phrase used in the President's broadcast of 2nd October, 1961, in which he also threatened to dissolve Parliament if its relations with the Government were to endanger political stability.

[3] *v. supra* p. 228.

Algeria. And even there, if Algeria does remain in association with France, there will be ample scope for disagreement, as the example of Tunisia has shown. If Deputies get as far as considering constitutional revision, all the evidence points to a revival of the arguments gone over again and again in 1945, 1946, 1950, 1955, and 1958, in the Press as well as in Parliament – arguments that M. Reynaud has complained of having listened to for the past twenty-five years.

But if the President decides himself to take a hand and mould the Constitution into something nearer his own views, what then? In the summer of 1962, according to rumour, he was contemplating a revision of the Constitution, in order to modify the composition of the Senate and to change the Presidential electoral system. It was said that he intended to transform the Senate into something much nearer his description of that organ in the Bayeux speech of 1946, and to substitute for the present Presidential electoral system that of universal suffrage. Both these proposals would be anathema to the majority of members of Parliament, the first as smacking of corporatism,[1] the second as recalling the path followed by Louis Napoleon just over a century ago.

What the views of the electorate would be regarding France's constitutional future are wholly conjectural. Nothing indicates, however, any substantial change in the political allegiance of the public since 1958. Certainly, there has been no evidence that the only two new, or relatively new, suggestions would have any following. The first is the proposal of some constitutional lawyers on the Left, first put forward in the last years of the Fourth Republic, for a form of Presidential system – but one having no relation to Gaullist conceptions.[2] The second is an isolated plea for pragmatic common sense.

'. . . since the future belongs to nobody,' it argues, 'it would be

[1] In the Bayeux speech, it was suggested that the Second Chamber should include representatives of professional and economic interests. This was, at first, proposed in 1958, but later abandoned in the face of some Trade-Union opposition.

[2] The best-known exponents of this view are professors Vedel and Duverger. A brief analysis of discussions along these lines is given in the author's article in Parliamentary Affairs, Vol. X, No. 1.

For the latest discussion of what M. Duverger calls 'scientific Presidentialism' *v.* '*La Ve République et le régime présidentiel,* (Paris, Arthème Fayard, 1961.

better to keep the existing Constitution. Its wording is supple enough to allow for evolution in many respects.'[1]

This was also the plea put forward on behalf of the 1875 Constitution by some Radical elder statesmen in 1945. It was not listened to then. Nothing in the past three years' experience of the 1958 Constitution indicates that it has any friends outside the narrow circle of the more dedicated Gaullists. Nor is there any evidence that the French taste for making and breaking Constitutions has given way to a belief in the merits of 'make do and mend'. The hopeful are looking forward to a Sixth Republic, the pessimists to a Third Empire, a military dictatorship or a popular democracy. But France has confounded prophets before and may do so again.

[1] Jacques Fauvet, *L'Avenir de la Cinquième* I—in *Le Monde* January 1962. M. Leenhardt, President of the Socialist group in the National Assembly, has also suggested that the best thing would be to keep the present Constitution, with some revision, as of, for instance, article 16, and articles dealing with the functions of the Constitutional Council.

APPENDIX

The French Constitution of October 4th, 1958[1]

PREAMBLE

The French people solemnly proclaim their attachment to the Rights of Man and to the principles of national sovereignty as defined by the Declaration of 1789, confirmed and completed by the Preamble to the Constitution of 1946.

By virtue of these principles and of that of the free determination of peoples, the Republic offers to those Overseas territories which express a desire to accept membership of them new institutions founded on the common ideal of liberty, equality and fraternity and conceived with a view to their democratic evolution.

Article 1. The Republic and those peoples of the Overseas territories who, by an act of free determination, adopt the present Constitution set up a Community.

The Community is founded upon the equality and solidarity of the peoples composing it.

TITLE I

SOVEREIGNTY

Article 2. France is an indivisible, secular, democratic and social Republic. It ensures the equality before the law of all citizens, without distinction of origin, race or religion. It respects all beliefs.

The national emblem is the tricolour flag, blue, white and red.

The national anthem is the '*Marseillaise*'.

[1] This translation is by William Pickles and is taken from his *French Constitution of October 4th, 1958* (Stevens, London, 1960).

The motto of the Republic is 'Liberty, Equality, Fraternity'.

Its principle is government of the people, by the people, for the people.

Article 3. National sovereignty belongs to the people, who exercise it through their representatives and by way of referendum.

No section of the people and no individual may claim to exercise it.

The suffrage may be direct or indirect in conditions provided for by the Constitution. It is in all cases universal, equal and secret. The right to vote, in conditions laid down by law, is enjoyed by all French nationals of either sex who are of age and in full possession of their civil and political rights.

Article 4. Parties and political groups play a part in the exercise of the right to vote. The right to form parties and their freedom of action are unrestricted. They must respect the principles of national sovereignty and of democracy.

TITLE II

THE PRESIDENT OF THE REPUBLIC

Article 5. The President of the Republic endeavours to ensure respect for the Constitution. He provides, by his arbitration, for the regular functioning of the public authorities and the continuity of the State.

He is the protector of the independence of the nation, of the integrity of its territory, of respect for treaties and Community agreements.

Article 6. The President of the Republic is elected for seven years by an electoral college which includes the members of Parliament, of the Departmental Councils, and of the Assemblies of Overseas territories, in addition to the elected representatives of the Municipal Councils.

These representatives are:

The Mayor for *communes* of less than 1,000 inhabitants;

the Mayor and first Deputy-Mayor for *communes* of 1,000 to 2,000 inhabitants;

the Mayor, first Deputy-Mayor and the municipal Councillor having received the highest vote in the municipal elections, for *communes* of 2,001 to 2,500 inhabitants;

the Mayor and first two Deputy-Mayors for *communes* of 2,501 to 3,000 inhabitants;

the Mayor, the first two Deputy-Mayors and the three municipal Councillors having received the highest votes, for *communes* of 3,001 to 6,000 inhabitants;

the Mayor, the first two Deputy-Mayors and the six Councillors having received the highest votes, for *communes* of 6,001 to 9,000 inhabitants;

all the municipal Councillors for *communes* of more than 9,000 inhabitants;

in addition, for *communes* of more than 30,000 inhabitants, delegates nominated by the Municipal Council at the rate of one for every thousand inhabitants after the first 30,000.

In the Overseas territories of the Republic, the electoral college also includes representatives elected by the Councils of the administrative entities, on the conditions laid down in an organic law.

The representation of member States of the Community in the college electing the President of the Republic is determined by agreement between the Republic and the member States of the Community.

The methods of application of the present article are determined by an organic law.

Article 7. The President is elected at the first ballot, if an absolute majority is obtained. If this is not obtained at the first ballot, the President of the Republic is elected at the second ballot by a relative majority.

Voting begins at the time fixed by the Government.

The election of the new President takes place not less than twenty and not more than fifty days before the expiry of the existing President's term of office.

If, for whatever reason, the Presidency of the Republic falls vacant, or if the incapacity of the President has been certified by the Constitutional Council, at the request of the Government and by an absolute majority of its members, the functions of the President, except those conferred by articles 11 and 12 below, are performed temporarily by the President of the Senate. When a vacancy occurs, or when the incapacity is certified by the Constitutional Council to be permanent, and unless *force majeure* has been certified by the Constitutional Council, the election of a new President takes place not less than twenty and not more than fifty days after the opening of the vacancy or the declaration of the permanence of the incapacity.

Article 8. The President of the Republic appoints the Prime Minister. He terminates his period of office on the presentation by the Prime Minister of the resignation of the Government.

He appoints and dismisses the other members of the Government on the proposal of the Prime Minister.

Article 9. The President of the Republic presides over the Council of Ministers.

Article 10. The President of the Republic promulgates laws within the fortnight following their final adoption and transmission to the Government.

Before the end of this period, he may ask Parliament to reconsider the whole law or specified articles. This reconsideration cannot be refused.

Article 11. On the proposal of the Government during Parliamentary sessions, or on the joint proposal of the two Assemblies, published in the *Journal Officiel*, the President of the Republic may submit to a referendum any Government Bill dealing with the organization of the public authorities, approving a Community agreement or authorizing the ratification of a treaty which, although not in conflict with the Constitution, would affect the working of institutions.

If the result of the referendum is favourable to the adoption of the Bill, the President of the Republic promulgates it within the time-limit laid down in the preceding article.

Article 12. The President of the Republic may pronounce the dissolution of the National Assembly, after consulting the Prime Minister and the Presidents of the Assemblies.

A general election takes place not less than twenty and not more than forty days after the dissolution.

The National Assembly meets as of right on the second Thursday following its election. If this meeting takes place outside the periods fixed for ordinary sessions, a session opens as of right for a period of a fortnight.

No new dissolution may take place during the year following these elections.

Article 13. The President of the Republic signs such ordinances and decrees as have been considered by the Council of Ministers. He appoints to the civil and military posts of the State. Councillors of

State, the Grand Chancellor of the Legion of Honour, Ambassadors and Envoys Extraordinary, Senior Councillors of the Court of Accounts, Prefects, Government representatives in Overseas Territories, General Officers, Flag Officers, Air-Marshals, Rectors of Academies and *directeurs* of Government departments are appointed in the Council of Ministers. An organic law determines the other appointments to be made in the Council of Ministers, as also the conditions in which the appointing power of the President of the Republic may be delegated by him and be exercised in his name.

Article 14. The President of the Republic accredits Ambassadors and Envoys Extraordinary to foreign powers; foreign Ambassadors and Envoys Extraordinary are accredited to him.

Article 15. The President of the Republic is Head of the armed forces. He presides over the Higher Councils and Committees of National Defence.

Article 16. When there exists a serious and immediate threat to the institutions of the Republic, the independence of the Nation, the integrity of its territory or the fulfilment of its international obligations, and the regular functioning of the constitutional public authorities has been interrupted, the President of the Republic takes the measures required by the circumstances, after consulting officially the Prime Minister, the Presidents of the Assemblies and the Constitutional Council.

He informs the Nation of these matters by a message.

These measures must be inspired by the desire to ensure to the constitutional public authorities, with the minimum of delay, the means of fulfilling their functions. The Constitutional Council is consulted about them.

Parliaments meet as of right.

The National Assembly cannot be dissolved during the [period of] exercise of the exceptional powers.

Article 17. The President of the Republic has the right of pardon.

Article 18. The President of the Republic communicates with the two assemblies of Parliament by means of messages which are read for him and on which there is no debate.

If Parliament is not in session, it is specially summoned for this purpose.

Article 19. The acts of the President of the Republic other than those provided for in articles 8 (*para.* 1), 11, 12, 16, 18, 54, 56 and 61 are countersigned by the Prime Minister and, where necessary, by the appropriate Ministers.

TITLE III

THE GOVERNMENT

Article 20. The Government decides and directs the policy of the nation. It has at its disposal the administration and the armed forces.

It is responsible to Parliament in the conditions and in accordance with the procedures laid down in Articles 49 and 50.

Article 21. The Prime Minister is in general charge of the work of the Government. He is responsible for National Defence. He ensures the execution of laws. Except as provided for under Article 13, he exercises rule-making power and appoints to civil and military posts.

He may delegate certain of his powers to the Ministers.

He deputizes for the President of the Republic, when necessary, as Chairman of the Councils and Committees referred to in Article 15.

In exceptional circumstances, he may deputize for him as Chair man of the Council of Ministers, by virtue of an explicit delegation of authority and with a specific agenda.

Article 22. The acts of the Prime Minister are countersigned, where necessary, by the Ministers responsible for their execution.

Article 23. Membership of the Government is incompatible with that of Parliament, with the representation of any trade or professional organization on the national level, with any public employment or professional activity.

An organic law lays down the conditions in which the holders of the above offices, functions or employments are to be replaced.

Members of Parliament are replaced in the manner laid down in Article 25.

TITLE IV

PARLIAMENT

Article 24. Parliament is composed of the National Assembly and the Senate. The Deputies of the National Assembly are elected by direct, universal suffrage.

The Senate is elected by indirect suffrage. It represents the territorial entities of the Republic. French citizens resident abroad are represented in the Senate.

Article 25. An organic law determines the length of life of each assembly, the number of its members, the payment made to them, the rules concerning qualification for and disqualification from election and the incompatibility of certain functions with membership of Parliament.

This organic law also determines the manner of election of those who, in the event of a vacancy, replace Deputies and Senators until the next election, general or partial, to the assembly in which the vacancy occurs.

Article 26. No member of Parliament may be prosecuted, sought out, arrested, held in custody or tried on account of opinions expressed or votes cast by him in the exercise of his functions.

No member of Parliament may be prosecuted or arrested on account of any crime or misdemeanour during a parliamentary session, without the consent of the Assembly of which he is a member, except when the member is arrested *flagrante delicto*.

Members of Parliament may be arrested when Parliament is not in session only with the authorization of the *bureau* of the assembly of which they are members, except when the arrest is *flagrante delicto*, when the prosecution has [already] been authorized or the final sentence pronounced.

Members are released from custody or their prosecution is suspended if the assembly of which they are members so demands.

Article 27. Any specific instruction to a member of Parliament [from an outside body] is null and void.

The member's right to vote belongs to him alone.

The (*sic*) organic law may authorize the delegation of the right to vote in exceptional circumstances. In these cases, no member may cast more than one delegated vote.

Article 28. Parliament meets as of right in two ordinary sessions per year.

The first session begins on the first Tuesday of October and ends on the third Friday of December.

The second session begins on the last Tuesday of April; it may not last more than three months.

Article 29. At the request of the Prime Minister or of the majority of the members of the National Assembly, Parliament meets in special session, with a specified agenda.

When the special session is held at the request of members of the National Assembly, the closure decree is read as soon as Parliament has completed the agenda for which it was called and at most twelve days after its meeting.

Only the Prime Minister can ask for a new session before the end of the month following the date of the closure decree.

Article 30. Except when Parliament meets as of right, special sessions are opened and closed by decree of the President of the Republic.

Article 31. Members of the Government have access to both assemblies. They are heard when they so request.

They may be assisted by Government commissioners.

Article 32. The President of the National Assembly is elected for the life of each Parliament. The President of the Senate is elected after each partial renewal.

Article 33. The sittings of both assemblies are public. A full report of debates is published in the *Journal Officiel*.

Each assembly may meet in secret session at the request of the Prime Minister or of one-tenth of its members.

TITLE V

RELATIONS BETWEEN PARLIAMENT AND GOVERNMENT

Article 34. Laws are voted by Parliament.

Laws determine the rules concerning:

- civic rights and the fundamental guarantees of the public liberties of the citizen; the obligations of citizens, as regards their persons and property, for purposes of National Defence;
- the nationality, status and legal capacity of persons, property in marriage, inheritance and gifts;
- the definitions of crimes and misdemeanours and of the penalties applicable to them; criminal procedure, amnesty, the creation of new orders of jurisdiction and the statute of the judiciary;
- the basis of assessment, rate and methods of collection of taxes of all kinds; the currency system.

Laws determine also the rules concerning:

the electoral system for Parliamentary and local assemblies;

the creation of categories of public corporation;

the fundamental guarantees of civil servants and members of the armed forces;

nationalizations and the transfer of property from the public to the private sectors.

Laws determine the fundamental principles;

of the general organization of national defence;

of the free administration of local entities, of their powers and of their resources;

of education;

of the law of property, of real-property rights and of civil and commercial contract;

of labour law, trade-union law and social security.

Finance laws determine the resources and obligations of the State, in the manner and with the reservations provided for in an organic law.

Programme-laws determine the purposes of the social and economic action of the State.

The provisions of the present article may be completed and more closely defined by an organic law.

Article 35. Declarations of war are authorized by Parliament.

Article 36. A state of siege is decreed in the Council of Ministers. Its prolongation beyond twelve days can be authorized only by Parliament.

Article 37. Matters other than those regulated by laws fall within the field of rule-making.

Documents in the form of laws, but dealing with matters falling within the rule-making field may be modified by decree issued after consultation with the Council of State. Such of these documents as come into existence after the coming into force of the present Constitution may be modified by decree only if the Constitutional Council has declared them to be within the rule-making sphere, by virtue of the previous paragraph.

Article 38. With a view to carrying out its programme, the Government may seek the authorization of Parliament, for a limited period of time, to issue ordinances regulating matters normally falling within the field of law-making.

(The) ordinances are made in the Council of Ministers after consultation with the Council of State. They come into force upon publication, but cease to be effective if the Bill ratifying them is not laid before Parliament by the date fixed by the enabling Act.

At the expiration of the period mentioned in paragraph 1 of this Article, (the) ordinances may be modified only by law, as regards matters falling within the field of law.

Article 39. Legislative initiative is exercised by the Prime Minister and by members of Parliament.

Government Bills are considered in the Council of Ministers, after consultation with the Council of State and laid before one of the two assemblies. Finance Bills are submitted first to the National Assembly.

Article 40. Private members' Bills, resolutions and amendments which, if passed, would reduce public revenues or create or increase charges on the revenue are out of order.

Article 41. If, in the course of legislative procedure, it becomes apparent that a private members' proposal or amendment does not fall within the field of law-making, or is in conflict with powers delegated by virtue of Article 38, the Government may demand that it be declared out of order.

In the event of disagreement between the Government and the President of the Assembly concerned, the Constitutional Council gives a ruling, at the request of either party, within a week.

Article 42. Government Bills are discussed, in the assembly to which they are first submitted, on the basis of the Government's text.

An assembly debating a Bill transmitted from the other assembly discusses it on the basis of the text transmitted to it.

Article 43. Government and private members' Bills are sent, at the request of the Government, or of the assembly then discussing them, to Commissions specially appointed for this purpose.

Bills of either type for which such a request has not been made are sent to one of the permanent Commissions, the number of which is limited to six for each assembly.

Article 44. Members of Parliament and the Government have the right of amendment.

When the debate has begun, the Government may object to the

discussion of any amendment which has not previously been submitted to the Commission.

If the Government so requests, the assembly concerned accepts or rejects by a single vote the whole or part of the Bill or motion under discussion, together with such amendments as have been proposed or accepted by the Government.

Article 45. Every Government or private member's Bill is discussed successively in the two assemblies with a view to agreement on identical versions.

When, as a result of disagreement between the two assemblies, a Bill has not been passed after two readings in each assembly, or, if the Government has declared the Bill urgent, after a single reading by each assembly, the Prime Minister is entitled to have the Bill sent to a joint Committee composed of equal numbers from the two assemblies, with the task of finding agreed versions of the provisions in dispute.

The version prepared by the joint committee may be submitted by the Government to the two assemblies for their approval. No amendment may be accepted without the agreement of the Government.

If the joint committee does not produce an agreed version, or if the version agreed is not approved as provided for in the preceding paragraph, the Government may ask the National Assembly, after one more reading by the National Assembly and by the Senate, to decide the matter. In this case, the National Assembly may adopt either the version prepared by the joint committee or the last version passed by itself, modified, if necessary, by one or any of the amendments passed by the Senate.

Article 46. Laws to which the Constitution gives the status of organic laws are passed or amended in the following conditions.

The Bill, whether Government or private member's, is not debated or voted on in the first assembly in which it is introduced until a fortnight after its introduction.

The procedure of Article 45 applies. Nevertheless, if the two assemblies fail to agree, the Bill may become law only if it is passed at its final reading in the National Assembly by an absolute majority of its members.

Organic laws relating to the Senate must be passed in the same terms by both assemblies.

Organic laws may be promulgated only when the Constitutional Council has certified their conformity with the Constitution.

Article 47. An organic law lays down the conditions in which Parliament votes Finance Bills.

If the National Assembly has not concluded its first reading within forty days from the introduction of the Bill, the Government sends the Bill to the Senate, which must reach a decision within a fortnight. Subsequent procedure is that provided for in Article 45.

If Parliament has reached no decision within seventy days, the provisions of the Bill may be put into force by ordinance.

If the Finance Bill determining revenue and expenditure for the financial year has not been introduced in time to be promulgated before the beginning of the financial year, the Government asks Parliament, as a matter of urgency, for authorization to levy the taxes voted and to allocate by decree the sums necessary for estimates already approved.

The time limits fixed by the present article are suspended when Parliament is not in session.

The Court of Accounts assists Parliament and the Government to supervise the application of Finance Acts.

Article 48. The agenda of the assemblies gives priority, in the order determined by the Government, to the discussion of Government Bills and private members' Bills accepted by the Government.

Priority is given at one sitting per week to the questions of members of Parliament and the replies of the Government.

Article 49. The Prime Minister, after deliberation in the Council of Ministers, pledges the responsibility of the Government before the National Assembly, on its programme or, if it be so decided, on a general declaration of policy.

The National Assembly challenges the responsibility of the Government by passing a vote of censure. A censure motion is in order only if it is signed by at least one-tenth of the members of the National Assembly. The vote may not take place until forty-eight hours after its introduction. Only votes in favour of the censure motion are counted, and the motion is carried only if it receives the votes of the majority of the members of the Assembly. If the censure motion is rejected, its signatories may not propose a further one during the same session, except in the case provided for in the next paragraph.

The Prime Minister may, after deliberation in the Council of Ministers, pledge the responsibility of the Government before the National Assembly on the passing of all or part of a Bill or a motion. In this case, the Bill or part of Bill or motion is regarded as having been passed, unless a censure motion, put down within the following twenty-four hours, is passed in the conditions provided for in the previous paragraph.

The Prime Minister is entitled to seek the approval of the Senate for a general statement of policy.

Article 50. When the National Assembly passes a motion of censure or rejects the Government's programme or a general statement of Government policy, the Prime Minister must tender to the President of the Republic the resignation of the Government.

Article 51. The closure of ordinary or special sessions is automatically postponed, if need be, in order to permit the application of the provisions of Article 49.

TITLE VI

TREATIES AND INTERNATIONAL AGREEMENTS

Article 52. The President of the Republic negotiates and ratifies treaties.

He is informed of the negotiation of any international agreement not subject to ratification.

Article 53. Peace treaties, commercial treaties, treaties or agreements concerning international organization, those which involve the State in financial obligations, modify the provisions of the law, concern personal status or involve the cession, exchange or addition of territory may be ratified or approved only by virtue of a law.

They take effect only after having been ratified or approved.

No cession, exchange or addition of territory is valid without the consent of the populations concerned.

Article 54. If the Constitutional Council, consulted by the President of the Republic, the Prime Minister or the President of either assembly, has declared that an international obligation includes a clause contrary to the Constitution, authorization to ratify or approve it may be accorded only after revision of the Constitution.

Article 55. Treaties or agreements regularly ratified or approved have, from the time of publication, an authority superior to that of laws, provided, in the case of each agreement or treaty, that it is applied by the other party.

TITLE VII

THE CONSTITUTIONAL COUNCIL

Article 56. The Constitutional Council has nine members, whose term of office lasts for nine years and is not renewable. Its members are appointed by thirds every three years. Three members are nominated by the President of the Republic, three by the President of the National Assembly, three by the President of the Senate.

In addition to the nine members provided for above, former Presidents of the Republic are *ex officio* life-members of the Constitutional Council.

The President is appointed by the President of the Republic. He has a casting vote.

Article 57. The functions of a member of the Constitutional Council are incompatible with those of a Minister or member of Parliament.

Other positions incompatible with membership of the Council are listed in an organic law.

Article 58. The Constitutional Council supervises the election of the President of the Republic, with a view to ensuring its regularity.

It investigates objections and proclaims the result.

Article 59. The Constitutional Council decides, in disputed cases, on the regularity of the election of Deputies and Senators.

Article 60. The Constitutional Council supervises the conduct of referenda with a view to ensuring their regularity, and proclaims the results.

Article 61. Organic laws, before their promulgation, and the rules of procedure of the Parliamentary assemblies, before their application, must be submitted to the Constitutional Council, which pronounces on their conformity with the Constitution.

For the same purpose, [ordinary] laws may be submitted to the Constitutional Council, before their promulgation, by the President of the Republic, the Prime Minister or the President of either assembly.

In the cases provided for in the two preceding paragraphs, the Constitutional Council decides within a month. At the request of the

Government, however, if the matter is urgent, this period may be reduced to a week.

In these above-mentioned cases, reference to the Constitutional Council prolongs the period allowed for promulgation.

Article 62. A provision declared unconstitutional may not be promulgated or applied.

Decisions of the Constitutional Council are not subject to appeal. They are binding on public authorities and on all administrative and judicial authorities.

Article 63. An organic law lays down the organization and methods of working of the Constitutional Council, the procedures to be followed in referring matters to it and in particular the time-limits within which disputes may be laid before it.

TITLE VIII

THE JUDICIAL AUTHORITY

Article 64. The President of the Republic is the protector of the independence of the judicial authority.

He is assisted by the Higher Council of the Judiciary.

An organic law regulates the position of the Judiciary. Judges are irremovable.

Article 65. The Higher Council of the Judiciary is presided over by the President of the Republic. The Minister of Justice is *ex officio* its Vice-President. He may deputize for the President of the Republic.

The Higher Council has in addition nine members appointed by the President of the Republic in the conditions laid down by an organic law.

The Higher Council of the Judiciary submits nominations for appointments to the supreme Court of Appeal (*Cour de Cassation*) and to the posts of First President of Assize Courts (*Cours d'Appel*). It gives its opinion, in conditions laid down by the organic law, on the proposals of the Minister of Justice concerning the appointment of other Judges. It is consulted on reprieves in conditions laid down by an organic law.

The Higher Council of the Judiciary sits as the Disciplinary Council for Judges. It is then presided over by the First President of the *Cour de Cassation*.

Article 66. None may be arbitrarily detained.

The judicial authority, guardian of the liberty of the individual, ensures respect for this principle in conditions determined by the law.

TITLE IX

THE HIGH COURT OF JUSTICE

Article 67. A High Court of Justice is instituted.

It is composed of members elected, from their own numbers and in equal parts, by the National Assembly and the Senate, after each election to these assemblies. It elects its President from among its members.

An organic law determines the composition of the High Court, its rules of operation and the procedure applicable before it.

Article 68. The President of the Republic is responsible for actions performed in the carrying out of his duties only in case of high treason. He can be indicted only by identical motions passed by the two assemblies in open ballot and by an absolute majority of their members; he is tried by the High Court of Justice.

Members of the Government are penally responsible for actions performed in the carrying out of their duties and classed as crimes or misdemeanours at the time when they were committed. The procedure set out above is applicable to them and to their accomplices in cases of plotting against the security of the State. In the cases provided for in this paragraph, the High Court is bound by the definitions of the crimes and misdemeanours and by the rules as to penalties to be found in the criminal laws in force at the times when the actions were performed.

TITLE X

THE ECONOMIC AND SOCIAL COUNCIL

Article 69. The Economic and Social Council gives its opinion, at the request of the Government, on such Government Bills, draft ordinances, draft decrees and private members' Bills as are submitted to it.

A member of the Economic and Social Council may be appointed by the Council to appear before the parliamentary assemblies and put forward the opinion of the Council on Bills submitted to it.

Article 70. The Economic and Social Council may also be consulted by the Government on any economic or social problem concerning the Republic or the Community. Any plan or programme-Bill of economic or social character is submitted to it for its opinion.

Article 71. The composition of the Economic and Social Council and its methods of work are laid down in an organic law.

TITLE XI

TERRITORIAL ENTITIES

Article 72. The territorial entities of the Republic are the *communes*. the *départements* and the Overseas Territories. Any other territorial entity is created by law.

These entities are freely administered by elected councils in conditions laid down by law.

In the *départements* and territories, the Government delegate is responsible for the interests of the nation, supervises the administration and ensures the observance of the law.

Article 73. The status as defined by law and the administrative organization of the Overseas *départements* may be modified by measures intended to adapt them to local conditions.

Article 74. The Overseas Territories of the Republic have a special organization which takes account of the interests of each within the framework of the general interests of the Republic. This organization is laid down and modified by law, after consultation with the Territorial Assembly of the Territory concerned.

Article 75. Citizens of the Republic who do not enjoy ordinary civil status, the only status to which Article 34 may be construed as referring, keep their personal status so long as they have not renounced it.

Article 76. Overseas Territories may keep their status within the Republic. If they express the desire to do so, by a decision of their Territorial Assembly, within the period fixed by Article 91, para. 1, they become either Overseas *départements* or, grouped together or separately, member States of the Community.

TITLE XII

THE COMMUNITY

Article 77. In the Community established by the present Constitution, the States enjoy autonomy; they administer themselves and manage their own affairs, freely and democratically.

There is in the Community only one citizenship.

All citizens are equal before the law, whatever their origin, race or religion. They have the same duties.

Article 78. The field of competence of the Community includes foreign policy, defence, currency, common economic and financial policy and policy concerning strategic raw materials.

It also includes, in the absence of a special agreement to the contrary, supervision of justice, higher education, the general organization of external and common transport, and telecommunications.

Special agreements may establish other common fields of competence or provide for any transfer of competence from the Community to one of its members.

Article 79. The member States come within the provisions of Article 77 as soon as they have made the choice provided for in Article 76.

Until the coming into force of the measures necessary for the application of the present Title, matters of common competence will be dealt with by the Republic.

Article 80. The President of the Republic presides over and represents the Community.

The latter has as its organs an Executive Council, a Senate and a Court of Arbitration.

Article 81. The member States of the Community take part in the election of the President in the conditions provided for in Article 6.

The President of the Republic, in his capacity of President of the Community, is represented in each State of the Community.

Article 82. The Executive Council of the Community is presided over by the President of the Community. It is composed of the Prime Minister of the Republic, the Heads of Government of each of the member States, and the Ministers made responsible, on behalf of the Community, for common affairs.

The Executive Council organizes governmental and administrative co-operation between the members of the Community.

The organization and methods of work of the Executive Council are determined by an organic law.

Article 83. The Senate of the Community is composed of delegates chosen from among their own number by the Parliament of the Republic and the legislative assemblies of the other members. The number of delegates from each State is fixed in a manner which takes account of its population and of the responsibilities which it assumes within the Community.

It holds two sessions a year, which are opened and closed by the President of the Community and may not last longer than one month each.

At the request of the President, it discusses common economic and financial policy, before the Parliament of the Republic and, in appropriate circumstances, the legislative assemblies of other members of the Community pass laws in this field.

The Senate of the Community considers the acts, international agreements, and treaties referred to in Articles 35 and 53, where these involve obligations for the Community.

It takes binding decisions in the fields in which power has been delegated to it by the legislative assemblies of members of the Community. The decisions are promulgated in the States concerned in the same ways as the laws of the territories.

An organic law determines its composition and the rules under which it functions.

Article 84. A Court of Arbitration of the Community gives rulings on disputes between members of the Community.

Its composition and powers are determined by an organic law.

Article 85. Notwithstanding the procedure provided for in Article 89, the provisions of the present Title concerning the functioning of the common institutions of the Community are revised by laws couched in the same terms passed by the Parliament of the Republic and by the Senate of the Community.

The provisions of the present title can also be revised by agreements concluded between all the States of the Community; the new provisions are applied in the conditions laid down by the Constitution of each State.[1]

Article 86. A change of the status of a member State of the Community may be requested either by the Republic, or by a resolution of the legislative assembly of the State concerned, confirmed by a

[1] Additions made by the revision of 4th June 1960 are given in italics.

local referendum, organized and supervised by the institutions of the Community. The methods by which the change of status is made are determined by an agreement approved by the Parliament of the Republic and the legislative assembly concerned.

In the same manner, a member State of the Community may become independent. It thereby ceases to belong to the Community.

A member State of the Community may also become independent, by means of agreements, without thereby ceasing to form part of the Community.

An independent State, not being a member of the Community, can join the Community, by means of agreements, without thereby ceasing to be independent.

The position of these States within the Community is determined by the agreements referred to in the preceding paragraphs and, where appropriate, by the agreements for this purpose provided for by paragraph 2 of article 85.[1]

Article 87. Special agreements concluded in application of the present title require the approval of the Parliament of the Republic and of the legislative assembly concerned.

TITLE XIII

AGREEMENTS OF ASSOCIATION

Article 88. The Republic or the Community may conclude agreements with States desiring to form an association with either, in order develop their civilizations.

TITLE XIV

REVISION

Article 89. The right to propose amendments to the Constitution belongs concurrently to the President of the Republic, on the proposal of the Prime Minister, and to members of Parliament.

The amending Bill, Government or private members, must be passed by the two assemblies in identical terms. The amendment becomes effective when it has been approved by referendum.

However, a Governmental amending Bill is not submitted to a referendum when the President of the Republic decides to submit it

[1] Additions made by the revision of 4th June 1960 are given in italics.

to Parliament, meeting as Congress; in this case the amendment is accepted only if it obtains a majority of three-fifths of the votes cast. The Bureau of the Congress is that of the National Assembly.

The amendment procedure may not be initiated or pursued when the integrity of the territory is under attack.

The Republican form of government is not subject to revision.

TITLE XV

TEMPORARY DISPOSITIONS

Article 90. The ordinary session of Parliament is suspended. The term of office of the members of the present National Assembly will expire on the day the Assembly elected by virtue of the present Constitution meets.

Until this meeting, only the Government has authority to summon Parliament.

The term of office of the members of the Assembly of the French Union will expire at the same time as the term of the members of the present National Assembly.

Article 91. The institutions of the Republic provided for in the present Constitution will be set up within a period of four months from the day of its promulgation.

This period is extended to six months for the institutions of the Community.

The powers of the present President of the Republic will expire only on the proclamation of the results of the election provided for in Articles 6 and 7 of the present Constitution.

The member States of the Community will take part in this first election in conditions appropriate to their status at the date of the promulgation of the Constitution.

The established authorities will continue to exercise their functions in these States in accordance with the laws and other instruments applicable on the date at which the Constitution enters into force, until the installation of the authorities provided for by their new form of government.

Until its constitution has been finally determined, the Senate consists of the present members of the Council of the Republic. The organic laws which will determine the final constitution of the Senate must come into existence before July 31, 1959.

The powers conferred on the Constitutional Council by Articles 58 and 59 of the Constitution will be exercised, until the installation of the Council, by a Commission composed of the Vice-President of the Council of State as chairman, the First President of the *Cour de Cassation* and the First President of the Court of Accounts.

The peoples of the member States of the Community continue to be represented in Parliament until the coming into force of the measures necessary for the application of Title XII.

Article 92. The legislative measures necessary for the installation of the institutions and, until that installation, for the functioning of the public authorities, will be taken in the Council of Ministers, after consultation with the Council of State, by ordinances having the force of law.

During the period prescribed in the first paragraph of Article 91 the Government is authorized to determine, by ordinances having the force of law and issued in the same form, the electoral system for the assemblies provided for by the Constitution.

During the same period and in the same conditions, the Government may also take, on any subject, such measures as it may consider necessary to the life of the nation, the protection of the citizens or the preservation of freedom.

The present law will be applied as the Constitution of the Republic and of the Community.

Index